STEPPING WILD

HIKING
THE APPALACHIAN TRAIL
WITH MINGO

D0920589

PHILL GROUNDS

outskirtspress

DENVER, COLORADO

The opinions expressed in this manuscript are solely the opinions of the author and do not represent the opinions or thoughts of the publisher. The author has represented and warranted full ownership and/or legal right to publish all the materials in this book.

Stepping Wild
Hiking the Appalachian Trail with Mingo
All Rights Reserved.
Copyright © 2015 Phill Grounds
v3.0 r1.1

Cover Photo © 2015 Phill Grounds

This book may not be reproduced, transmitted, or stored in whole or in part by any means, including graphic, electronic, or mechanical without the express written consent of the publisher except in the case of brief quotations embodied in critical articles and reviews.

Outskirts Press, Inc.
http://www.outskirtspress.com

Paperback ISBN: 978-1-4787-4950-9
Hardback ISBN: 978-1-4787-4241-8

Outskirts Press and the "OP" logo are trademarks belonging to Outskirts Press, Inc.

PRINTED IN THE UNITED STATES OF AMERICA

Thank you
To Judy Trishman. She motivated me
and gave great input about the book.

In loving memory of a dear friend Julie Bryce,
trail name Pony Express.

Contents

Introduction

PREPARING TO HIKE the Appalachian Trail was like starting any adventure. I had absolutely no idea what I was doing! I read books, took notes, and tried to get every bit of available information about the trail. But, once on the trail, I said the same thing every hiker says: "It isn't what I expected." I was clueless.

The trail can be hiked by a totally inexperienced and unprepared hiker, while another hiker, who is stronger and better prepared, can find the trail impassable. Hiking one day can be the most hazardous day of your life. Yet, hiking another day can be so eventless it is forgotten in obscurity. This was an adventure!

How do you prepare for such a range of experiences? This book gives only one example. Here you will read of the adventures I endured as "Mingo," making my way from end-to-end of the Appalachian Trail.

To show how each hiker's experiences are different, let's start with the basic need for shoes. Some hikers use only two pairs of shoes to complete the entire trail. Then there are hikers like me. I went through eight pairs of shoes and never really got a pair that worked well.

Without a doubt, I should have been smarter at planning and executing my hike. My life experiences should have given me an exceptional edge. But as I explained before, the trail can be easy for one hiker and difficult for another. The entire trail is never easy for anyone. If anyone ever says otherwise, they are lying. During my hike I made some tremendous mistakes.

A quick word of warning: reading this adventure will take you through some hard times and some fun times. You will experience a roller coaster ride with me, so hang on! This trip cost me more blood, sweat, tears, and pain than I ever expected. Both my body and soul paid a high price.

Having the correct gear for a thru-hike is essential. Of course, I started with all the wrong gear. My hope was to hike with old gear and save money. That idea caused my problems—well, not all of them. Trying to hike cheaply ended up costing me more money. I went through two sets of hiking poles, eight pairs of shoes, four backpacks, two tents, four sleeping bags, three sleep pads, three water filters, two stoves, two hats, and several other items.

During the hike, I lost forty pounds. My feet went from completely numb to severe pain and back to numb again. My body was injured from falls, cuts, sprains, strains, and multiple other injuries.

Let me take a moment to set the stage. Hiking the Appalachian Trail is a "walk" of over 2,181 miles in the woods. Okay, most of it is in the woods; there are parts of the trail above the tree line, and some of the trail goes through towns. But, most of the trail is in the woods. While 2,181 miles was the distance of the known trail at the time I started, there are other factors to consider. The hiking distance to a water source can be a half mile or more from the trail. The hikes to towns for resupplies can be as much as seven to twelve miles. The trail has detours, reroutes, and other reasons that cause a change in course. Oh, and getting lost and having to find your way back to the trail adds miles to a hike. The entire hiking distance was well over twenty-two hundred miles.

Preparing for the Trail

MY PLAN WAS simple. I was going to start the trail on March 29, 2011, and finish in four months. That was "the plan." For months in advance I spent days and evenings researching books and maps. Daily miles were planned. Each stop for lunch and for a night's rest was carefully planned. I would hike twenty-seven miles a day for four days then take two days off. That was the plan . . . talk about being naive!

I packed boxes and boxes of food for resupply. My research books and maps gave me the directions and addresses for sending my care packages by mail. My wife would send the packages on certain dates. This was a fully and properly planned adventure; nothing was left to chance. Each meal, each step, and each stop had been planned. Contingency upon contingency was prepared to ensure success. The one thing I didn't count on was the Appalachian Trail. The trail has a "life spirit and way" of its own.

Someone once asked me why I thought I could easily hike the trail. I grew up in West Virginia; hiking in high hills is nothing new to me. I am also an ex-Special Forces soldier. Special Forces soldiers are often referred to by the hat they wear, the "Green Beret." After serving eight years in the Army Special Forces, I became a police officer in Columbus, Ohio. My passion has always been to set personal challenges and succeed in them, and in the past I have even run marathons. Taking on this task did not seem to be anything too great.

I was in for some real learning experiences. A big slice of humble pie was waiting for me in the woods! Nothing seemed to happen according to plan. The difficulty started even before the first day. My mistakes began weeks before the trail and continued all the way to the end of the trail.

Preparing for the daily hikes should have included some sort of hiking or walking. Instead, my goal was to relax and wait till I was on the trail and get fit there. My gear was not what one would recommend. I thought I had all that would be needed.

Not owning a backpack that was large enough to hold all that I felt I needed, I ordered a pack on-line. When the pack arrived, trimming excess straps to lower its weight began immediately. Loading it was carefully planned. The weight carried is one of the most important factors on the trail. Most hikers cut all tabs off their gear and clothes. Toothbrushes have the handles cut off to a shorter size, the tops of socks are cut off, pant cuffs are removed. Any extra buckle or strap is cut away. Ziplock baggies are used for wallets.

The maps for the trail were separated into my care packages so that I would carry only three maps at a time. Sections from a guidebook were torn apart and packaged the same way as the maps.

Gearheads are those hikers who focus way too much on the latest and greatest in light-weight gear. Good for them if they want to go that route, but as for me, an old pup tent resewn with added zippers to close the front was good enough. My forty-degree sleeping bag and a fleece liner would be good for sleeping. Simple gear, not new high tech equipment, was the plan. My water filter was about twenty years old, but it had never failed me before. I was ready—or, at least, I was getting ready.

Prior to leaving for the trail, I decided to do some remodeling in our house. I tore a wall out to join two rooms to make a larger bedroom. I removed the floor, and my wife wanted a bamboo hardwood floor to replace it. So for a couple of days I worked at laying the hardwood floor.

Before I finished the floor, my first trail mishap occurred. While nailing the floor, I missed the tongue of the tongue and groove on a floorboard. When I say I missed it, I mean I missed it with the nail gun. The nail, a two-inch nail, hit the top of the floor. The nail then ricocheted off the floor and into my knee! It was okay, because there was a pair of pliers sitting close by. My knee ached. Finding the head of the nail was difficult at first, as it had counter sunk all the way into my knee.

After grabbing the head of the nail with the pliers, I tugged. The nail didn't give. I gritted my teeth and tugged harder. I pulled the nail free from deep inside my left knee. That kinda hurt! My worry at the time was only an infection. In hindsight, I should have gone to the hospital for a shot or something. No time for that, I had a floor to get down before going to hike the Appalachian Trail. Now I was going to start the hike temporarily crippled!

Setting Out

ON THE MORNING of my departure from home for Georgia, my wife and I were up before four o'clock. Deb was up boiling eggs to put in my pack for added protein. That was a great idea. By the way, fifteen boiled eggs are heavy. Deb added a pair of running shoes to my pack as well. Carrying extra shoes sounded like a horrible idea, but to make her happy I consented. We had bought a pair of boots just for the hike so I really didn't want to take extra shoes.

The boots were perfect. They were heavy duty and designed for cold weather. The last thing I wanted was cold feet. My new boots had an extra thick Thinsulate lining. The outer shell was a rubber waterproofing topped by leather. These boots were great. They cost a little extra, but my feet were going to be both dry and warm.

My buddy Dave, or Puff, as we call him, came by to drive me to Georgia. Springer Mountain is the southern terminus of the trail in Georgia. Puff was going to drive me down in my truck, we would stay the night, and then he would drop me off the next morning and return home to Ohio.

During the entire drive to Georgia, Puff kept laughing at me. Snow was falling almost the whole way on our drive south. He kept promising me he would come back to Fontana Dam to pick me up. Puff teased that I could make it only to Fontana Dam. The farther south we drove, the heavier the snow covered the ground.

When Puff and I arrived in Georgia, we went to the trailhead. There is a back road to get to a mile from the beginning of the Appalachian Trail. Another option is to hike what is called the approach trail from Amicalola Falls. The approach trail is about eight extra miles. Some hikers do the approach trail and some don't. That is one of the first divisions of the type of hikers on the trail.

My choice was not to do the approach trail. Puff and I drove on the back road to find Springer Mountain. We wanted to see the area so we could find it the next morning. A small parking area is at the trail and road crossing. The road is a dirt, unimproved back road but it was smooth enough for even a car to drive on. There was a light mist in the air as we arrived.

I wanted to go to the top of Springer Mountain to get that first mile done. That way, Puff would be there to take a picture of me at the beginning. He resisted the idea of hiking up a hill in the rain, but my persistence paid off. Puff followed and complained in a comical manner all the way to the southern end of the Appalachian Trail.

Litter marked the trail; an abandoned sleeping bag was stuffed under a rock. Dark mud outlined every rock along the way. There was nothing green to see; all the trees were dormant for the winter and the forest bed was blanketed by dead leaves from seasons past.

After some hiking, we arrived at an area with carved plaques embed-ded in the rocks. These plaques announced that we were at the southern terminus of the Appa-lachian Trail. We took our pictures and looked around. There wasn't much to see.

While on Springer Mountain, the misting rain continued to fall steadily. The wind was not as strong as it could have been, but it was gusty from time to time. A young man in his late teens or early twenties showed up, hiking northbound from the approach trail. He was a clean-cut young man. His pack was obviously new. It still had creases from being packaged at the store or warehouse. This young man wore a military-style camouflaged hat, and his clothes were a similar fashion. He was sweating from a hard hike. He looked as if he had been over-exercising.

We studied our first hiker as he approached. Then, without being prompted, the young man said, "That's it! I quit!" Puff asked, "Hey, how far were you going?" The tattered hiker replied with dread in his eyes, "Katahdin." Mount Katahdin is the northern terminus of the Appalachian Trail. This guy had planned to hike the 2,181 miles plus the eight miles of the approach trail. He quit at the end of the eight-mile approach trail.

I missed a great opportunity. As bad as I felt for the guy, I should have asked to buy his food. He probably had an excess of Mountain House food. In his condition he may have sold his gear at a sweet rate. The least I could have done was find out his shoe size. That was an opportunity missed. He had quit and was headed home with food and equipment enough for at least four—maybe five—months on the trail. Someone on eBay was going to get lucky.

Puff and I hiked back to my truck and were off to find our hotel then lunch. As we were leaving the parking lot we saw a young female hiker. She was standing along the dirt road with her hiking poles held horizontally in front of her. A good-looking young lady, she appeared to be staring at her poles as if in some kind of trance or meditation. I figured she was

conducting a personal ceremony or prayer before going off on the trail. Her mother and father were standing in front of her gazing with concern and pride. Puff and I each wondered what she must have been doing.

We drove directly to the hotel. An old army buddy of mine from Virginia, Ken, happened to be in the area. Ken called and came by the hotel parking lot as we pulled in. We talked for about five minutes, took a couple pictures, then parted ways. It had been at least eight years since we had last seen each other.

I slept well that night before setting off on the trail. Puff kept me laughing with his incessant pestering about picking me up at Fontana Dam in four months, which was less than a couple hundred miles away. The next morning would come and my life would be forever changed. My life's focus would embrace survival and continual progress hiking the trail. Sounds simple, doesn't it?

The morning came and we were up before dawn. The skimpy continental breakfast didn't feed us well. The coffee was good, though. We had to go to a restaurant for a real breakfast. After a quick eat and a final check of my pack, we were headed to the back road and trail crossing.

Day One

THE MORNING WAS still dark; a light, misty rain was still falling. This was a rain like the kind you find in Seattle, Washington. We waited in the truck as daylight slowly pierced the morning rain. Fog rolled through the woods carrying more mist. The time had come. This was it! I was getting out of my truck and putting on my pack and heading north to Maine. The goal was still to get there in four months.

I set my pack on my back and adjusted the straps. The pack did not feel right. The adjustments were not comfortable. I had a lot to get used to. As I headed into the woods I could hear the diesel engine of my F-250 rolling away. Puff was leaving. That was the end of my chance to turn back. I was alone. The whole Appalachian Trail lay ahead of me and here it was, a wet trail with heavy fog.

As I started my hike the pack just would not fit correctly. The pack was overstuffed. My two single-liter nalgene water bottles did not fit in the pack. I put those bottles in my jacket pockets. My jacket was fleece-lined, made of cotton canvas, and loose fitting. The water bottles swung and bounced against my legs as I hiked.

The straps on the pack dug deeply into my shoulders. Creases on the jacket pinched my skin under the weight of the pack. Worried the rain would soak my pack, I decided to cover it, so I took off my jacket and put my pack back on. Then I put the hood of the jacket on my head and swung the jacket over the backpack. The water bottles swung wildly, much more than before. I looked a mess!

Starting my hike was as uncomfortable as it could possibly have been. My knee ached from the nail-gun wound, the water bottles swung and banged against me, the rain made the ground slippery, and I was out of breath quickly. It takes time for a hiker to get what is referred to as "trail legs." Usually, trail legs develop after the first four hundred miles. Once you get to Damascus, Virginia, you will have them.

The body goes through many changes while hiking. At first, it is shocked by the torture of carrying a backpack all day long. The calories needed for a successful hike could be as high as six thousand calories a day! The feet take a beating from the constant pounding on the ground. Twisting ankles is almost a daily event. "Pain and rain" are two absolutes you endure while hiking the Appalachian Trail. I learned about them on the first day.

I did not make the time or mileage I had planned, but I made excellent time compared to most. Most hikers start hiking a moderate and smarter five to eight miles a day. I tried to do twenty-seven but ended with thirteen to eighteen miles a day. That's not twenty-seven miles a day, as planned, maybe because I shot myself in knee or because I was so far out of shape, weighing in at a healthy two hundred and five pounds. That much weight on my short five-foot-eight frame was way too heavy.

It is all uphill and downhill along the beginning of the trail. It wasn't long before realizing my boots were way too heavy. My boots were apparently good for the twenty-degree weather in Ohio, but that was not what was needed in Georgia. I know what you're thinking, "Who would have thought?" I asked the same thing. The boots were so heavy that after ten miles my knees were blasted. It was too painful to take another step, and both of my knees were now swollen.

Having "shot" myself in the left knee caused me to favor it, so the right knee really took a beating from overuse. After I figured out the boots were too heavy, I changed shoes. Deb had forced me to take a pair of running shoes. Those shoes saved my butt. If it weren't for them I would not have been able to walk any further. Taking the running shoes out of the pack did not free up enough room for the boots, so I tied the boots laces together and hung them over my neck, situated in front of me.

Having the water bottles swing wildly was uncomfortable enough. Now, the boots were doing the same thing. The boots felt as if they weighed ten pounds apiece. They were for arctic weather, not hiking long distances. While changing into the shoes, I stopped for a bit of lunch.

I wasn't hungry, but knew I needed to eat. After having some water, I searched the map to reassure myself there would be water ahead. To my surprise, there was water everywhere! Streams and springs were all along the trail. Because the weather started wet with steadily falling rain the streams stayed full of rushing water. Each time I passed a stream I would think about how refreshing it looked and remember I was carrying two liters of nasty-tasting tap water. Time and time again the trail passed water; all the while, I was carrying water.

A couple of guys showed up while I was having lunch. They were hiking to the next "shelter." Shelters are found along the Appalachian Trail, or sometimes a short hike just off the trail. A shelter is a three-sided building with a platform off the ground, large enough to allow at least six hikers to sleep on it. Some shelters hold more hikers and a few are even two stories or more. Each shelter is different.

The two hikers kept asking questions about me and my plans for hiking the Appalachian Trail. Their inquiry soon grew embarrassing. I was not proud of the situation in which I found myself. My background and experiences were not serving me well. I guess I was over confident and did not heed good advice.

The last thing I wanted to do was tell people about my time in Special Forces while they were seeing me as an out-of-shape, unprepared slob. I wanted to hike but I hurt. The hikers moved on after I stopped talking to them. I wasn't trying to be rude. I just wanted to be left alone.

After the two guys left, a female hiker with a dog showed up. She was talkative as well, but much less inquisitive. She volunteered information and offered advice about hiking. Her trail name was Aunt Bear. Aunt Bear and the other hikers kept asking me what my trail name was. I had none. A trail name is the name that you are known by while you are hiking the trail.

Hikers may give themselves a trail name or let other hikers give them a name. The latter is more risky. Either way everyone respects the trail name. In the shelters are notebooks used for journals. Hikers write in the journals to tell stories, leave notes, and communicate with other hikers. The journals are always signed using the trail name. On a rare occasion a hiker will not get a trail name, usually for a reason.

After lunch, I hiked with Aunt Bear to the next shelter. Pride kept me from complaining about my knees. Upon arrival at the shelter, it was evident the shelter was already full. The surrounding area was spotted with tents, tarps, and hammocks. The woods were full of people attempting to hike the Appalachian Trail. Each year over three thousand people attempt to make it the whole way; around three hundred actually make it. I hoped to be one of the people who made it.

I found a semi-flat spot to set up my tent. The ground declined slightly downhill; that is where my feet would go. Aunt Bear had a nice tent site. The rain had stopped but the air was heavy with moisture. The ground was wet. Hikers were all talking and talking over one another. Each had a story of grandeur about their adventure that very day.

After filtering water and having dinner I set my gear inside my tent. I lay the sleeping pad out with my sleeping bag and fleece liner out on top of the pad. My legs were beginning to cramp and I was tired. A quick check of my cell phone indicated there was cell service in the area. Verizon has the best service coverage over the trail from Georgia to Maine. I sat in my tent, taking inventory of food and equipment, trying to come up with better options for my pack.

Someone outside my tent called out, "Does anyone have trash they need carried out?" This was cool! A local hiker was going to help us by carrying trash out so we wouldn't have to carry the extra weight. I asked him if he could take something heavy. He asked how heavy. He was a bit surprised when he saw my boots. They had ten miles on them and were obviously new. He said he would give them to charity. That was a great idea.

Sleep came quickly as I was extremely worn out. That first night in my tent I dreamed I was swimming in a pool with fins on. In my dream I finned and finned. The harder I finned in my sleep the louder the splashing

faster in the wet and cold made me both tired and sore. Aunt Bear hiked with me for most of the day. We made it to another shelter, where other hikers were already setting up for the night.

On the second night there was no doubt staying in the tent would be a bad idea. Everything I owned was soaked through and through. The shelter had several young hikers who were full of glee. That's old speak for "they were too happy for their own good." These young folks brought a good laugh and they took it upon themselves to find me a trail name. I was worried.

Never let someone else give you a trail name. At least, don't do it if you don't want a name that needs explaining. One gal had seen me taking a nap on a rock along the trail earlier that day. She tried to name me "Nap Time." Later that night, two of the gals were talking about doing laundry together at Mountain Crossings Hostel at Neels Gap. Then, they were talking about their gear and having the same undergarments. I was trying to be helpful and asked how they would tell their clothes, the undergarments, apart when they were washed together. Some dude, Fish Head, cupped his hands together and sniffed as if sniffing panties. It was a joke!

Well, the joke was almost on me, because the gals pointed at me and said my trail name would be "Panty Sniffer." No way! As quickly as I could, I shot down that idea, shot it down like a clay pigeon on a skeet range; I blew it to dust! How could I ever explain that name to my wife? These kids were crazy. One of the crazies was the pretty, meditating gal whom Puff and I had seen the first day. Later, when asked, she explained she was making sure her poles were set to the same length. That made sense. I didn't have poles, so I didn't think of that.

I told an old story about when I was a police officer in Columbus, Ohio. The story was of an incident when I was working plain clothes. Once, I stood on a street corner, after being talked into it by the other officers, to pose as a male hooker. After being propositioned by another guy, the arrest team didn't arrive as planned. They sat in their car laughing at me. The hikers had a good laugh at the story and dubbed me with the name Hooker. The other hikers were Fish Head, who wore a hat that had an embroidered fish on it; Benz, who got her name when she was dropped off by her parents in a Mercedes-Benz; and Ruth, who took her name after the candy bar Baby Ruth. She shunned the name Shit Foot. She almost got that name when she twice nearly stepped in doo-doo before getting onto the trail. And the meditating fox, she didn't have a name yet; it would later become Mouse.

I slept in the shelter. The young ones were a bit worried about me freezing to death. There wasn't a dry anything about me. The air was cold and the wind was constant, but with this group of hikers it was easy to laugh almost all night; really, they were crazy. Tons of fun they were.

The morning came with heavy clouds but no rain. The air was heavy-laden with moisture. My knees were swollen, and I was beginning to get chafed. One lesson to learn is: cotton kills. My pants were flannel-lined and the cotton flannel was causing damage that I would soon regret. This day was to be highlighted by a mountain called Blood Mountain. That's a cool name. I figured that if the weather was bad I would take the Freeman Trail that went around the mountain, but as my luck was holding out, the weather wasn't bad, so over the Blood Mountain I went. Is that like losing for winning or what?

A hostel was waiting at the end of the day for me at a place called Neels Gap. I think the name of it was Mountain Crossings. Catchy name! At the hostel, a group was giving out apples and cooking hamburgers. That was my first taste of "trail magic." It was perfect. Trail magic comes in many forms.

The trail magic here was grilled hamburgers and apples. Trail magic is fun to find, when you are lucky enough to find it. Usually, the trail magic is for thru-hikers. Unfortunately, section hikers and day hikers will help themselves to the magic, also, leaving thru-hikers without any magic.

Trail People

I'LL TRY TO explain a little about the culture of the trail. The trail has its own society, culture, classes of people, and language. My feeble attempt to explain these may make you merely confused, but I will do my best.

Let me start with the classes, or types, of people found on the trail. There are day hikers, section hikers, thru-hikers, nobos, sobos, yoyos, slack packers, purists, blue blazers, yellow blazers, green blazers, ridge runners, rangers, and trail angels. Each of these persons has a purpose, because you cannot have the good without the bad. Not that any are bad, but you will see.

Day hikers are those folks who come to the trail for a day hike. Some bring their kids to teach them to respect the forest. Other day hikers are college-age and they come out yelling in the woods, throwing plastic bottles and paper on the ground with no respect for nature. You have to wonder why they are even out here. Never trust them; they will never give you correct information, partly because they don't understand distances or steepness. The worst of the day hikers bring their dogs and don't leash them.

I came across too many dogs. On one occasion, a dog had its hair standing on end and the owner just sat there and said, "He don't bite." As a matter of fact, they all said that. Don't they know their dog won't bite them, but will bite? That's what dogs do. I learned to answer with a kind, "Get your dog. If it bites me I will kill it, hurt you, and then sue you. I bite." That often got their attention. If you don't want someone being rude about your dog keep it under control.

Section hikers are the folks coming out for a week or even a month or two to hike. They usually have trail names as well. They carry way too much stuff. Section hikers brag a bit too much, but they mean well. Most section hikers do not have their trail legs or trail stomach, and they certainly do not have "the look." Some claim to be thru-hikers, but after a few questions they are quickly revealed for who they truly are.

Thru-hikers! Now there is a crew for you. Those guys are a bit off the deep end . . . or so I am told. Those nut jobs are hiking all the way from Maine to Georgia or Georgia to Maine. You can usually tell a thru-hiker by "the look." They look like a vagabond, a bum, a gypsy, a beggar, or a tramp. Most never shave, never comb their hair, hardly ever wash, and will eat food right off the ground. When a thru-hiker finishes eating, he or she washes the dishes—often just a single small pot—and doesn't throw the wash water away. They drink it. Yup, they drink the dish water. It's okay, they don't put soap in it, and they need the water and calories. Aw, the life of a thru-hiker, how sweet it is.

A nobo is a type of thru-hiker. That's the guys and gals going northbound. Get it? Nobo is short for northbound. Anyway!

Can you guess what a sobo is? The thru-hikers going from Maine to Georgia, or southbound. Point of interest: section hikers also claim nobo or sobo as well. They share all the same language and ways of a thru-hiker. They aren't doing the full trail in just one attempt. They may finish the AT but they do it in sections at a time.

So what about a yoyo? I hear you. *No! I am not a yoyo! Very funny!* A yoyo is someone who walks through from Georgia to Maine then turns around and walks back to Georgia. Now that is just weird! So, they are yoyos; they go forth and back. I admire the few who can do that.

Slack packers are an interesting crew. Anyone may be a slack packer. A slack packer is when you get someone to take the weight of your pack from one road crossing to the next. You carry hardly any weight at all, just food and water. There is no need for a full pack. You can make some serious miles slack packing. Some folks are against it. But others say,

"Hey, you are still hiking the trail." Me? I say do what it takes to get the job done.

A purist hikes every inch of the AT and nothing less. The Appalachian Trail is marked by white blazes, or white paint marks, on trees and rocks. These marks are two inches by six inches and are called blazes. A purist will hike where only the white blazes are. The problem with that is that the trail changes all the time from reconstruction or avalanches or beaver dams flooding the trail or for whatever reason. I chose to not be a purist because I didn't want someone else to decide what I see or where I go.

Blue blazers are not purist. There are blue blazes that show side trails, short cuts, and hazardous weather alternate trails. A blue blaze is often the old white blazed trail that has been painted blue. Some blue blaze trails go from one point of the trail to another. These will have better views and more water falls. Now that's what I am talking about!

Yellow blazers are viewed as cheaters. These are just hitchhikers. I am not talking about hitchhiking into town for a resupply. I am talking about hitchhiking from one section of the trail to another, skipping large sections. There isn't any other way around it: they are cheating. If you take a car to skip part of the trail then you really didn't hike the whole thing.

Green blazer was a new term I learned. That's the crazy idiot who sees that the trail made a switchback and jumps over the hill to the other trail section. He will also walk off the trail and through the woods to cut out sections of the trail and to save time. Green blazers take a huge risk of getting lost in the woods. They are not the smartest "bean bags" in the woods. Green blazing is also bad for the environment. That is a lesson I learned late on the trail.

Ridge runners are an aid to the rangers. Rangers are law enforcement and are rarely ever seen. Trail angels are those people who come out to a road crossing to give hikers food, water, pop, beer, rides, and information such as weather reports.

That is pretty much most of the people on the trail and some of the language. Now, I will attempt to explain trail magic a little better. Trail magic is often given by trail angels. You know, the food, water, pop, and beer. Sometimes you will be hiking along and walk upon a cooler in the woods. Trail magic! In the cooler will be candy bars, Twinkies, PB and J sandwiches, pop, water, and/or beer. Other times you are late and the magic is already gone. With the magic is often a journal in which to write a thank you or to let other hikers know you were there and to leave messages. The shelters have journals, also. Hikers write in the journal as a way to communicate. I have even read a song written about me in a journal.

For me, trail magic had a familiar feeling about it. I could not place my hands on that feeling, until one day it dawned on me why it was so familiar. Trail magic is like being a Free and Accepted Mason. That might sound corny to some, but when you are a Mason then you know what I mean. You give to those who are in need whether they ask for it or not, and most often they did not ask for the help but you give it anyway. Trail magic as a Mason is going to the widow's home and helping make her life a little better that day. Trail magic as a Mason is hearing a brother needs a ride to the hospital and taking him there. Hopefully I explained it well enough and you get the point.

The two are different groups, with different goals, who exist separately but have one huge commonality: doing good for humanity. Brotherly love, relief, and truth are the three great tenants of Freemasonry, but it seems the same is true for the Appalachian Trail culture. I felt at home on the trail. Every day brought another experience that warmed the heart.

There are also different methods of camping. Staying in the shelters is one way. Tenting is setting up your tent to sleep in. Hammock camping is sleeping in a hammock, of course. Stealth camping is hiding in the woods to set up camp. Cowboy camping is sleeping in your sleeping bag without a tent. You are basically sleeping outside.

Back at the Hostel

BACK AT THE hostel in Neels Gap, I took a shower and used a towel to dry off. Oh, my, how nice it was to be dry. Then, I went to the outfitters and bought a one-man tent, a Hubba. Fish Head and Mouse each carried a Hubba tent as well. After cleaning my water filter and doing a little maintenance on my other gear, I packed as much unneeded gear in a box as possible and mailed it home. Prior to gearing down, my wet pack was sixty-five to seventy-five pounds. After gearing down, my pack was a whopping twenty-eight pounds. There wasn't a happier hiker out there than me.

That night in the hostel the hikers were all telling about the start of their hikes so far. Everyone had a story. Then, I explained how my knees were not holding up too well and how I had considered doing the blue-blaze Freeman Trail around Blood Mountain if the weather had been bad. To my surprise, somebody said, "If you are weak you don't need to be on the trail." Man, that struck a chord with me.

I started toward the guy. My mind was made up he was going to get his tail kicked. I told him, "I know you aren't calling me weak!" My hands clenched to fists as I quickly sized him up. My body was hurt but he would crumble quickly. I was seeing red. As quickly as he could the knucklehead took back his idiotic statement. He went by the name Moonshine. Fighting on the trail is way uncool, but he needed to learn respect. It was obvious he had none.

Who on earth would tell someone they didn't have the right to walk on a public trail? Man, that guy put my undies in a bunch. The arrogance of his statement was epic. He had done some time with the US Marines. Later, he worked for Blackwater. According to him, he saved the whole mission in Iraq with his superior guidance and experience. Oh my, how the second lieutenant Butter Bar was so mistaken when he crossed me.

So, morning came at the hostel. Off I went with dreams of traveling faster and farther than before. My pack was lighter, my belly full of food, and I was dry and had a new tent. Still, I didn't realize the cotton flannel lining of my pants was causing me great harm.

The trail went up hills and then down. Up hills hurt my thighs as they were getting worn out, but the down hills were the worse. My knees ached and ached. Having shot my left knee, I favored it. Favoring the left knee caused the right knee to swell and become sore. So, then I was favoring the right knee and the left was really taking a beating.

Heck, at one point, the map showed level ground, but the spot, Hogpen Gap, was anything but level. The trail went straight up nine hundred feet or so, in what seemed to be no distance at all. It was like going up endless stairs. But what goes up must come down, and the trail did just that. The down was steep. Steep hurts. By the end of the descent my knees were like two swollen balloons.

Facing Changes

ON MY THIRD day of hiking, bears stole food bags from hikers farther down trail. The only attacks against me had been two-inch to four-inch thick branches crashing from the treetops and landing next to me during the high winds. Oh joy! It was windy out—very windy. For a while, I thought for certain I was going to be taken out by a falling branch. It seemed to me that every five minutes another branch was falling from the trees landing right next to me. Luckily, the ones that hit me were only the small ones. For the record, small branches hurt, too. Hiking in the windy weather has its thrills, but wind also made every step ache because it was cold out there.

Fish Head, Mouse, and I hiked together for a while. We played leapfrog, catching and passing each other. Fish Head was a fast hiker. We got to Tray Mountain. There we met a Boy Scout troop, Troop 24/605. They were making hamburgers and hotdogs and other food for us hikers. It was awesome trail magic. Man, the hot foods hit the spot. After eating, we decided to go back a ways on the trail to set up our tents. It was cool to watch. We each had a Hubba tent. Under my tent I laid a piece of Tyvek house wrapping. I had bought it for ground cover to protect my tent. It cost one dollar and fifty cents per foot. Ouch!

After we set up our tents, we looked like a Mountain Safety Research (MSR) advertisement with our three bright yellow tents. We dubbed ourselves the Hubba Hubba Hubba Crew. Then Fish Head and Mouse went back to the boy scouts for more food. There was a promise of apple crisp. I volunteered to stay back with the tents. The truth be told, I was in pain and could not walk. My inner thighs were so freaking chafed from the cotton flannel lining in my pants. There was that lesson I didn't listen to: "cotton kills."

My thighs were raw and swollen, but that wasn't the worst of it. The seepage from the chafing was drying then cracking. The open cracks in my skin were getting infected. The infection smelled badly. This is the worst my thighs have ever been in my lifetime. I wondered how I was going to make it over two thousand miles, when I couldn't seem to walk just a few days.

The next day we headed off to spend the night at Deep Gap. Things had gotten worse. Fish Head gave me some powder for my chafing; that turned out to be a bad idea. I had already lost several layers of skin. The chaffed area was like a road rash and it burned like hell. The powder didn't dry things up; when I applied the powder the seepage mixed with the powder and caked up into hard lumps. Then, when I tried to walk the caked-up powder turned into an abrasive. Yup, it was as if I were wearing sandpaper! This was not my best moment.

I bet I lost another six layers of skin. There was so much skin lost I was able to peel it away. The skin came off like sun burnt skin. If that wasn't bad enough, my legs had swollen even more. My thighs went from being red to being bluish and bleeding. Both knees seemed not to want to support my weight anymore when going downhill, and the rains began, again.

Something had to change. I made a new plan. Medical aid was needed; there was no other way. My plan was to get up at five in the morning, hike slowly with baby steps to get to a road, hike into a town, find a pharmacy for meds, and find a hotel with a bathtub for an Epsom salts bath. The distance I needed to hike in the morning was three and a half miles. My pain was extraordinary, and that was the longest three and a half miles of my life. It took me two hours and thirty minutes to go that short distance. I could take only three-inch steps. Oh yes, it hurt.

A hike without sore knees or chafing filled my hopes and dreams. Once I made it to a road, there was a van waiting. A local hotel sends a

van to drop off and pick up hikers. What a great idea. They were a godsend. I was now headed to Hiawassee, Georgia.

I stayed at a hotel called the Hiawassee Inn. The hotel has a pharmacy across the road. I bought Epsom salts and patches for the chafing. At the hotel, I had a bathtub to soak in. I made my way back to the pharmacy and bought a scrub pad and bleach. There is no way I was going to soak in an unknown tub, not with my open wounds—especially with where the wounds were. After two hours of sanitizing the tub, I was soaking in Epsom salts.

While in Hiawassee, I received the first of twenty planned resupply packages. This was exciting. My food supply had been getting low, so now I had plenty to eat. While in town, going out for food would have been easy enough if I could have walked. But in my condition, it was a chore. I bought food to take back to the hotel room so I wouldn't have to walk as much. There was no way I could keep walking. I needed rest!

A second day in Hiawassee may help me get to a better condition for hiking. I had to take a zero. That meant I was not hiking any miles that day. The day before, when I arrived at Hiawassee, my hike was only three and a half miles. That's called a "nero," meaning near zero miles.

There were a few other wounds I needed to heal as well. My hopes were that the next day, when I headed out again, that I could make better time. Everyone hikes his own hike. Not many appreciated my hiking style or goal: I wanted to go as fast as I could. It was a personal challenge to make as many miles as possible each day, but so far, I hadn't made too many miles in a day. I wanted to, and should have been able to do more. Pleasure hiking isn't my style, but being an endurance challenger was. The harder I push the more fun it is to me. I can have all the fun in the world on the trail.

While in Hiawassee, Georgia, I met Two Chicks and a Dog. They had tried to hike the year before, but one of the chicks became injured. I also met Ompah, a hyper European. When it came to hiking, he was good. Fish Head and Mouse stayed at a hostel farther away. I couldn't stay there, as they didn't have a bathtub, which I needed. I really enjoyed the Hiawassee Inn; it had all I needed. It was perfect for me. Fish Head, Mouse, Benz, Baby Ruth, and a gang of other hikers, including Coyote, Two Beards, and Rebel, came to the hotel to find me. We went to find a place for dinner. We had a good time.

North Carolina

ON THE SECOND morning at Hiawassee Inn, I was taken by the shuttle van back to the trail. Fish Head, Mouse, and the others had all left before me. North Carolina wasn't too far away. This was going to be my first state line. Now, that was exciting. The condition of my legs, back, and mind put my most probable finish date at around August 20. That was slower than what I had planned; I had wanted to finish by the end of July. At the very latest, I needed to finish by August 29. That is a special and private date for me; I could not go past that date.

Starting the day I was dry, well fed, and showered, with clothes laundered, wounds dressed, hot spots wrapped, and food resupplied. I was packed up, all ready to go, and I was rehydrated.

North Carolina was getting closer. What a feat! It was exhilarating; I  was reaching my first state border. The day greeted hikers with clear skies and cool air. The sun shined bright across the sleeping forest. My steps grew more and more rapid as I craved seeing North Carolina and getting the heck out of Georgia. The trail headed up a hill, as it so often does.

I found the border—or at least, a marker for the state border. There was a small wooden sign on a tree to mark the state line. The sign read only: "NC/GA." That was it! Not much to see, no fanfare, and no party. But for me, it was as exciting as could be. My first state line! Hot dog!

While taking my own pictures at the sign, a couple came by. We talked for a while, but not long. They were in a big hurry. Apparently they were a brother and sister from Ohio. They were staying with their father, who met them at each road crossing. They hadn't even slept in the woods yet. Off they went in a blur, hiking at a rate to be admired. I figured I would never see them again. I wished them luck.

After trudging up a ridge, the trail angled to the right and the ground leveled off. The trees were still bare. Hardly a green leaf could be seen high or low. The trail appeared wide. Then, an odd tree lay in the middle of the trail, or, it stood in the middle of the trail; actually, it did both. The tree came out of the ground from its roots then made a large hump and went back into the ground then curved back up from the ground and spread its limbs out like antlers on a deer.

The tree was really unusual to see. My first thought was to mount the tree and ride it like a rodeo bull. If I had a big red ball I would have turned this tree into Rudolph. While riding the tree I swung my hat in the air wildly as if being bucked at a rodeo. Anything for a thrill!

Riding the tree was as fun as watching paint dry.

Unfulfilled by the tree my eyes searched for something more. A cut grape-vine near the "Reindeer tree" provided a few moments of fun. Pictures show me successfully swinging on the vine. What is not seen is the vine I found first. That vine failed to hold my weight and I crashed to the ground and rolled down the hill. There were pictures of that first event but they were quickly erased.

Well, the night was rapidly approaching, so I stopped three miles later at Muskrat Creek Shelter. But, before reaching the shelter, the trail turned to some serious hills. The steepness totally blew my right knee out. Walking was again painful. I needed a knee brace and hiking poles.

The evening started getting colder as night began to fall fast. The number of hikers on the trail at this point was still a considerably high number. There were over twenty-five hikers throughout the shelter area. The crowded condition did not make for pleasant camping.

The next morning, I arose early and headed out to go as far and as fast as I could. Camping with a large group was not what I had in mind for a fun hike. Groups of hikers tend to form what are called bubbles. The bubbles take on their own characteristics. I have seen party bubbles, where the members of that bubble tend to drink and party all night. That isn't a fast-moving bubble and it is costly.

I have seen a gearhead bubble. The members of the gearhead bubble compete over who has the latest and greatest gear. Gearheads go a bit overboard with the gear talk. When you first meet them they will ask what kind of pack you are carrying and why. Then they will unabashedly let you know why you are wrong. My gear was crap; I knew that, I was okay with it. I was doing my hike my way.

There are many other types of bubbles. There are feuding bubbles, in which everyone argues, pious bubbles, in which everyone is a bible thumper, young bubbles and old bubbles; they all have their own persona. If you are not in a bubble then you could be in the envelope. The envelope is the space that doesn't have the crowds. Here, you really do hike alone. That's where I wanted to be.

I needed to be away from this bubble. The people I enjoyed hiking with, Fish Head and Mouse, were long gone. My knee was feeling a little better. The chaffing hurt but was bandaged. I couldn't run, but wanted—hell, I needed—to do big miles. My hike was way behind schedule. A map reconnaissance revealed the trail was taking a large horseshoe-shaped path. A blue blaze, or side trail, cut across Standing Indian Campground. That way could save me nearly twenty miles.

I had thought about this decision all the night before. *Should I take the blue blaze through Standing Indian or not?* My final decision was to take the Standing Indian Trail. The trail changes every year, and I am not a purist. My plan was still to hike all the way to Maine. This wasn't yellow blazing. My hike was still my hike. By the way, a couple of other terms include aqua blazing and pink blazing. Aqua blazing is getting off the trail and taking a waterway by renting a canoe or kayak. Pink blazing is having sex on the trail.

Once across Standing Indian—a nice place, by the way, with lots of water falls—I met Rebel at a road crossing. Rebel was injured and could not hike. He had yellow blazed to the road to give trail magic to Coyote, Two Beards, Benz, Baby Ruth, Fish Head, and Mouse. He offered me a beer, which I gladly accepted. Rebel may have yellow blazed, but he was honest about it and he made the hike a little easier for others with trail magic.

Once back on the white blazes, I met another hiker named Milo. Milo was a heavyset young man. He professed being a cook and dreamed of one day opening his own deli. Milo always had a smile on his face and saw the brighter side of every situation. His hike was dedicated to veterans who needed some form of reconstructive surgeries. Milo set a strong pace, which I could keep. We hiked the second half of the day together.

We arrived at the shelter called Siler Bald. The shelter was a good distance away from the trail. The shelter was empty, but down the hill from the shelter were several tents, so Milo and I went down to the tents to chat with the hikers there. They were an interesting bunch.

This group of young men was from Louisiana, specifically the New Orleans area. They were the Crazy Cajuns. They had long hair and spoke of crawdads, the bayou, and alligator meat. I fully expected their trail name to be the Swamp Rats and for the group members to have names like Gator, or Cotton Mouth. They asked our names. "My name is Milo, and this is Hooker," answered Milo. "What are your names?" I asked. "How'd in tarnation did ya git Hooker fer a name?" they asked.

I went through the same silly story about the event that had happened eighteen years ago and how that got me my name. They had a good laugh, but then they realized that years ago I was a police officer. They stopped laughing and just sat quiet. "So, guys, what are your names?" I continued. I was shocked! Guessing the names of this crew would have been impossible. They introduced themselves as Story Time, Once Upon A Time, and Dear Diary. The gal who was with them was Dream Catcher.

Dear Diary was the most sociable one in the bunch. He and I talked for a long time. He had lost an arm in a lawn mower accident when he was four years old. That didn't slow him down, though, as it shouldn't. Dear Diary was a highly confident young man and easy to get to know. The other two sat down by a piece of paper that they had inked squares onto and played chess.

Darkness settled in as four other hikers showed up at the shelter. Milo and I went to say hello. The hikers were two guys and two gals. They, too, were young, in their early twenties. They were not couples, just hiking friends. The guys acted overprotective of the female friends. They didn't need to be; the gals were more aloof than other hikers had been. One of the gals seemed colder than all the others. Her name was PC, short for Politically Correct.

We wished them a good night and went back down the hill, wondering why they were so snobbish. They must have had a bad experience before meeting us. Milo and I were polite and we were hiking a good hike. We figured we would never see them again.

Milo's pace the next day was extra difficult for me. He may have been heavier, but he was younger and could hike fast. I did my best to keep up.

It was an enjoyable day, a good day to hike. We stopped for lunch at Cold Spring Shelter. Not much was there, so after a quick lunch away we went again.

We hiked eighteen miles that day. Eighteen miles are big miles at that point of the trail. We made it to Wesser Bald Shelter. No sooner had we arrived at Wesser Bald and taken our packs off than my left leg started to cramp. The calf muscle started knotting up. I jumped to my feet to grab my calf and stretch it out, then the hamstring muscle cramped. The hamstring was curling up into a tight ball.

Grabbing my leg and squeezing the muscles made my forearms and hands cramp up. At this point I was worried. I must have dehydrated myself, and I was paying a big price. If I didn't get the muscle cramps under control, and soon, I was going to have to be carried out of the woods. Milo went to get my pack to find the salt I kept in the top of my backpack. As he searched, my toes crossed in both feet; I yelled in pain. This was the first time I had yelled in pain in public while on the trail.

Heck, it was the only time I had yelled in pain while in public. Once, years ago, I fell and broke my left foot and right arm in the same fall. I had laughed at my dumb luck, but never yelled in pain. This was different. I yelled. Looking back, I feel like a wimp.

Milo got the salt out for me. I swallowed a large pinch of it. Salt is carried on the trail just for muscle cramps. Water would have washed the salt down and made it reach my muscles faster, but I could not move. There I was, doubled over, with my calf, hamstring, forearms, hands, and toes all cramping at the same time. I ate more salt, hoping to make my mouth water. What seemed like hours went by in seconds. Slowly, the cramps eased up.

I set my tent up, crawled in, and cramped more. A blister started to form on my toes but I could not get to it. Every time I tried to reach my foot to apply a bandage my leg muscles cramped. That was one rough night for me. Worry filled my mind again about being able to finish the trail.

The muscle cramps actually caused damage to my legs. Starting off in the morning was difficult. Milo and I decided we would stop at the

Nantahala Outdoor Center (NOC). The NOC was only five miles away, at the Nantahala River, and mostly downhill. There is an outfitter's there and I could buy hiking poles instead of using sticks from the woods. They have a hostel there, too, and we could get food and other provisions. "Today is a nero!" The sound of that made hiking easier.

The first thing Milo and I did once we got to the NOC was to stop at the store and grab a beer. Next, we went to a restaurant for a big lunch. We sat our packs down and hiked around the area; it was interesting. There were kiosks selling hiking equipment and giving out information. We sat back and started people watching. There was a strange bunch of people in the area. One couple had two pit bulls on a leash that they could barely control. The dogs dragged them up and down the sidewalks. Later, I heard one of the dogs got away and ran off into the woods.

Some hikers were soaking their feet in the river and watching kayakers float by. I joined them, and that was relaxing. Milo went to find a room or bunks in the hostel. He reserved our bunks, so we were good for the night. At the outfitters, I bought hiking poles and had my water filter repaired. Once in the hut, we unpacked and set up our sleeping areas. There was room for four people in the hut. We got a towel and washcloth with the bunk.

Cargo

ANOTHER HIKER WAS in the hut with us, Bubbles. We were talking about not wanting some other hiker to show up and be an asshole. You never know whom you'll get as a roommate. We were so hoping the fourth bunk would not be used. Then, before we left to go eat dinner, another hiker entered the hut.

This hiker carried crutches. He was overly extraverted. "Hey, is this my bunk. My name is Cargo!" We made our introductions. He had injured himself on a horse prior to getting to the trail. His calf muscle was torn, so he started the trail on crutches. Cargo was frank about his past. I pretended not to listen but was gripped by every word. His past sounded all too familiar.

Cargo went into the Army in 1980. I went into the Army in 1980. Cargo was infantry, and I was infantry. Cargo went to jump school, which is paratrooper training, and I went to jump school as well. He went on to become a Ranger and I went to Special Forces. Later, I went to language school in Presidio of Monterey, and he did, too, around the same time. We were instant friends, comrades, army buddies. We had a fourth person in the hut and he was not an asshole; his name was Cargo.

To make our friendship better we went to dinner then off to buy some beers. There was a bluegrass band playing that night. Hikers and kayakers alike gathered around to drink beer and hear the music. It was a pleasant night. I needed the rest because the next morning I was going up Sassafras Mountain. That is a three-thousand-foot climb in elevation.

Cargo stayed at the NOC the next day to hear speeches from old thru-hikers. They were giving advice and telling how to hike ultralight. I probably should have stayed as well. I could stand to learn a thing or two; my hike wasn't going so hot. As a matter of fact, I was really screwing up.

Milo and I continued hiking together. The climb up Sassafras hurt a little. Well, it hurt a lot. It wasn't long before my legs were cramping again. Each step caused another cramp. I could barely stand. Time and time again I would fall to the ground, despite the fact that I had hiking poles. I needed to stop and could no longer keep up with Milo. My hike was finished. To add to the mix, I got another blister.

Fontana Dam

AS I REACHED a road I stopped to rest. There was a jug for water off to the right. Being out of water I went to the jug with high hopes. It was empty! I was near the end of my food supply, also, but there was a phone number on the jug for a ride to a cabin. Staying indoors again would suit me just fine. My legs were getting chafed again. The bandages on the inside of my thighs needed to be changed.

I called the number but could not hear the person on the phone. The wind was blowing too fast to hear anything. When I tried to crawl inside the woods away from the wind, I lost the cell signal. I went back out to the road for a better signal and huddled inside my jacket to make the call. Successful, a ride was on its way and I was staying in a cabin.

Up early in the morning, I took another shower. One can never shower too often. Having had a hot cup of coffee in the morning was a welcome change. I didn't have any eggs for breakfast, so I ate my jerky and instant potatoes. That was all I had left. While eating breakfast, the television flashed with warnings, the weather person excitedly pointing at areas on a map. A large storm front was headed this way from the west and was coming fast. This storm was going to hit when I was in the Smoky Mountains. My gear was dry, so I packed it neatly and was ready for my ride to the post office. That day I would get a full resupply at Fontana Dam.

The lady who owned the cabin arrived on time, as previously promised. After loading my gear into the truck, we were off. The roads were windy and she was full of conversation. My mind was focused on my re-supply. There was going to be more weight in my pack, and I did not look forward to more weight, but I needed the food.

The post office at Fontana Dam is not conveniently located. The drive was much longer than I suspected. My plan to hike back to the trail from the post office was dashed. The lady offered to drive me back to the trail after I got my resupply package. Into the post office I ran. The post office is a small, one-story wooden building. It is part of a shopping mall, although small and quaint. It reminded me of the wooden buildings in Norway.

A lady behind the counter assisted me. I gave her my driver's license and she brought back a white box. This was a beautiful box. It had blue and red stripes. Sure, it was the same flat rate shipping box I had packed at home, but now it was here at Fontana Dam. That made the box beautiful. To make it seem even more beautiful, I was hungry.

Not wanting to waste any time, I grabbed my box and headed straight for the door, gripping my prized possession tightly. Quickly, I returned to the front seat of the truck and off we went, headed to the trail. The ride took me back to Fontana Dam. There was not a car in sight. The large parking lot was deserted. The park was closed; the ranger station was all locked up. But somehow, I needed to register to hike through the park.

Hoping someone would come by sooner or later so I could ask where to register, as is required in the Great Smoky Mountains, I sat down and opened my resupply. I set-aside some breakfast bars to eat on the spot. After emptying my pack and having the box's contents spread out before me, the task of repacking began. Once my pack was fully loaded, the box and other trash needed to be thrown away.

There were no large dumpsters, but the trash cans in the area were empty so I tore the box into small pieces and threw it away. As I was work-ing on destroying the box a green pickup truck pulled into the parking lot with four older men. They were all wearing the same utility-type green uniform and the truck had a park symbol on the side. These guys would know where to register for hiking in the park.

I walked up, smiled, and said, "Good morning." But the response I hoped to get was not coming. There was no greeting, no smile, and no feeling of being welcome. At first, the four guys tried to just ignore me. Look, I was the only living creature in the middle of the large open parking lot and these guys were trying to pretend they didn't see me? This wasn't going to go well.

After getting closer, I yelled, "Hey! Excuse me, but I have a question!" Then these guys actually tried to drive away. So, I yelled, "Stop!" They stopped. "What do you want?" They glared as if I were in their way. Let me interject a little here. There are people out of work today. There were people out of work that day. If these guys couldn't find the time to answer a little question and be nice, then fire them! Hire someone who will represent your park better. There was no reason for them to act the way they did.

Feeling they wanted to be anywhere but there answering my question, I made it quick. "Where can I register for hiking in the park?" The four talked among themselves. One said he didn't know, another said the park was closed, and a third said, "Who cares?" Without answering me, they drove off. *Honestly, are they that secure in their jobs, not afraid of being fired?*

While riding into the park I had seen a fenced-in area just off the road that read, "Police Only." There had to be someone there who would know where to register. I hiked back up the hill. It was a bit of a hike, especially with the added weight of a fresh resupply. I entered the "Police Only" area and instantly smelled pancakes. My mouth watered.

Sitting in what appeared to be a garage for servicing the police cars was a heavy set man watching a morning television show. I quickly introduced myself and asked where I could register. Now, this guy was helpful. He explained that on the backside of the closed park office building, where I just was, is a self-register box.

We chatted a while. He had questions about my hike and shared advice based on other hikers he had met. Then it was off to register, without any of the pancakes. The register box was packed full. There wasn't any way this box was going to be useful. What a total waste of time! I registered all the same. I also left a bit of a note expressing my displeasure with how the park was being run.

I hiked across the dam, down a road, and then into the woods. The trail went up steeply. Small flowers were starting to peak out from under the ground cover of dead leaves. Bugs were beginning to show life as well. Periodically, small flies would show up in mini swarms. The first hill was steep, a climb of about two thousand feet.

While headed up, I met a couple of hikers coming down. We sat down and chatted a bit. That was a good rest for me. They gave advice about what to expect farther up the trail. We smiled, shook hands, and hiked on in opposite directions. Then I came upon another hiker, a ridge runner. This was the first ridge runner I had met so far.

A ridge runner is a paid employee who hikes the trails and helps others by giving directions. They also clean areas that have been abused by people. They have contact with rangers and the head office. I don't think they have law enforcement powers, but they are certainly an asset to the trail.

This ridge runner was a tall gentleman dressed in all-green military fatigues. He was much bigger than me and you could tell he knew it. I think he tried to use his size to intimidate me. I don't know why, but this dude tried to stand over me and preach, "If you pack it in, you pack it out." He continued his rant about fire safety and more about picking up trash and on and on, while blocking my path.

Here I am, trying to hike up a steep hill, and this tall, oversized ridge runner is standing in my way. He stood uphill from me and prevented my passing. Having heard enough, I finally told him to, "Get the hell out of my way!" He took on a look of shock as if I had just swallowed a live mouse. As he started walking down, partially at my side, I walked past him. He had to brush me with his shoulder. He just couldn't let me go on by without incident. Being on the uphill side now, I had the advantage. He tried to order me to listen to more of his asinine rants. So I snapped out my patented smart response, "Get your ass on down the road."

He turned and asked what I said, as if I would not repeat it. Oh, I repeated it, and added that he could preach to someone else and never block my trail again. For a moment he acted as if he wanted to take some kind of action against me. That was okay by me, my patience was gone. He made another remark, wanting the last word. His having the last word meant nothing to me; I hiked on.

The Great Smoky Mountains

MY MAPS WERE old maps that I bought through EBay. They still worked, but some things had changed. For instance, the first shelter in the Smokies used to be Birch Spring Gap Shelter. Now, there was no shelter at that spot as shown on my map. I made note of the shelter being gone and continued my hike. At the peak of the ridge small white flowers covered the ground, giving the appearance of it being snow covered. The air was still warm but the wind began to grow stronger, picking up speed.

After going only nine or ten miles from Fontana Dam, I came upon a shelter, Mollies Ridge Shelter. This shelter was packed full with people on top of people inside. A large blue tarp hung over the entrance to help keep the wind and impending rain out. The surrounding woods were spotted with tents and hammocks. The area was quickly taking on the look of a refugee camp.

After a quick survey, I found a level spot to set up my tent. Oddly enough, the wind was blowing from east to west, but having seen the news that morning I knew a storm was coming and it was blowing from west to east. I set my tent up with the fly opening to the east so the wind would not blow rain into my tent if I had to get up in the night.

The other hikers had their tents set up with openings to the west or on the downwind side. I explained a strong storm was coming and the wind would be blowing the other way. No one took heed; none of the others changed their tent openings. At least I tried. My feet were blistered, my left leg kept cramping severely, and to make matters worse, I was tired and had not eaten since my resupply. This was the roughest day of hiking so far.

That night the storm hit. Thunder shook the earth, strong winds blew, limbs broke from the high treetops and fell to the ground. The rains came and pounded every tent down a few inches. The ground flowed with streams where no stream had been. Thoughts of Noah's ark came to everyone's mind. The temperature dropped as fast as the rains fell from the sky. This storm was a record breaker and we were camping in it.

Next morning came and the air was frozen, as was the ground, and the water. Ice covered the earth, but rain continued to fall. It was a freezing rain that would turn to ice as soon as it hit the ground. The ground leaves would break and crunch loudly as they were walked upon. The wind howled, blowing both high and low.

The high winds continued shaking limbs from the treetops while the low winds blew cold air into my tent, causing any built up heat to escape. I shivered inside my sleeping bag. This was going to be one difficult day, and the goal was to both get warm and stay warm. After a small breakfast, I went out to dig a hole in the ground. There was no privy or outhouse at this shelter.

Returning to my tent, I was pleased with the direction it was facing and my forethought when setting it up. The wind was blowing from west to east. My tent's fly was downwind and the rain never got in when I opened the fly. A nap after breakfast was in order. Getting my feet warm was the most difficult. The hot water bottle trick fixed that.

The hot water bottle trick is to boil water, then pour it back into the water bottle, tightening the top on securely. Then, you simply throw the bottle into the sleeping bag at your feet. This is a trick used during cold nights. I used the hot water bottle trick often. By the time I woke up, the bottle had usually made its way to my chest. I would sit up and drink the still warm but not hot water.

After a long nap, it was time to go back outside to pee. As soon as I stepped outside I thought everyone had left. Nearly every tent had been taken down and was gone. One hammock remained hanging between some trees, but it was not occupied. It hung open and was filling with water. Wanting to be helpful, I went to the shelter to find the owner of the hammock.

As soon as I passed the tarp protecting the residents in the shelter I found that no one had left the area. Those who were tenting had taken down their tents and moved into the shelter. The shelter had been designed to hold up to sixteen people. There were over thirty people in sleeping bags huddled together inside the shelter. The dirt floor had hikers sleeping on it.

A hiker claimed the hammock and quickly ran out to pour the water from it. His sleeping bag was soaked. After he returned to the shelter, the wind flipped his hammock again, allowing it to fill with rain. The hiker gave up trying to protect it.

The shelter was alive with conversation. Each hiker had a story to tell and each wanted to ask and know about the others. In time, the questions came my way. I explained some basics about myself. Then the topic of languages came up. I mentioned I spoke a few other languages. One hiker quickly asked what languages and I answered that my strongest language was Thai.

Now, here I am, huddled in an overcrowded shelter nine miles from Fontana Dam in the Great Smoky Mountains, hiding from a record-breaking storm. The word "Thai" had no more than passed my lips before I heard the guy standing beside me to my left blurt out a long explanation about himself in Thai. He explained how he had learned to speak Thai when he was in the Peace Corps. He had just come from Thailand a few days earlier. He went on to explain some of the places he had visited while in Thailand.

Of all the times and places, what were the odds two guys would be standing in a shelter, hiding from the cold rains, and be able to speak the same foreign language. We talked a bit in Thai, then the other hikers began feeling uneasy. They felt we might be talking about them; we were. Sorry, dudes!

My Thai-speaking friend was named Crop Duster. My first guess was he flew a small plane for farmers. That guess was wrong. Crop Duster explained how he got his name. He got it from, well, let's just say he is not the guy you want walking in front of you when you are going uphill! He was known for being gassy. Nice guy, though. Crop Duster was also the owner of the hammock that kept getting full of rainwater. He was a strong, fast hiker. I don't think I ever saw him again. He was always a day to five days ahead of me, according to the shelter journals.

Heavy rains kept coming down and the winds refused to relent. The temperature stayed below the freezing point. From time to time rain shared the sky with snowflakes. Everyone stayed at the shelter. I stayed in my tent. This day was a zero day. There would not be any miles hiked this day. I was in pain; my left leg still cramped, my feet still blistered, and my knees were swollen. A nurse who was hiking the AT and was staying in the shelter offered me a large handful of Motrin.

That second night at Mollies Ridge was not a good restful night. Try as I might, there was no getting comfortable. The next day would have to be better. My plan at this point was to hike only five miles a day after the weather cleared. If it were warmer, then it would most certainly be better. I lay in my tent hoping the morning would bring a better hike.

Morning came bringing high winds and cold air. The clouds seemed to be low and blowing through the trees. The hike would hopefully still prove easier than before. I filled my water bottles and had a hot breakfast of oatmeal and dehydrated apples. With a full stomach, I began my hike. My hope was to separate from as many people who were at the shelter as possible. They were okay, but I preferred to hike mostly alone. The crowd at Mollies Ridge was a large group of hikers, so I headed out early hiking alone. My knees still hurt, especially the left leg.

Both legs hurt but my left leg was extremely painful. Could it be because I shot it with a nail gun? Having a two-inch nail countersunk into my knee wasn't the best way to start my hike. However, even on the first day of the hike, my right leg had begun swelling and hurting from over use. Trying to hike was just inviting more pain. Pain would go from one spot to the next. As soon as one injury healed a new one began. Hikers with blisters change their gait and often end up with shin splints.

To explain how one leg can be favored over the other, when hiking downhill, the bad or sore leg is extended first. All the weight and effort is put on the other leg as it bends and lowers you down the hill. Do that a few hundred times a day and you will find which leg is strong and which is weak.

Keeping notes on my maps, I wrote that finishing the trail might not be possible. I may have wanted to quit. If anyone ever wants to do a long-distance hike my first advice would be to start only if both knees are healthy, and by all means stay away from nail guns. Other advice would include getting the right gear. My gear was so wrong for what I was attempting to do. I can admit that now.

So, on with the hike: that first day in the Smokies had taken me about nine to ten miles into the Great Smoky Mountain National Park. The second day was a zero—no miles hiked—because of the tremendous storm. Now, on the third day, I was rested and ready to hike. The first five miles went by well. It was noon by that time. Granted, five miles is not a long distance, but my legs needed to heal. So, I stopped at a shelter and ate lunch.

After lunch, I set out for the next shelter, Derrick Knob. The plan was to hike slow and easy. The distance was only seven miles or so. The terrain was not difficult and the trail was more of a path. Despite the easy terrain my left leg was not getting any stronger. It cramped with every step. Pain shot through my leg from my knee to my brain. The sharp, stabbing feeling followed each failed attempt to apply weight to the leg.

I made it to Derrick Knob. My mind wondered at my pitiful condition. Here I was, deep in the woods, and I could barely walk. From my calculations, I had hiked about a hundred and ninety miles. That left me with just under two thousand miles to go. Grief and despair began filling my heart, but I was not about to let self-pity take over. So, I crawled into the shelter and lay there thinking. There had to be a way to do this hike.

I wondered how others made the hike look so easy. They didn't seem to get chaffed as much. They didn't seem to get swollen knees. Some had blisters on every toe, though; and I did see a guy with shin splints so bad his legs were swollen and it looked like a bag of water was under his skin. But, my concern was how I was going to make it through to the end of the AT.

A new plan was formed. I would hike what I could and listen to my legs. When my legs hurt, I would stop hiking. That night I did not sleep. I heard every sound of every branch and leaf being tossed by the wind. Counting sheep did not help. If I lay on my back, my hamstrings cramped. When I lay on my side, my hips pressed uncomfortably into the shelter platform. Sleeping on my stomach was impossible without a pillow. I tossed and turned all night, and twice in the night I had to dig for my emergency salt pack to stop the cramps from hurting the muscles in my legs. This was not a good night. I continued to worry about being able to finish; I had find a way . . . I would find a way!

The next morning was a new day! And a new day brings a new idea. My daily hikes would be shorter. I must give my body a chance to heal. Off I headed to Siler's Bald. It was a short hike, about four miles, then lunch. During lunch I stretched. My legs were hurting, but today I would take it easy on them. Two miles more and I would stop at Double Spring Gap.

The two miles to Double Spring Gap were odd. The trail was a razor-back ridgeline. Nowhere for the entire two miles could I find a place to dig a hole to relieve myself. There wasn't a place to even pee. During those two miles a person stays exposed to the wind. "Rocks piled upon rocks" is the best description of the trail at this point. No problem, Double Spring Gap reportedly had a privy.

Double Spring Gap had only two other hikers present when I arrived, Gun Runner and Curmudgeon. Gun Runner got his name early, when he started his hike. A female hiker had stopped for lunch on the trail and they'd had a short conversation. The female hiker had packed up her gear then headed off to hike.

Gun Runner noticed the female hiker had left a gun behind. Most hikers do not carry guns. A gun is weight that isn't needed. Most of my friends and family advised me to carry a gun, but I decided against it. Seeing the gun, Gun Runner took it and ran to catch up with the female hiker. He had to run hard and fast to catch her, so, you get the picture; he ran with a gun so he is the Gun Runner. No one ever claimed hikers are smart or clever.

Gun Runner was the kind of guy who always looks as if he just got out of the shower. He was always clean. He wore a khaki-colored shirt and pants. His clothes resembled that of a boy scout. Gun Runner was clean-shaven, but most hikers stop shaving on day one, present company included. I heard Gun Runner had to leave the trail, days later, after a tornado hit his father's house.

Double Spring Gap Shelter filled up fast. Hikers started arriving in small groups. My tent was set up just to the front of the shelter and closer to the trail. The water source was two springs. Bet you couldn't guess that from the name of the shelter. One spring was better than the other; that was because one spring was next to the privy. It was good to have a privy, but even better to have a spring away from the privy.

The temperature dropped that night. Despite the cold air and high winds I slept pretty well. The ground where I set up my tent was soft, and the tent site was in a ravine that shielded me from the wind. So, fresh spring water, a wind barrier, the hot water bottle trick, a privy, and soft ground were all that I needed for a good night's sleep.

Clingman's Dome

I WOKE UP refreshed and ready to go. My plan was to hike only five miles a day for the next week. That should give my legs all the rest they needed, and that should help rejuvenate my mind and body for the rest of the hike. To make things even better, today's hike was taking me to the top of Clingman's Dome, the highest point on the Appalachian Trail. With an optimistic outlook, I hiked up the trail toward Clingman's Dome.

Upon leaving Double Spring Gap, I hiked with a section hiker. He was knowledgeable about the area and the trees. His name was Dave. Dave worked a seasonal job with the Park Service. His current job was treating evergreens dying from some kind of infestation. Dave knew this area of the trail well. He explained how he got his job, hiked, and also explained how he was getting back home from his section hike.

The first mile was an uneventful and pleasurable hike. A light breeze blew through the woods. The sun rose in the east and lit the sky brilliantly. That mile went by quicker than I expected. We took a short break and had a quick snack, then we were off again.

The trail turned into more climbs and a rougher terrain. Rocks on the trail made hiking more difficult. The hill became steeper as we headed up to Clingman's Dome. Our steps grew shorter as the difficulty of the hike increased. The wind went from a light breeze to a tempest. Clouds floated along the ground as ghosts the size of elephants. They passed through the trees without resistance.

The clouds brought higher humidity and a rapid temperature drop. The sun had disappeared. From time to time a cloud would hit us with ice hidden inside. As the clouds blew faster, ice hit us harder. Soon, visibility shrank to mere feet. Conversation with Dave became nearly impossible. The wind shrieking through the trees was deafening.

Oddly, my right ear became sore, not just from the noise but from being frozen by the wind! We scampered across rocks, and at times hid behind trees to catch a breath before returning to the onslaught of the clouds. Sheets of ice crashed down that could have destroyed anyone or anything in their path. The limbs of the trees helped break the falling ice, but when we were exposed to the open sky we were easy prey to the weather.

Being in higher elevations made hiking in the clouds more likely. This had been the case for most of the trail to this point. Our visibility became even less than a few feet. At one point we stopped, because the trail had disappeared completely. I reached out one hand and it disappeared into the fog. Visibility was zero. We paused for a moment to let the thick cloud blow by. We pushed on through the fog and ice that became compounded by heavy rain. Climbing Clingman's Dome was harder than I had expected it to be.

We reach a parking lot that had a building at one end. There were a couple of vehicles parked, but too few. Somehow, we had missed the trail that went to the top of Clingman's Dome. The path we had followed took us to the park station. A paved path went up to the top of Clingman's Dome and back to the trail. Dave had had enough misery for one day and was going to try to find a ride back to a town. I hiked up the paved path to find the Appalachian Trail and the top of Clingman's Dome.

My first thought was, "A paved path should be an easy walk." But weather conditions had changed the path. The cold winds and ice storm pounding all around put me in a dangerous place. The wind nearly blew me over as I attempted each step. The clouds were thick and I could see only ten feet away. My body shivered from the cold. I thought about stopping and wrapping up in my tent, but gave that up for fear of freezing to death.

That fear brought a new worry: hyperthermia! My body shivered uncontrollably, even though I was walking and carrying a pack. The physical exertion of hiking uphill should have been enough to keep me warm, but it wasn't. My teeth chattered. My mind worked, considering every option. Hide in the woods? Set up my tent on this path? Wrap my sleeping bag around me? Turn around and hitchhike out of here? Keep going higher to the top of this mountain? Just keep moving forward? I shivered and shook. My eyes watered from the cold, icy rain. My hands were swollen from the cold. If my knees hurt, I didn't know it. My head hurt from the cold. This was the first time I had ever had an ice cream headache without the pleasure of eating ice cream.

I decided to keep moving. Somewhere, somehow, this wind would stop. I had to keep moving. The winds were blowing sixty miles an hour and the gusts were higher than that. Ice cut into my skin, threatening to shred me apart. I hoped other hikers were doing better than I was at this point. Higher up I hiked, until I reached the top.

On the top of Clingman's Dome was a lookout tower. The way up to the tower is a giant ramp that winds round and round to the top. A ridge runner and four other hikers stood at the foot of the ramp. It was PC and her three friends; we had met before. The clouds and winds had slowed, but not much. The ridge runner agreed to stand by our packs as we ran to the top of the tower for a quick picture then back down.

We took our pictures. The batteries in my camera had frozen and there was enough charge for only one picture. The winds began blowing harder. We tried to run back down to our waiting packs. The ridge runner was talking to rangers on the radio. The rangers were ordering everyone to head for shelter or get out of the woods. The park was closing. The weather was bad now, but it was going to get much worse. The current conditions were winds of sixty miles an hour with gusts. The temperature was forty degrees. Rain, sleet, and ice were falling.

I threw my pack on and headed for the trail. Once I crossed to the downwind side of the mountain the wind stopped blowing; or, at least, the wind was blocked by the mountain. Being out of the wind was a huge relief. I could hike faster and I stopped shivering. Then, I started feeling dizzy. *Were my eyes deceiving me?* The feeling was like being raised up a few feet and floating in the air; that was followed by a sinking feeling of falling back to the ground. I shook my head and walked on.

After walking a few feet, I had to stop and look back up the trail. Something just wasn't right. That feeling of rising up was too real. I thought the cold air was freezing my brain so much I was developing vertigo. As I looked back up the trail, the winds blew hard through the treetops. A tree bowed in the wind. As the tree bowed it roots were separated from the earth and its root ball lifted from the ground. The root ball was about twenty feet across and the trail had gone directly over it. The part of the trail that was on the root ball rose up as the wind blew the tree over. The rising feeling I felt was me standing on the root ball as the tree was being blown down.

That was a relief; I was not losing my mind. Mother Nature had played a trick on me. What a ride! Happy that I didn't get tossed away in the wind by the tree, I hiked on. I decided to hike farther than previously planned. The first plan was to go as far as Mount Collins Shelter, which was about six miles. But the impending storm changed all that. I decided to go four and a half miles more to Newfound Gap. There, I could hitchhike into town.

Most of the trail to Newfound Gap was shielded from the wind by being on the downwind side of the mountain. I seemed to gain strength as I hiked. The idea of a warm bed certainly gave me renewed vigor. The last few feet in the woods were protected from the high winds, but once I stepped onto the road at Newfound Gap the wind tore through every stitch of my clothing. The rain and ice assaulted me again. This was not a good place to be.

Gatlinburg

THREE OTHER HIKERS were huddled near a sign depicting Newfound Gap's historically important sites. We talked and they explained that a ride would be coming there in a couple of hours. A couple of hours felt like an eternity; that was too long to be out in this weather. I went to the road to try my luck at hitchhiking.

To hitch a ride from Newfound Gap to Gatlinburg is supposedly the easiest hitchhike on the trail. That was promising. I stuck out my thumb as cars and trucks drove by. Then I went to the edge of the roadside parking lot to hitchhike there. That would make it easier for someone to offer me a ride.

A newer white SUV came from the parking lot. I smiled, stuck out my thumb, and hoped for the best. A young man drove the vehicle. He appeared to be in his thirties. He was well dressed and clean-cut. A beautiful lady in her mid-thirties sat in the passenger seat. She was charming and dressed in a classy fashion. They appeared to be well-to-do.

I made eye contact with the lady. She smiled a big smile at me as I smiled back with my thumb extended. My hopes for a ride increased as she raised her hand and waved slowly. This was it; I was going to get a ride out of the high winds, heavy rain, and ice. They were going to save me. Just as I was certain of getting a ride, the lady rotated her waving hand so that the back of her hand was to me. She then stopped waving and dropped all fingers but the middle one. She flipped me off!

The desire to flip her back was strong, but I resisted. If anyone saw me flipping her off or acting irrational it would ruin any chance for a ride. They drove away and left me there. Two guys in a small red car drove by quickly; the driver stuck his finger out at me as well. I could not believe it! I was flipped off twice in one minute.

Other cars and trucks drove by, but no one even slowed down. Perhaps the wet weather had something to do with their reluctance in giving me a ride. About five minutes lapsed when another car came up from the parking lot. A couple was in the front, with the guy driving and a lady passenger. In the backseat was another couple. The backseat couple laughed at me as they flipped me off. Now, this was getting downright silly.

I could not figure out why these people felt the need to flip me off. I was wet and cold and tired. Sure, I hadn't shaved in a while, and my clothes needed washing, but I was a thru-hiker. There was no reason for their actions. I made every effort to look clean and be polite.

Then, a small green pickup truck came by. The truck stopped right in front of me. The driver was looking for oncoming traffic so he could get onto the road from the parking lot. What appeared to be his teenage son, who sat in the passenger seat, looked at me then waved with the one-finger salute. I was pissed. Enough was enough. As the truck drove on I memorized the license number. The last three were 222. I won't give the rest of the plate number but I remember it.

My plan, once in town, was to look for the truck and pound the driver into the ground. He could then ask his son why he got his ass handed to him. I never did find the truck, but I looked. Being flipped off four times in less than ten minutes was enough for me to stop hitchhiking. I went back to the other hikers and waited for a ride.

A green SUV pulled up and the driver asked if he could give us a ride down to Gatlinburg. We were all delighted. That was absolutely wonderful. The driver was the ridge runner whom I had met standing at the base of the lookout at Clingman's Dome. He was awesome!

We arrived at Gatlinburg from the highest point on the AT, Clingmans Dome, six thousand two hundred feet above sea level. The wind was gusting at sixty miles per hour, the temperature was forty degrees, sheets of ice were falling from the skies, the threat of hypothermia was likely, and the rangers were warning all hikers to seek shelter because it was getting worse. So, we came into town. In the past days I sort of kept pushing distances too far. The need to slow down was evident. I had promised myself to take it a little easier and the rain would help me keep that promise.

There are several all-you-can-eat places in Gatlinburg. Those were my favorite places to eat. After checking in at the Grand Prix Hotel, I weighed myself. The scales showed I had lost twelve pounds already. That sounded like a high amount of weight to lose, but after talking with other hikers it was average.

I bought a six-pack of beer and a bucket of chicken for dinner. The next morning I found the perfect place for breakfast. The restaurant had an all-you-can-eat deal for breakfast. I thought for certain they were going to kick me out. Most places will ask you to leave after your seventh plate of food. They let me stay. They were awesome.

It was so comfortable in Gatlinburg that I had to take a zero. The hotel was full of hikers coming in from the bad weather and some hikers headed out in the bad weather. They were going to have it rough. Looking up into the hills I could see the dark clouds engulfing the trail with rain and ice.

I did some extra shopping. There were only a couple outfitters. One was rather small but fairly priced and stocked for hikers. I bought a couple items there. The other outfitter was quite large. They had gear for kayaking, fishing, climbing, and a small amount of gear for hiking. While there, another hiker, Bismarck, gave a tube of lip balm to the gal behind the counter. He carried it from the Nantahala Outdoor Center, NOC, in Wesser, North Carolina. If you bring it to this outfitter they give you free trail bars.

Seeing the box of free trail bars and not having a tube of balm I chose to "Yogi" a trail bar. Yogi-ing is the art developed by the great Yogi Bear. To Yogi, the hiker goes to someone who has food and stares pitifully, or compliments the food, or tries any technique that gets you some of their food. I commented how cool it was that the outfitter created such a great gimmick. That didn't work. I gave my saddest look. Strike two! "Hey, it would be so cool to get a trail bar from someone as hot as you!" I told the girl behind the counter. Now that was cheesy, but it worked. I got two trail bars. Yogi Bear would be proud!

I finished my zero with beer, chicken, and Motrin. The second morning I went back to the all-you-can-eat for breakfast. They seemed happy about my return. I had an excellent breakfast, again. I ate and ate. When I got back to the hotel to check out, I weighed myself again. Surprised, I had gained six of my twelve pounds back.

I had adjusted my food supply. Some foods are better than others for hiking. Peanut butter gives needed proteins and adds a good kick in calories. Spam is an excellent source of fats. Fats are needed more than one may think. Hydration packets are a must, as they keep muscles from cramping so badly. A hydration packet is something I made before I left home. It was easy. Six teaspoons of sugar are added to a half-teaspoon of sea salt. Six teaspoons of powdered Gatorade or other sports drink is mixed with the sugar and salt mixture. Then, you seal it in a waterproof packet. When needed, just add the full packet to one liter of water.

Several people were headed back to the trail. Most of the shuttles were full. I decided to try my luck at hitchhiking again. I was a glutton for punishment. Getting flipped off four times in ten minutes wasn't enough. So, off I went, headed out of town with my backpack on and my thumb out.

It wasn't long before I was out of town. An SUV stopped. Holy Crap! Did they stop for me? Was hitching going to be easy this time? I ran to the SUV. I hoped they knew where the trail was. When I got to the SUV I was asked if I was a thru-hiker. I said yes, and was settled in the SUV to be taken to the trail.

The driver said he was a hiker as well. His trail name was Shenanigans. His father sat in the front passenger seat, and Shenanigan's fiancé, Fancy Pants, sat in the back to my left. They asked my name and I had to explain how I got the name Hooker. Here I was, telling that same stupid story again.

Happy to be getting a ride, I continued entertaining them by telling them my trail stories. I told them about the other names suggested for me. Fancy Pants recoiled when I told them about "Panty Sniffer." Again, it wasn't me who pretended to be doing that! I was being nice. Poor Fancy

Pants looked repulsed. She made herself as small and as far away from me as possible. Even after the explanation, she looked as if she wished I were gone.

Knowing that any silence at this point would be more uncomfortable, I continued telling them my stories. Hearing the two up front laugh set me at ease. Fancy Pants didn't laugh anymore. She would look, smile, then quickly look away. I can't blame her! I looked a mess, they didn't know me from a hill of beans, and she was stuck in the backseat with me.

I arrived at the trail at Newfound Gap and thanked Shenanigans for the ride. He was a nice chap. His dad looked like an older Paul Newman. I suggested the trail name for him to be Cool Hand Luke. We parted ways, and I was back on the trail again. My foot had a blister, but no big deal. I had Motrin and was taking it. My knees were sore but the Motrin helped.

There weren't many scenes to view because low clouds hid them. The several items I got rid of from my backpack didn't seem to lighten the load. Of course, that could have been all the water weight from the rain. I was happy, healthy, and feeling good about completing my hike. All in all I had no complaints, just a few challenges. Physically, I had started to change . . . stronger legs, sore back, and my feet were starting to ache.

Still plugging away, I had passed the point where I had less than two thousand miles to go. The pace seemed slow to me, but I decided to give it a couple weeks then try to pick it up. For now I was pushing on through the second half of the Great Smoky Mountains.

Razorback Ridges

THE SECOND HALF of the Smoky's was much different from the first half. The trees and terrain were more interesting to see. Ice was still on the ground as I climbed higher and higher. The trail followed the border of Tennessee and North Carolina. Lunchtime came and I sat down in Tennessee and looked over into North Carolina eating my lunch. It was a good lunch: Fruit Loops and Spam. I took a picture of lunch because it was that good.

Lunch went down quickly, and it was back to hiking. Soon, I came upon a short, stocky guy smoking a cigar and wearing an oversized pack. He wore blue jeans, which are not recommended by hikers. As a matter of fact, he was the only person I ever saw wearing blue jeans on the trail. He had every earmark of a section or day hiker.

He said his name was James. When asked, James said he was a thru-hiker. I was shocked. How on earth could he get this far with a pack that heavy, smoking a cigar on the trail, and wearing blue jeans? This didn't make sense to me. James then said he started hiking at Newfound Gap. Well, that was only a couple miles back. I had gone over one hundred and eighty miles.

"James, the trail starts in Georgia!" I offered. He responded with his logic, "Well, yes, but I figured I would start here." "Umm, okay." I was stumped by his casual answer. He was a thru-hiker, but had skipped Georgia. He had skipped an entire state. He tried to keep up with me but couldn't.

I hiked on, hoping he would go back and prepare better for his goal. At least he could ask someone about hiking. Soon, I found the trail had led me to some razorback ridges. These ridges were sharp. I wanted to test the steepness on each side so I chose a scientific way to measure just how steep they were. The trail was on the border of North Carolina and Tennessee. I turned to the left facing Tennessee and drew a formable loogie, or spitball. With an extraordinary force, I launched the said specimen into the air. Zeus would have been proud, as it probably looked like Thor throwing his hammer.

As the spitball flew into the air I dubbed it "Thunderbird One." It flew far into the air and landed well into Tennessee, hitting the ground with a thunderous smack. Not that I heard it, but if I were close, I bet it would have been loud. Anyway, I gave it a SWAG. SWAG is a technical term for Scientific Wild Ass Guess. The SWAG was about five hundred feet down into Tennessee.

Continuing the experiment, I created a second specimen, "Thunderbird Two." I then faced North Carolina to the right and launched "Thunderbird Two" with what could be described as the same force used by Mr Winter in the claymation of Rudolph The Red Nosed Reindeer. "Thunderbird Two away!" I called out.

The estimated flight of Thunderbird Two was four hundred feet into Tennessee. Yes that's right, Tennessee, not North Carolina. There was a strong wind blowing from right to left. But, hey, I had the presence of mind to say a loud, "Hello" as Thunderbird Two flew back, only inches from my nose and into Tennessee.

The experiment was truly an unqualified success. NASA would have been proud. I proved that spit does not have the proper aerodynamics needed to fly in winds blowing from right to left. The experiment ended without injury, despite the fact I was not wearing goggles and Thunderbird Two could have put an eye out. And my hike went on.

Pecks Corner Shelter was way off the trail; the hike downhill to the shelter seemed to last forever. It was not surprising that the shelter was full. The weather had caused a traffic jam of hikers clumped together. After setting up my tent, I felt great. My legs didn't cramp and my knees were not swollen. I did take Motrin and drink a hydration packet, just to be safe. This was going to work.

That evening, James showed up at the shelter. He was grossly unprepared. He was carrying two hardback books. One book was *A Walk In The Woods* by Bill Bryson and the other was *It* by Steven King. This was weight no thru-hiker would willingly carry. Heck, we cut our shoelaces down to save weight.

James wasn't prepared to camp out, either, so other hikers squeezed him into the already overcrowded shelter. He hung his pack up off the ground. Apparently, he didn't have a sleeping bag; he instead used blankets or a poncho liner. Neither would have been sufficient this cold night.

In the morning the shelter was all astir. Hikers who were normally quiet sorts were swearing. Others were obviously stomping mad. They'd had a bad night. I asked if someone had snored loudly. They said that didn't matter. An alarm clock had gone off in someone's pack around two in the morning and kept going off every hour. They were pissed!

James finally admitted it was his alarm clock; this guy was set on by the wolves. They were chewing him up for breakfast. He earned that ass chewing. While defending his actions he kept exclaiming he knew everything there was to know about hiking the Appalachian Trail. He knew everything because he had read Bill Bryson's book three times. "Dude, Bill Bryson didn't make it! He rented a car!" was yelled in unison by the thru-hikers.

James decided it would be best if he turned around and went back. He was spent. His legs were not ready. His pack was way too heavy. The other hikers gave good, solid advice on how to better prepare and sent him back with the hopes of trying again. They also gave him emphatic instructions: if you are a thru-hiker, you can't just skip the state of Georgia.

Steam and Moonshine

THE MORNING WAS cold. A female hiker, Moxie, hiked with me. We talked and got to know each other a little better. She was an attorney from California taking time away from work hoping to complete the trail. Moxie had met a guy on the trail. That happens often. She also had a friend who was a nurse. The nurse was awesome! She was the one who gave me the Motrin! My legs thank her.

Moxie was a fast hiker, so I was soon left behind. I was left behind until the next shelter, anyway. By the time I arrived at Tricorner Knob Shelter, Moxie and her two friends were already there and halfway through their lunch. The distance between Pecks Corner where we started and Tricorner where we had lunch is only five and one-half miles.

Only five miles had passed and lunchtime had arrived; that was super slow. But I had been hiking in pain and did not want to make matters worse, so I was slowing down and enjoying my hike. It was lunchtime, and the sun was out in full force. The heat felt outstanding, refreshing my sore body.

I sat on an embankment just outside the shelter. There didn't seem to be too many options for finding a flat piece of land. As I sat down I rather enjoyed the soft plush moss under my butt. The moss had soaked in the heat from the sun. It was warm and felt like a heating pad. I lay down to get my sweaty back on the ground away from the wind.

After a minute on my back, the moss support began shrinking away.

Without noticing, I sank lower into the ground. The moss had supported me above water, which was flowing over a rock. Now, cold water started flowing down my back, filling my shirt, and down my pants. The cold, icy water ran across my backside and down both legs. My body shivered uncontrollably.

I sat up. It was too late to stop from getting wet, so I stayed there and ate my lunch. More Spam! The sun felt so warm compared to the water, which was so cold. Lunch went down quickly, as did the rest of my drinking water, so I went looking for more water.

Not far from the shelter were two large steel boxes painted brown. These boxes are for forest workers to keep their tools locked away. As I walked past a box I touched it. The sun had made it hot. That gave me an idea.

My pants and shirt were soaked in the back. So, I sat on one of the boxes as other hikers watched curiously. Steam rolled up from both sides of my hips as the wet pants sizzled upon the hot box. I was ironing my pants while wearing them! It felt awesome! Not wanting to burn my hair, I put a cloth under my head as I lay back. The heated box caused so much steam it was difficult to get a full breath of air.

The sizzling sound of the shirt being ironed was loud enough to be heard from the shelter. My eyes closed as the heat penetrated my body. All my chills and every cold part of my body were being soothed by the steam. The heat relaxed my legs, back, and mind. The sun kept the rest of me warm. Time stopped. All sounds disappeared. Nothing mattered. The miles planned for the rest of the day had vanished. This was where I wanted to be. It felt great having my own personal sauna.

But then a cloud rolled in and stole the sun away from my exposed body. The metal box had lost its heat as well. Time had slipped away. It seemed to be much later than when I sat down. I must have fallen asleep. Go figure, me taking a nap. Moxie and the others had hiked on. I was left alone.

There was a small flat area near a steep ravine just in front of the shelter. It looked like a freshly dug grave and had stones outlining the plot. By the size of the area and from the looks of it by the arrangement of the stones, it was possible this was a grave for a horse. Well, the horse wouldn't mind, I thought. So I set my tent on it.

Hey, this was a flat spot—the only flat spot. After setting up my tent I felt tired again, so I crawled in and took another nap. Now, this was living! I needed that second nap. Later, I was awakened by a hiker asking, "Is the shelter full?" Staying in a tent is not permitted unless the shelter is full. I responded, "If you are a ranger, then yes, it is full. But if you are a hiker, there is lots of room."

Behind him were other hikers, and the shelter soon filled up. The area was crawling with more hikers than it was designed to hold. Hammocks, tents, and cowboy campers littered the area. Each new hiker cursed the overcrowded area and was jealous of my spot.

After a warm dinner, several of us stood around a small fire, trading stories of our great adventures. Then, as if from heaven, a hiker walked up to our group and interrupted us. "Hey, can you guys do me a favor?" My thoughts were that he was going to need food, or someone to get him water. I was ready to volunteer. Many of us were ready to volunteer. We said sure, and asked what he needed.

He reached into his pack and withdrew a Mason jar. The jar was full. He explained he had brought moonshine for a friend to try. He needed to lose some of the weight he was carrying and needed us to drink all but an inch-worth from the bottom. I smiled. This guy was my new best friend. His name was Thigh Master.

The first hiker took the jar and sipped from it. "Wow, that's strong," he rasped, handing the jar to the next hiker. The young man took it and with a great amount of apprehension took a mouthful and swallowed. He tried to talk but couldn't. Bent at the waist, he handed the jar to his left where I stood. Smiling, and remembering that Thigh Master needed the moonshine taken to a lower level, I raised the jar. It was my duty to help a friend and fellow hiker. I did my best.

"Damn, Hooker!" the other hikers yelled, shocked at the four gulps I had taken from the jar. I blushed, not from embarrassment but from the alcohol. As the next hikers each took sips I watched with thirsty eyes, hoping the jar would come back again. My stomach felt warm, comfortably warm. Sip after sip was taken from the jar until it was returned to Thigh Master. Each hiker again exclaimed shock at the amount of moonshine I had thrown down.

Thigh Master held the jar up high. He smiled and extended his arm, holding the jar out toward me. "Dude, did you not see how much I drank the first time?" I asked. "Yeah, but I need to get rid of all but this much," he said as he showed the inch level at the bottom. I smiled. That meant there were at least six more good-sized gulps to go.

Taking the jar, I proudly explained, "I can do that." But before drinking the final gulps, I offered to share. To my delight, there were no takers. I drank carefully, not to drink more than what Thigh Master wanted left. The moonshine warmed my stomach more and more. Then, it started warming my mind. Even my fingernails started feeling both warm and numb.

After finishing the sixth gulp, I return the jar, with its diminished contents, to Thigh Master. He held the jar high again, smiled brightly, and thanked us all for our help. It was the least I could do for a new friend. That night I slept better than any night on the trail to date. I was finally warm. Others complained of high winds and freezing temps. Not me! I was warm inside and out. Best sleep ever.

The Routine

AT THIS POINT along the trail, or long before, hikers have fallen into a daily routine. Routines help get hikers where they need to be without hurting themselves and without losing gear. My mornings would start by waking inside my tent. My feet were usually cold—too cold. While still in the tent I would sit up and drink a half bottle of water. Then, I would reach for my food.

After sorting my food to inventory what is left, I would carefully choose what to eat for breakfast. A flour tortilla with a coating of chunky peanut butter washed down with sips of water would then be followed by a handful of jerky. Before getting out of my sleeping bag, I would grab a few small candy bars. After breakfast, I packed my gear and got dressed.

Getting dressed and packing my backpack inside the tent was a job for a contortionist. I then would pack all the debris from breakfast away in a Ziploc bag. All the waste would get set-aside, then I would pack it last in case I found a trash can and could lighten my load. Next, I would roll up the sleeping bag and stuff it in a small cinch bag, then stuff it into the backpack.

Small items were collected and stowed away, items such as my glasses, a lighter, the flash light/phone charger combo, duct tape, Body Glide, Motrin, and my phone. The map for the day's hike was set outside the tent under the vestibule. Outside the sleeping bag I was usually freezing cold, and before getting dressed I had to prepare for the day. This ritual was not pretty! I would start with my feet. I had to decide between duct tape or Body Glide to put on my toes. If a blister had formed, then duct tape won. My knees came next. A quick massage with Icy Hot indicated how much pain to expect during the day.

When my knees were painful, I would grab a Motrin or two, depending on the severity of pain and the difficulty of the trail ahead. Body Glide worked well on the upper thigh region. It helped prevent chaffing. I would then check my back for blisters caused by the pack and apply Body Glide as needed.

I then grabbed my toothbrush and put a bit of salt on it. After cleaning my teeth, I would go ahead and wash it down with a swig of water. The salt would help prevent muscle cramps! Then, I'd search for ticks. A search for ticks was made before bed and after I got up. All wounds, bites, and scratches were then cleaned with an alcohol pad and treated as needed.

I would lie down to put on my shorts or pants that I wore the day before. They were usually still damp with sweat. The shirt, whether it was a button-up type or a t-shirt, would smell of body odor. It was still wet from the previous day's hike as well. My body would shake uncontrollably after donning the cold, wet shirt. Needed body heat was quickly lost.

Putting socks on was quite a job. The socks stiffened up during the night. Old sweat and whatever else got into them caused a stink. Because the socks could stand up by themselves, I would rub them together to loosen them up, then flip and fling them around to shake out all the debris. Having polluted the air with sock dust, I would put the socks on. Ready at last, I would grab my hat and put it on. Why was I wearing it? The hat was colder than the air and also still wet from sweat. Fully dressed, I would then get out of the tent.

Putting shoes on in the morning hurt. During the night, my feet would swell and the shoes would shrink; whatever causes socks to stiffen also stiffens shoes. I would open the shoes wide and check for spiders—always check for spiders! With shoes on, it was time to stand up. Then, it was off to the woods, or if lucky, a privy. Before leaving, I would grab the plastic sealable bag that held "TP" and hand wipes.

The walk to the privy was strange to behold. My body was humped over and I walked stiff-legged. This caused a "wobble." The walk is called a "hiker's wobble." Hikers can walk just fine if they have a backpack on and are "making miles." Take their packs off and they look like people walking on eggshells.

After the privy visit, it was time to resupply water. I would grab my water filter and bottles then head to the water source. Oftentimes, if the source was a spring, I would trust it without filtering; but I always filtered water from a stream. Well, that was if my filter would work. You never knew what was going on upstream; some animal could be having a dump in the water.

Returning with water I would set the bottles aside. Next, tent pegs would be pulled and placed in a small bag. Then, I took the sleeping pad out of the tent and put it on the ground. I grabbed the maps and put them in a pocket. Finally, I would take the tent down. I would release the fly and shake it out. I shook the fly, the tent cover, to remove all the bugs and condensation. Water from condensation builds up on the inside of the fly. After shaking it thoroughly, I would roll and stuff it in its bag.

The final parts of the tent were the mosquito netting and poles. Before removing the poles, it was always a good idea to open the door as wide as possible, then pick up the tent and shake out all debris, dirt, and leaves. I would check the tent for bugs, such as ticks and mosquitoes, then shake them out as well. Popping off the poles, I would fold and roll the tent and poles together then stuff them in a bag. I then rolled my sleeping pad into a tight roll and wrapped a bungee around it.

After all items were placed in their proper position in my pack or in my pockets, a final inventory was completed. Finally, a search for anything left behind was done. I would then check the campsite to ensure that it showed little sign of anyone being there. Thru-hikers leave the smallest impact on the environment. Well, good hikers do, anyway. Before heading off, I would look at the map and mentally prepare for the day.

Finishing the Smokies

MORNING HAD COME. I was packed and had many miles to make on the day's hike. There was no time to waste. I was headed out on a mission. Miles were going to fly by my feet this day. I was going to attempt to get the heck out of The Great Smoky Mountains. Eight miles later I stopped for lunch. My buddy Milo was hiking with me. He had enjoyed the moonshine the night before as well. After lunch, he hiked on ahead of me.

Still hiking alone, I had stopped and was getting a drink of water. While standing on the trail I enjoyed the view of the woods. My back was at the uphill side of the trail. To my surprise, a little bird had her nest beside the trail. It just happened to be directly behind me. The bird flew out of her nest between my legs chirping loudly. That startled me so much that I flapped my arms wildly and attempted to fly! I must have jumped three feet in the air. After a loud, high-pitched scream, I landed back on my feet and ran away. Bravely!

Lucky for me, Milo wasn't hiking with me then or he would have laughed at me. That little bird scared the crap out of me. After lunch, we were off to Davenport Gap. This was the last shelter in the Smokies. This was also the last fenced shelter. Get this: the park service thought it was a good idea to put chain-link fencing in front of the shelters. This was to keep bears out of the shelters as the hikers slept.

That sounded like a good idea. The fence covered the front from ground to roof. There was a gate that could be tricky to open and close. What the rangers didn't count on were stupid people. Now, I am not being mean; it is the truth. There were people who took advantage of the fence as a way to "safely" feed the bears. You got it! They stood inside this caged shelter and fed the bears though the fence. The bears would then camp out in front of the shelter, trapping the stupid people who were now out of food!

The scene plays out this way: a hiker feeds the bears, the bears stay, the bears get hungry and want more, the bears get mad, the hiker gave his food to the bears earlier, the hiker has no more food, the bear wants more food and the hiker wants food, too, and the hiker can't escape. Bad hiker! I guess the park service didn't really think that idea through. The rangers took all the other cages down in the park. Davenport Gap Shelter is the last caged shelter and the bears know it.

Later that night a hiker came running in needing help. He was suffering from severe leg cramps. His name was the Cape Crusader. I gave him one of my homemade rehydration packets. They work great. They are as good as a fresh IV. They really do work, and are good for hangovers, too. The Cape Crusader drank the mixture and was off in a flash.

On another note, I heard that another hiker later came through during his attempt to thru-hike. He had a medical problem and died at Davenport Gap. He would be the first hiker of 2011 to die on the Appalachian Trail, but not the last. I heard many good things about him.

Hot Springs

IF THERE IS one thing I had learned by this time, it was that I enjoyed hiking in the mornings. I love getting up early. So, morning at Davenport Gap came and I was up at 4 a.m. I had a quick, cold breakfast, packed all my gear, and off I went. The moon was bright. Staying on the trail was easy. Critters scurried about on the forest floor; some sounded quite large. I figured they were more afraid of me than I was of them.

Before daylight, I reached a road. The trail was not well marked and finding where it crossed the road was difficult. Clouds rolled in, hiding the moonlight. There were flashing moments when it was bright out, clear as day. That was when lightning crossed the sky. A storm loomed just beyond the last ridge. It was catching up to me. I was stuck until I could find the trail again. Large rocks were arranged along one side of the road. I sat on one and called home.

While talking to Deb, light pierced the storm clouds and revealed the trail. It was a stair climb uphill. I was back on the trail again! Later, I stopped for lunch at Groundhog Creek Shelter. Milo caught up to me there and passed me. The rest of the day was a steady uphill climb. The trail followed a fifteen-hundred-foot elevation increase in seven miles.

I reached a large, open area just as another storm cloud rolled in. The open area was a "bald" named Max Patch. I had been hiking alone for some time and rather enjoyed the experience. While on Max Patch, I set up my camera and took a few photos.

Just beyond Max Patch, and as soon as I reentered the woods, campsites were all around. I thought about hiking on, but the area was too inviting. The storm seemed to be stirring up something fierce. So, I set up camp. This was my first night camping solo, so I  had to take photos of the event. Sleeping alone—I love it.

It was a good night's rest on Max Patch. I slept soundly. My morning started long before daybreak again. Breakfast consisted of a hot bag of oats and warm water. I packed up, but really wanted to stay. After checking my map, my goal was to make it to Hot Springs, North Carolina. This was to be a twenty-mile day, but at the end of it would be a warm, soft bed, hot food, and cold beer.

Apple trees were covered with white blossoms and the aroma made hiking quickly through the area impossible. I stopped again and again to breath the fresh, sweet smelling air. Streams flowed with fresh water from the storms the night before. Bees buzzed in the apple blossoms. The trail was slippery, but long before dark I was in Hot Springs. The trail went straight through the middle of town.

There is a coin laundry in town with a "hiker box" inside. A hiker box is a container in which hikers put food and gear they no long want or need. Other hikers scrounge through the box and take what they need from it. It is a good system. My search through the box didn't offer much. I took a pack of cheese and crackers to eat while waiting for my laundry to dry.

Also in town is a Dollar Store, the best resupply store on the trail! Hot Springs is a hiker's paradise, boasting restaurants, pubs, and hotels. I arrived on a Thursday evening and immediately secured a hotel room. Places like this fill up quickly. The post office was still open and had a resupply package for me from home.

My plan for Friday was to take a zero. It had been a while since I had e-mailed home about my hike, so I figured Friday was a good day to go to the library and send an e-mail to family and friends. Friday was a good day . . . too good. It was actually "Good Friday," and the library was closed. Just my luck!

During breakfast, I met Shenanigans again. I sat with him, Chicago, and Alien for a quick bite. Shenanigans was the guy who gave me a ride back to the trail from Gatlinburg. I had met Alien at a shelter. He was a large Irishman, actually from Ireland. I guess he was about six foot three and probably weighed in at over two hundred fifty pounds. Once, when I was walking out of a shelter, he was walking in and mowed me down like a Mack truck hitting a deer. To make matters worse, he was eating and talking and accidently spit food on me. I was pissed and wanted to clobber him, but that was then; I got over it. They were working out a slack pack deal and would end up miles ahead of me; I would never see them again.

I wandered around town, shopping for gear, doing laundry, and drinking beers. Milo found me and said Cargo was in town. That was great news. We could hit the pubs that night and have a great time. I was delighted to see Cargo. Besides, I owed the guy a beer!

That night, we hit a pub early. Walking to the pub we met other hikers. One guy introduced himself as Comfortably Numb. He had thru-hiked before, more than once so it seems. He was a tall, thin, quiet guy. He tried to keep to himself. If he did talk he was quick and to the point. When it comes to thru-hikers you know you can trust them. It was easy to see you could trust Comfortably Numb.

A pub stood along a stream in Hot Springs. There was a covered deck out by the water. A pool table sat out there as well. Cargo and I sat and drank our beer with the young brother and sister couple from Ohio. They had slack packed all of Georgia with their father's help. I thought I would never see them again, but their father had gone home so they were out hiking like the rest of us. The sister had her husband visiting her. It was good to see them again.

Later that night, drinks started landing on the floor from too much partying. Two hikers were shooting pool. One, called the Spaniard, was from Spain. His buddy was some chunky, chubby drunk. Let me tell you, the one thing that gets my goat worse than a drunk is a mouthy drunk, and that was him!

Cargo and I were trading Army stories, drinking beer, and having a good ole time. The Spaniard was shooting pool poorly. He kept throwing his pool cue on the floor after missing each shot. Warren Zevon's song "Mohammad's Radio" played over the speakers. Being a fan of Warren Zevon, I commented that Stevie Nicks sang vocals for Warren in that song.

"No, she didn't!" was heard from the crowd. I focused on the crowd from where the voice was coming. "Yes, she did," I baited. "No, she didn't!" stated the drunken friend of the Spaniard. "Yes, I know she did!" "No, she didn't." What a complete ass! Then the drunk had enough liquid courage walked up to me. Oh joy!

He was really sluggish, so I had plenty of time to plan my next move. Hell, I had time to plan several scenarios of what to do next. As he stood swaying in front of me, I decided on a simple plan.

My plan was to throw the bottle through the window of the bar, distracting everyone. Then, when all eyes were on the window breaking, I would bend down, do a fireman's carry, and lift the drunk, hoisting him over the railing and into the river. No one would ever realize he was gone! The most it would cost me was a new window. Too easy? My beer was empty. I gripped the bottle tightly; my eyes landed on the spot where I would aim it across the patio.

I drew the bottle back. My plan was in action. Sensing I was up to something, Cargo stepped forward and started pestering the drunk. Cargo's comments and mannerisms were perfect for defusing the situation. He saved the fool from a midnight swim. I laughed as the idiot swayed and staggered. This guy was a jerk when he drank and was still a jerk when sober. Poor slob!

As the bar closed, we all headed off on our own way. I bid Cargo good night. He was staying the next day for a zero, but, I was going to get up early and start before daybreak. Milo would catch me later. He was going to start in the morning also.

The Toilet Paper Run

UP EARLY, OFF I went. My hike started well enough. My pack was heavy with a full resupply. Having had a good zero, I was well rested. The trail didn't have too many obstacles and was well maintained. The moon provided good lighting. Without tripping or twisting an ankle, I hiked well into daybreak.

I stopped at a small dam. The fog was thick over the scum-filled stagnant pond. The site had an eerie look about it. The fog reflecting from the pond carried a green glow. Putting my pack by the side of the trail, I took out my camera and took a couple of pictures. After a couple of quick snacks and a good rest, I headed off-trail up the hill, away from the pond to dig a hole.

It was easy to find a private spot to dig a hole to relieve myself. The ground was soft and gave away easily.

Holding onto a small tree provided perfect balance to safely take care of my business in the woods.

After cleaning my hands with a handy wipe, I loaded my pack, took a final look at the pond, and headed up the trail. The miles went by quickly. The trail was pleasant. The weather was cool enough to allow for rapid hiking. I was delighted at the pace of my hike. The day was going well. To make things even better, I didn't see another person the entire morning.

It was early midday when I came upon a small, fast flowing stream that crossed the trail. The stream was a good spot to get a cold drink and to rehydrate. This was a good site for a break. With expert precision, and a bit of cockiness, I swung the pack off my back and landed it by the side of the trail. There was a large stone near the trail for me to sit on and relax.

My eyes fell back on my pack as if it were calling me. There was something odd about the pack; something was different. I stared at my pack as if it were a puzzle. Then, the lightbulb came on; puzzle solved. I crouched forward and grabbed the unzipped pocket on the side of my pack. The side pocket is where I keep toilet paper. My hand searched and my eyes darted into each corner of the empty pocket on my pack.

Leaning even more forward toward my pack, I yelled, "No!" Could my cry of displeasure somehow right this horrible wrong? My mind raced; what was I to do? Repeatedly, I searched the side pocket. Each search ended with the same result. The pocket was empty; my TP was gone! "Woe is me!"

Thinking back, I remembered the pond where I had dug a neat little hole in the ground. That was the last place I remembered seeing the toilet paper. I had just gotten my resupply, and there was no way I was going several days without toilet paper; no way! I had to act fast. I had to find my toilet paper.

Without any further thought, I pushed my pack onto its side on the trail. Then, in a flash, I was running at full speed. The start of the run was easy; it was slightly downhill. The distance to the "toilet paper prize" was about three miles. Each curve on the trail, each hill and memorable sight was replaying in my mind. I hoped to reach the pond soon.

Every step got me closer and closer to the pond. My pace increased. The effort was great, but to me, it was worth it. I needed the toilet paper! Soon, the pond came into sight. The fog still lay heavy over the water. I regretted the time I had spent here. I blamed this ominous site for having stolen my toilet paper. Actually, it did cause me to be distracted enough to lose my toilet paper.

Following my tracks, I left the trail and hiked up the hill. I was careful not to disturb the site where I last used the toilet paper. The low, arched tree still stood firm. After a careful search of the site, I still didn't find the toilet paper. Maybe I left it where I had originally stopped to take pictures?

I went back to the pond. My heart was pounding from the run and I was out of breath. Usually, a short three-mile run would not be too much for me, but my legs were now accustomed to long hikes. The run took more energy than I realized. I continued searching the trail along the pond. Every site where I had stood and stared at the stagnant water was investigated. Each log and rock was searched.

Finally, I came to the realization that some squirrel had come out of his tree nest and taken my toilet paper! That stupid squirrel will have the softest bedding of any squirrel in the neighborhood. Well, good for him, damn squirrel, I thought.

As I realized there was no recovering my toilet paper, my mind shot like a rocket back to my pack. Oh crap! My money, my ID, my food, my tent, everything I owned was in that pack. It was lying on the trail, out in the open and miles away. It had not been the smartest idea to leave it behind. Losing my toilet paper wasn't too bad now that I was at risk of losing everything.

My feet hit the trail faster than before. I was tired, but this was almost as bad as it gets. I had to get to my pack at all costs. This felt almost as bad as a life or death situation. My heart pounded in my ears and my breathing was heavy. Familiar sites were passed and cursed as they were not the site of my pack.

While running, I needed to develop a plan for how I would handle seeing someone with my gear. Would they be digging into my pack? Would they be carrying my pack away? Would someone have scattered my pack all over the trail searching for my money? Even worse, would a raccoon or bear have my pack, dragging it into the woods and tearing it apart?

I would have to just handle the situation when I got there. Should I slow down so I will have some energy left to get my pack back in case someone else has it? I wondered. Should I run faster to beat anyone else to my pack? I hadn't seen anyone all morning. That was a plus, but now it was midday and people were out hiking. A local could also have come across my pack. I just got resupplied with provisions and that included getting more money. I had to find my pack and quickly!

Motivation made me run and run. Finishing was the most difficult part, as it was a slight uphill incline. As I rounded the last bend in the trail, I saw my pack, untouched. Not even a mouse had visited the pack. What a relief. I sat on a large stone next to my pack, panting, trying to get my breath under control and get my heart rate slower. My chest heaved; I was dizzy and totally exhausted.

I sat there gripping my pack, really thankful to see it again. But that stupid squirrel had my toilet paper! Getting my breath was difficult; I panted for several minutes. Now, instead of just rehydrating I would also have to replace the calories lost from the run. A six-mile run is not what a hiker ever plans to do. This was one tough day.

My decision was to rehydrate and slowly eat a large lunch to regain lost energy. Water would serve me well. After I had cooled off, I would eat a lunch. Sweat dripped from my brow. My water filter was kept inside the pack, on top. Easy access was important. I opened my pack to retrieve the water filter and my eyes widened. My mouth dropped open as a low groan came out. "No," I whispered in fright, in anger, and, certainly, in major disappointment.

There in the top section of my pack sat my toilet paper! I had put it in the wrong place. When I thought the toilet paper was lost I had only searched my pack where it should have been. I sat there in total disbelief and panted, "I will not do that again. I will not do that again." My new mantra. This was repeated over and over, once for each step it took to get to the pond and back.

I ate my lunch, had a long rest, and rehydrated. When I repacked, everything was put back in its correct place, checked, and then rechecked. My miles hiked that day were not going to be as many as I first thought, but my feet were back on the trail and my hike continued.

Easter Sunday

THE SUN WAS setting across the sky. It had been a clear day. The wind had blown steadily, keeping the air cold. I had gone only fifteen miles but my body was spent. Recovering from the TP run was going to take some time. Ahead, the trail crossed a road just after Allen Gap.

Three hikers were standing by the road. When they saw me they called out, explaining there was trail magic about three hundred yards up the road. I needed to hike to the home of two thru-hikers, Hercules and Fall. They had opened their home to other hikers.

Getting to the home of Hercules and Fall was easy enough, except their driveway was steep. They offered food, drink for rehydrating, and a place to relax. Then, Hercules explained the "deal." Option one: I could eat all I wanted and then continue my hike. The second option: I could eat quickly, then get a ride in the van ten miles up the trail and slack pack back. All for free!

Whoever took the slack pack offer had to spend the night. Fall would wash their clothes. There was plenty to eat and drink. The showers had awesome water pressure and the water was hot. The next morning all the slack packers would be taken to Easter service. After church, we would all go to a Chinese buffet, each paying for his own meal. Later, we would be taken back to the trail, up the ten miles we had slacked.

I opted for the slack pack. A little church service might do me some good. I needed someone to be on my side when things got tough. The slack was an easy ten miles. Dinner, laundry, and every other aspect of our care were perfect. No one knows how to take care of hikers better than a thru-hiker. Hercules and Fall obviously knew how to prepare us for our hikes in the days to come.

The Chinese buffet was good, but the food prepared by Fall was better. Our gear was clean, packed, and ready. Returning to the trail and hiking was easier this time than any time previously. My legs were getting stronger.

Stronger legs or not, when I returned to the trail I hiked only six miles and stopped at the next shelter. The large volume of food I had eaten slowed me down; there was no chance for a long hike. But, hey, it was okay, because I had the ten-mile slack, so this was more like a sixteen-mile day.

There weren't as many hikers as I had expected at the Jerry Cabin Shelter, where I stopped. After fixing dinner and getting fresh water, I went to bed in my tent. The following day I hiked down to Flint Mountain Shelter for lunch and a noontime nap. There was a "headstone" along the trail. It had been erected by the descendants of Millard Haire. That fact wasn't too interesting, then I read the dates.

Millard F. Haire was born in 1850. He died on July 1, 1863. I had to think about that for a while. This guy died at the age of twelve or thirteen. But, the interesting fact is that he had descendants, at thirteen! Either way, that was a rough time; he died during the Civil War.

My hike was going well. In the afternoon, I tried calling Deb but a storm blew in and lightning started striking the ground. I put my phone away. That night I slept soundly. I no longer had a blister. My knees did not hurt. My ankles did not get twisted all day and were not swollen. There wasn't any chaffing on me at all. And, I did not have a single muscle cramp all night. I was in great shape. My sleeping bag was perfectly suited for the temperature. I couldn't have been more comfortable.

The next morning, when I started my hike, Shenanigans came running by me. He was moving rather quickly. I kept pace with him to chat and see how he had been. We talked as we hiked. The uphill portions were done at a fast mall-walker pace. The downhills were quite different. Shenanigans took off running, and I followed.

Shenanigans and I ran the trail. Every pathway that was level or down-hill, we would run. This was fun. Shenanigans ran much faster than I could and he often left me behind. When I saw him coming back toward me, but farther down the hill, I realized he had gone through a switchback. Instead of hiking down the trail and back, I did what hikers should not do. I jumped off the trail and went through the woods for a short cut. After cutting Shenanigans off, he was surprised to see me ahead of him. We continued running down the trail. The pace was brutal but we made a great many miles. Without a break, we ran and ran. Running isn't too difficult, but running in the woods, on an uneven trail, with a pack on your back, is.

We came to a road crossing with a fast moving stream nearby. We stopped for a quick drink, a check of the maps, and a snack. We wondered if we could make it to the town of Erwin or if we would have to stop at the shelter seven miles before Erwin. No Business Shelter is small, and the last shelter before Erwin, Tennessee.

Mice and Tornadoes

AFTER FILLING MY water bottles, I was ready to move on. Shenanigans indicated he would catch up, so I ran ahead. Shenanigans was much faster and would catch me easily. At this part of the trail there were a couple of spots where some hikers could get on the wrong trail and a couple of spots that were risky. Shenanigans would be fine, though.

I ran till I made it to No Business Shelter. A couple of other hikers were already there. Doc Boom was building a fire to rid the area of the mosquitoes. Freight Train, the only female there, was setting up a tent. Night was coming on quickly. I ate dinner while waiting for Shenanigans. Two other hikers showed up, Romeo and Juliet.

One of the other hikers was setting up an "AT bear bag," a method to keep food safe from bears using string, a snap link, and a stick. I put my food bag up with the other hikers'.

Shenanigans was still not at the shelter and I was still seven miles away from Erwin. Nighttime had blanketed the woods. The fire gave off a decent glow into the shelter, allowing us to see well enough to care for our gear and set up for the night.

While setting up, I placed my gear in a specific order so I could get up early and make a run for Erwin. If I got there early enough I could take advantage of getting a ride and doing a slack pack. After the slack pack, I would stay at the hostel in town, Uncle Johnny's. It was supposed to be close to the trail.

Because I was getting up early to make a run for it, I decided to sleep in the shelter. The fire died out and the sky was cloudy. Inside the shelter it was completely dark. Three other hikers were sleeping in the shelter as well. They were already in their sleeping bags as I was crawling into mine.

We had a lively conversation as I set up my area. The conversation was about the pros and cons of sleeping in a shelter. I adamantly expressed my displeasure at sleeping in a shelter. This was my third or fourth time overnight in a shelter. "I can't stand to sleep in a shelter!" I said. "Why not, Hooker?" came a question in the dark. "Because they are dirty and full of mice," I replied as I lay my head down on the floor of the shelter. Squeak! Squeak! Squeak! A mouse yelled as my head landed right on it. "Sorry, little dude," I quipped as I picked the dead mouse up by the tail and tossed him into the dark toward the fire pit.

The shelter filled with laughter. The other hikers joked and laughed at the timing of my bitching about mice just as one met his doom under my head. That made falling asleep even more difficult. I knew that as we slept, critters would be running over us like free-range horses galloping over hills. We were the hills; the mice herds were coming. I just hoped they didn't bite.

The next morning, I was up before daylight. I threw my gear into my pack by feel. Checking the silhouette of the food bags against the morning twilight sky, I found mine. Tugging on the line worked as it was designed to work. After getting my food, I reset the "AT bear bag." If I had left the food down, a morning bear could have gotten it. That was the way my luck was going, so I wasn't taking any chances.

With my gear packed and my food ready, I headed for Erwin. The trail was easy and the weather was perfect for a morning run. After the first mile, I saw Erwin, six miles away. Seeing the town so soon after leaving the shelter often confuses and depresses hikers. They believe they are close to town, but it is still two hours away for a fast hiker and three hours away for an average hiker.

I kept running. The thought of a slack pack and a warm bed both appealed to me, but what really kept my feet moving was that Erwin had a Kentucky Fried Chicken with an all-you-can-eat deal. I wanted that! So I ran . . . and ran . . . and ran . . .

The trail was fairly easy. When I reached a road, I looked left and right for a blaze marking to show me which way to go. There wasn't a blaze in sight. I sat by the road, waiting for a vehicle to come by. Maybe someone could give directions. As I waited, I looked around the area. A sign downhill at the end of the road caught my eye. It read, "Hostel."

I went there and found Uncle Johnny's hostel. I asked if it was too late to get in on the slack pack. It wasn't too late, but it was twenty dollars. I found my money and paid the twenty dollars. Then, one of the employees started yelling at everyone, telling us if we were not in the van in two minutes he wasn't waiting for us. He kept yelling. I asked where I could leave my gear so I could pack a minimum for the slack pack. A fellow hiker threw a Honey Bun to me.

The idea of a slack pack was to carry only food and water. I was told to leave my gear on the deck. The deck was a wooden platform with picnic tables for the guests to use. I threw gear from my pack, looking for my water bottles. I found my water bottles empty! One of the other hikers informed me that water was at a spigot on the other side of the building. After letting the driver know I needed water, he replied, "You had better hurry up!"

Once again, I had to meet an asshole. This guy was talking down to every hiker he met as if they owed him money. He was speaking to me like I was a nine-year-old child. That didn't suit me too well. "Just wait till I get water!" then off I went. After I got my water, we were headed to Iron Mountain Gap. My frustration was setting in as we went up the road. Who in the hell was this jerk? He kept complaining about hikers as he drove. In a moronic fashion, he berated the same hikers who were paying him. On the upside, Alien was in the van. He had done the slack pack the day before, and now he and Chicago were headed to the trail to continue their hike.

The driver continued his rants against hikers as he stopped the van. I politely asked him to check for openings at the hostel for me. I wished to reserve a bed and stay there that night. He said he would check for me. Shortly after entering the woods, I took my pack off to inventory it to see how much food I had left.

The pack was in front of me on the ground when I opened it. A mouse squeaked and ran from inside my pack and disappeared into the leaves in the woods. Startled by the mouse, I looked into the pack for other furry hitchhikers. None were found. But there wasn't any food in my pack, either! In my haste I had taken the food out and kept a pair of pants and a rain jacket.

Disappointed, I strapped the pack tightly to my body and ran. The distance to cover was twenty miles to get back to food. Another option would be to hitchhike back to the hostel, but that wasn't happening. I had already run seven miles and had not eaten yet, except the one honey bun. Hiking and running twenty more miles should have been easy enough, but my reserves were going to be spent today. There was no time to waste. I had to get back to Uncle Johnny's. My anger at the driver grew as I ran.

My pace was strong and I ran the first five miles nonstop, all the way to the top of Unaka Mountain, which was well over a thousand-foot elevation increase. That was the highest point on my hike for the day. The drop in elevation was going to be thirty-five hundred feet in the next thirteen miles. My body was strong and I was feeling my trail legs. This is how a hike was supposed to be, except it should be with food.

When I made it back to the hostel, a small crowd of hikers was on the deck cheering me on. It was obvious they knew how far I had come: seven miles with a pack and now twenty miles slack packing. Finishing the trek was a feat in its own. It was around three o'clock in the afternoon when I crawled in. My body was totally spent. A fellow hiker offered a beer, which I gladly accepted.

Two quick gulps of the beer took it down to a half a bottle. My mind was swimming from the run. The beer was helping me feel no pain. By the time the beer was gone, I was dizzy. A couple, who were section hikers, showed up in a car. The wife offered me a beer. Halfway through that beer,

I was drunk. Man was I a cheap date.

After a quick check for a bunk I found that all the spaces were rented out. The driver had lied to me. He did not hold a bunk for me as he said he would. Lawn space was fifteen dollars a night to set up a tent; that was my only option. I set my tent up next to Taz and Walk-About-Roo, an Australian couple from Tasmania.

After I set up my tent, I had to hurry into the van for a ride to town. The all-you-can-eat KFC was calling my name. Hunger pains mixed with the beers caused my head to swim. Dreams of chicken legs made me smile ear to ear. It wasn't long before I was in KFC, causing severe damage to the dessert tray.

The chicken legs were out, but I love to eat dessert first. My first plate was filled with lemon wedge pies. These sweets were lemon flavored and came off a flat cookie sheet. They had a white icing on top and a cookie base. My plate was filled with them, but just for a moment.

On the second round at the buffet my plate was filled with fruit and Jell-O. It was then, as I was coming back to my seat, that I noticed Shenanigans was in the KFC as well. Fancy Pants was sitting with him. Shenanigans explained that he had caught a ride to Uncle Johnny's the night before and Fancy Pants had come to visit. He was going to go back to make up the miles missed then spend some time with his fiancé, Fancy Pants. My third and fourth plates were chicken only. I needed the protein.

That night the area was all a buzz. Tornadoes were coming through. A terrible storm was going to cross most of the United States and we were in a direct path of the tornado-producing storm. Deb called me and was worried about my staying in the tent. I tied the tent to a nearby tree with a piece of string, as if that would have helped.

While we were preparing for the storm, a car stopped outside of the yard just where our tents were set up. The driver let a large dog out of the car and walked the dog to the yard where we were. The dog squatted to poo. It stunk. Who the heck was this guy, bringing his dog to poop in the area where we were set up to sleep? I yelled at the guy and told him I would eat his dog if he didn't get it the hell out. He left quickly.

That night brought a terrible amount of wind and rain. Several times that night thunder and lightning woke everyone up. My tent held up well. Best of all, I stayed dry! This was a relief. Tragedy struck our nation, though, as two hundred and fifty people died from tornados on April 27th, 2011.

This was the last time I would see Taz and Walk-About-Roo. My slack packing took me twenty miles ahead of them. We said our farewells and parted ways. After a breakfast, it was back in the van and back up to Iron Mountain Gap. Two other hikers and I were headed north. The other hikers were faster and stronger hikers, but that was okay; the day prior had taken most of my energy.

Roan Mountain Pains

ONCE I GOT to Hughes Gap, the trail turned straight up a mountain, Roan Mountain. There were no switchbacks to make the climb easier. There were no plateaus, nothing to give any relief from the climb. The trail was washed out rocks. It suffered from severe erosion. The trail appeared more like a creek bed than a hiking trail.

My shoes were old and wearing thin. In my mind, I felt every rock under foot. Even the leaf stems seemed to be felt through the soles of my shoes. Each step made my feet ache more and more. To make matters worse, the trail was nothing but rocks—sharp, jagged rocks. They must have been put there to test the pain level of my feet. My knees were not faring any better than my feet. I was in severe pain and could barely walk.

My plan for the day had been to hike twenty miles or more, but Roan Mountain hurt my feelings. The difficulty of the climb resulted in only sixteen miles to Stan Murray Shelter. While on the top of Roan Mountain, I stopped to offer a moment of silence for all those who died the night before in the storms.

That night in Stan Murray Shelter I was freezing cold. The wind cut through to the bone. It may well have been the long distance running the day before, but I had no resistance to the cold air. That night, only one other hiker, Next Year, stayed at Stan Murray. Next Year set his tent up away from the shelter. I wanted a better windbreak and set my tent up inside the shelter. That was the one and only time I did such a fool thing, and I still froze my butt off!

Setting a tent up in a shelter is just dumb. There is a better way. Cargo later taught me to wrap the tent around me inside my sleeping bag for added warmth. That frees up space in the shelter and adds protection from the cold more efficiently.

Another hiker arrived while I was sleeping deeply, and, sadly, snoring extremely loudly. She arrived during the night and stayed in the shelter. She tried to sleep but gave up and left before I woke up. Next Year talked with her for a while before she headed out. He told me she was attractive and we would never see her, Snorkel, again. She was attempting to set a record for the fastest unsupported thru hike. *Sorry for the snoring, Snorkel!*

The morning started as cold as the night before. The cold temperature was brought in by fierce winds. Limbs fell from the trees, like crooked arrows being fired at me. They missed, at least, the bigger ones did. Some of the smaller branches hit the top of my head, just as in the beginning of my hike. It didn't take long to figure out that looking up was a bad idea. One limb in my eye and I had learned my lesson. Ouch!

As the day went on, the winds grew stronger. Little Hump Mountain looked safer to climb because there were no trees with falling branches. It is a bald mountain. A few hikers were ahead of me as I climbed. They were quite a distance ahead, but I felt strong and thought I could catch them. I hiked faster. My feet ached from the rocks on Roan Mountain and the paper-thin soles of my shoes offered no protection.

The higher up the hill I hiked, the higher the winds gusted. The wind hit forcibly, like getting pushed by a pickup truck. Glancing uphill, my hat nearly flew off. Holding my hat down with one hand, trying to shield my eyes from the wind with the other, I looked for the three hikers ahead of me. They were gone.

Did the wind blow the hikers away? Gusts kept me from staying on the trail. I staggered like a guy on a three-day bender. From time to time I fell but had to get up and keep going. At least it wasn't raining.

Near the top of Little Hump Mountain, several boulders lined the sides of the trail. The howling winds deafened nearly all other sounds, but I did hear a faint voice piercing the wind: "Hey, down here! Get out of the wind!" I looked down between some boulders and saw the three missing hikers tucked away from the wind.

I jumped down into an empty crevice. In an instant the wind pressure in my ears released, they popped, and the howling stopped. The cold chills rapidly faded, replaced by warmth from the sun. This felt good.

We talked a bit. The hikers were watching people come up the hill, laughing at how much they staggered like drunks. One hiker asked about a ring I was wearing. "What's that stand fer?" "It's a military ring, Special Forces." He looked at his hiking companion and said, "Oh great, another one." My first thought was that there are too many people out there who lie about being in Special Forces. It is a lie I have heard quite often. They must have met one of "those guys" earlier.

I asked, "Did you meet a guy saying he was SF?" They answered, "Yeah, we meet him every day." "He is a bit of an ass." They all laughed. Then it dawned on me, one of them must be an ex-Special Forces soldier. He introduced himself. We talked and had an interesting conversation.

They asked where I was headed, then they suggested I stop at a nearby hostel, Mountain Harbor. That sounded like a good plan. Six miles later I would turn left onto a road crossing the trail and head to Mountain Harbor Hostel. There I could recover from Roan Mountain's rocky trail.

Following the directions, I stopped at a large house and knocked on the door. A lady carrying a load of laundry answered the door. "You gotta hostel here?" I asked. She pointed at the large barn, which had horses and sheep coming in and out of it. It was a hundred-year-old two story barn. There wasn't any way this was going to work, I thought. "Trust me! Go look at it then decide. Go in around back and up the stairs," she pointed.

Filled with doubt, I walked around back of the barn, went up the stairs, and looked inside. Damn! This place was perfect! Bunks, stove, a shower, and everything a hiker needs was there. They also had resupplies available. It was totally awesome. I unpacked, set up in a bunk, took my shoes off, and relaxed.

Other hikers showed up and settled in as well. Later that evening, one of the three hikers I had met hiding from the wind on Little Hump

Mountain came by. "Hey, Hooker!" "Yeh!" As we met again, the hiker handed me a six-pack of beer. This was an unexpected treat. With gratitude and a handshake, I accepted the beer. Later that night, I shared the beers with the other hikers staying at the hostel.

We received a phone call at the hostel asking how many of us wanted to stay for breakfast. Yes, the hundred-year-old barn had a phone. Told you it was a cool place. We all decided to stay for breakfast. Little did we know how wonderful it would be. Mary, the hostess, got up at 4 a.m. to start cooking. She had a full-course spread on the tables for us. Eggs were prepared multiple ways. Breads were freshly baked. Potatoes were fried and casseroled. There was more food than we could possibly eat. Remember, hikers can really eat! Spoiler alert! This was the best home cooked meal I'd had on the trail and it was never topped.

Being full, showered, and well rested, with clothes washed, I was ready for the trail again. There were a few inclines along the trail but it was easy hiking. The winds had calmed down considerably and the sun warmed the air. This was a good day to hike. To make things even better, I was finishing my fourth map and starting on the fifth one. That is always a good benchmark. It feels good to progress to another map, or another state, or another hundred-mile mark.

The day's hike went by uneventfully. There wasn't a limb falling for me to dodge. There was no wind blowing me off the trail. I never met another hiker the entire day. My legs were strong, my pack felt good. The breakfast was awesome. My hike was good. That night I stayed at Mooreland Gap Shelter. It, too, went by uneventfully.

Mingo is the Name

AROUND NOON THE next day I met another hiker, Boy Scout. Boy Scout was a young man, a bit hard to get used to, but okay. We reached a waterfall and went exploring. The falls were pretty. The water was cold and it felt good to be near them during the heat of the day.

Farther up the trail was another hostel. This hostel was one which no hiker should pass by. Kincora Hiker's Hostel is a popular place for thru-hikers. It is run by Bob Peoples, a hero to many hikers. He organizes and develops trail maintenance and improvements through a program called Hard Core. Bob's reputation gets even better as the hostel is a popular hangout for thru-hikers.

Upon arrival, I was informed to pick a bunk and put my gear on it. Fairly quickly I found an empty bunk. The hostel was filling up fast. When I arrived, it was already pretty full. Most of the hikers here were taking a zero or two. Crazy Legs, whom I had met at Davenport Gap, was standing in the kitchen, exerting an OCD habit on the cabinets. Good thing, because the kitchen was totally disorganized. Not anymore!

The rules were simple. A ride was provided to town for shopping and resupplies. Any food you wanted to eat you bought then. The kitchen was free to use. You could write your name on food for yourself, but if no name was on the food it was open for public consumption. Showers were available, as were fresh towels.

It wasn't long before the ride to town took off. I bought a dozen eggs, a pork chop and baskets of strawberries. My shopping was done before the others, so I went out to the truck to wait for the ride back to the hostel. While waiting by the truck, a lady who had just filled up at a nearby gas station was eyeing me. She drove by me, stopped, then looked me up and down. This chick was undressing me with her eyes. She smiled and motioned for me to come over. She adored the way I looked.

Like a schoolboy I smiled, winked and waved at her. My head tilted to the side as I blushed. This was as far as I was willing to go. The lady drove off, looking back, hoping I would change my mind. Looking in the window at my reflection made me laugh. What the hell was she looking at? I looked a fright.

We returned to Kincora. Our groceries were thrown into the fridge after being appropriately marked. Then, a familiar voice came from the living room. I paused; a familiar laugh rang throughout the building. The voice was that of none other than Cargo. "Hey, Cargo!" Cargo was sitting, holding an ice pack on his legs. He had shin splints. They were so bad they had caused his legs to swell. Cargo was back on crutches.

It was time to join the crowd in the living room. I sat, crouched low on a couch cushion, almost reclining. As we talked, a young female hiker sat down to my left. Socks, the gal to my left, decided she needed to go shower. She had a little dog with her, Doobie. Socks hoisted Doobie in the air and landed the dog onto my lap. "Here, Hooker, I am pimping my dog. Doobie will keep you warm." I surmised that was thru-hiker lingo for, "Watch my dog, please."

Crazy Legs had finished her work in the kitchen and completed some embroidery work for Cargo. Crazy Legs was talented. Her embroidery work was detailed. Other hikers jumped in line to get their hiker names and the AT logo on their clothes. Crazy Legs had her work cut out for her.

While shopping, a hiker had bought several chickens, sweet potatoes, and green beans. He fixed dinner for everyone. This guy could cook. We ate well that evening. There wasn't heat in the building, but with all the hikers in there, heat wasn't needed. We ate, we talked, and we laughed. Kincora is an earthly paradise for thru-hikers. It is great for all hikers, really.

Other hikers kept arriving. When the place was full, the other hikers camped out in the woods next to the hostel. As introductions were made, it became clear that I needed to change my trail name. Telling the same silly story over and over was getting old. The name "Hooker" had to go. Cargo and I thought of a couple of names, but nothing felt right. Still, "Hooker" had to go!

The next day we were taken to town for a post office run. I received a resupply package. Then, it was back to the trailhead, and away we went, hiking north again. The weather turned better. Sunny skies and a slow breeze greeted our day. The breeze helped keep bugs away.

I caught up with Socks and Doobie. Doobie hiked better than a little dog should. He was one tough pup. Socks was as cute as a button. She was short with a little baby fat that made her more attractive, and she always had a smile. Socks turned out to be a good hiker as well. As we hiked together we chatted. As it turns out, she grew up a few miles away from my home! While at home I pass her house often. Hmm! It is a small world.

Cargo and I stopped for lunch and discussed possibilities for my new trail name. We decided it would be "Mingo." Mingo is the name of my Masonic Lodge in Ohio. I planned to carry the name Mingo and to try to do a good deed each day. Good plan! My wife is part Cherokee, as was the TV version of Daniel Boone's Indian friend Mingo. There is a Mingo County, West Virginia, not too far from where I grew up. Mingo was to be my official trail name. As of Virginia, I would no longer answer to "Hooker."

Cargo hiked on and stopped at a shelter to make an entry in the shelter journal. I arrived long after he was gone and I read the entry. The crazy coot wrote a song titled "Mingo." Funny, it had the same tempo as the song about a farmer with a dog named "Bingo." Cargo's song started, "There was a hiker who had a ripped shirt, and Mingo was his name, oh! M-I-N-G-O." Well, you can figure out the rest.

I made my entry in the journal after Cargo's. This made my name change official. I was no longer Hooker; my name was Mingo. "Mingo" sounded good. The more I heard the name the better it felt. It wasn't long before I had the persona of Mingo. Everyone graciously accepted the name change. I am Mingo.

Hoping to see Cargo at Iron Mountain Shelter, I hiked on. After I arrived, I was greeted by a hiker who had met Cargo. He greeted me as Mingo. Cargo had hiked on an extra eight miles to Double Springs. He was headed for Damascus, Virginia, the next day, but because the hour was late, I was stopping here at Iron Mountain Shelter. If I wanted to make it to Damascus the next day it would be a twenty-six mile day. A twenty-six mile day is a marathon day. Marathons hurt, but I would be in town when I finished.

The next day started with that challenge in mind. It was twenty-six miles to Damascus, Virginia. Cargo had hiked farther than me the day before. He wrote in the shelter journals, stating the times he was at each location. Twenty-six miles, a marathon day, was my continuous concern. My hike started late and I hesitated, wondering if I could do it.

During the hike to Damascus I stopped at a shelter for lunch, food, and water. While at the shelter I found a cell phone. Wanting to do my good deed for the day, I took the cell phone, hoping to recharge it and track down the owner. After wolfing down a quick lunch and drink of water, off I went. This was the day I would reach Virginia.

Damascus is only three miles into Virginia. My hope was to do another good deed, but that was getting difficult because I didn't see anyone else on the trail. I had the cell phone, but that was a shot in the dark as a good deed. Everyone at the shelter had left before me. Cargo would certainly be at Damascus. He made most of his miles the day before. Chaffing held me back from making more miles. Chaffing was slowing me down, again.

I hiked and hiked, then hiked some more. The hills weren't too difficult and the trail was not rocky. There were several slippery spots where I was lucky enough to bust my butt, repeatedly! The woods were quiet. The first buds on the trees had started making their appearance. The winds slowly picked up as the day went on. Twenty-six miles with no time for a second lunch, I hiked on.

The Virginia line is coming today, I thought repeatedly. Another state, now that was a big deal. Virginia is a big state for the Appalachian Trail. One-fourth of the trail is in Virginia. Ten miles went by quickly. Then fifteen miles had gone by. Once I was twenty miles into my hike, the winds kicked up big time. Limbs were flying off the trees and it seemed to me they were aiming right for me.

Up a hill I hiked. *Any moment now and I will be in Virginia.* That was my mantra, my motivation, but the state line wasn't where I thought it should be. The hill had no sign indicating the Virginia line. I wondered if there was even going to be a sign. Another hill and again, no sign; another hill, still no sign. This pattern was repeated again and again. With each hill, my steps slowed down. Fatigue was setting in and it looked as if it was going to get dark soon.

Just as I was convinced there would be no sign for the Virginia line, I found it! The sign was huge. The sky opened up and the day almost became bright again—or was that just my imagination? No! It was brighter. The clouds parted for a bit as I gazed upon the Virginia State line. As quickly as the sky had opened, it darkened again. This time the sky got really dark and rain began falling.

The rain didn't start slowly then pick up. No, it just came down full-blown and stayed that way. The rain brought darker skies, which made seeing the trail more difficult. My thoughts focused on the fact that it was only three miles to Damascus. It should only take one more hour to get there. As my steps picked up in pace, I fell, slipping on the wet trail.

Closer and closer I came to Damascus. Tents started appearing along the trail. Hikers had set up tent sites to escape the rain. At one point, the rain was coming from the sky like a waterfall. Along the trail was a string hanging from a tree. This was a bear bag line, but there was no food bag on the line. I called into the nearest tent, asking if whoever was there needed their food bag hung up. He did, so I hung the food bag. Now the hiker, One Step, did not have to get out of his tent in the heavy rain. This was another good deed for the day.

After hanging the bear bag, I continued on to Damascus. The rain poured even harder. The cold winds cut through to the bone. There was no escape from the rain. It was like being in Washington State. Night came on quickly; the rain continued into the evening. Oddly, while hiking down the hill into town, an odor of barbeque filled the air. My stomach grumbled, my steps grew quicker, and my feet ached. I slipped again and fell onto the wet, muddy trail.

While walking through the town of Damascus, I wondered where everything was located. I had no map of the town. There were no signs showing which way to go. A small shelter, like the ones on the trail, was in a small field. I ran to the shelter and considered setting up and staying there that night. It was a thought.

After retrieving my phone, I called Cargo. He gave me a couple directions, so off I went into the night, hiking into a strange town in the pouring rain. I soon found a pizza shop, restaurant, and bar all in one. There were hikers hanging out, shooting pool. This was a good spot. The hikers all greeted me as Mingo. Cargo bought me a beer. Dinner was excellent.

Lotat was one of the hikers shooting pool. He was young, in his mid-twenties, and kind of a tall dude. Heck, he looked more like a college student than he did a hiker. Lotat always greeted you with a smile and was friendly enough. We played a game of pool as he explained his trail name, Lost On The Appalachian Trail, LOTAT. That was catchy.

After dinner and pool, Cargo showed me the hostel called The Place. It was a simple place with basic rules. I took an empty bunk, setup my sleep pad, and tried to sleep on the plywood bunk. My ankles ached and blisters prevented me from getting a good night's rest.

The next day I bought a sleeping pad that was an air mattress. What a difference! This would help tremendously. The way I saw it, if I got a good night's rest I should be able to heal faster and hike longer each day. That should help me make more miles.

Fiber One

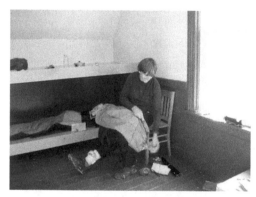

MUSCLE CRAMPS, HEAD-ACHES, shoulder ache, tendinitis, Achilles heel, Plantar Fasciitis, and other body malfunctions are all a problem, but one problem I didn't know I needed to watch for was a helpful friend. My buddy Cargo and I both got a resupply at the post office in Damascus. As we unpacked and repacked our food we kept sharing supplies with each other. When I thought the amount of food I could carry was reached, I said, "That's it, no more." Now it was time to fill my water bottles before I forgot.

The water spigot worked well enough. The water was clean, but tasted funny. I filled my bottles anyway. When I returned to my bunk there were several trail bars next to my pack. Cargo had left the bars for me, so I figured, why not go ahead and pack them? They didn't weigh that much more.

Cargo and I went to a Dairy King for breakfast. While eating breakfast, another hiker, Moonshine, the guy who had called me "weak" in Georgia, tried to start a political conversation about President Obama. We were not interested in politics, and certainly not his politics. Cargo made it clear he didn't want to hear his rhetoric. Then Moonshine decided he would drag me into a debate with "I want to see his birth certificate. Am I right?" referring to President Obama. Seeing Moonshine waiting for an "Amen," I shut him up with, "Hey, I voted for the guy." Moonshine stopped his incessant political rant and quit talking to us. This wasn't the time or place for political debates, as I agreed with Cargo. If it were an argument the guy wanted he was going to get more than he bargained for. I think he got the hint, because he left us alone.

Breakfast wasn't a complete loss. A tall, large man walked into the deli. Compared to me, the man was a giant. He sat down not far from us. He heard me and Cargo talking; I guess he heard my voice and recognized it. As he approached from the side, I grabbed a fork for defense, just in case. He asked in his booming voice, while standing over me, "Hey, are you Mingo?" My mind raced, wondering if I had done something to piss this guy off.

Thoughts of defense and fight scenarios flashed through my mind. My feet were firm and flat on the floor, my weight equally distributed for rapid movement and a quick counter attack. The only way I could beat this guy was to go on an offensive attack. What on earth did I ever do to him? He would get the first swing. He was standing too close for me to stand up and could easily knock me down if I tried. I would get to my feet after he tried to hit me; that would be my only chance.

"Yes, I am Mingo. What's up?" was my response as I watched his hands. He reached his right hand forward in a slow movement. I responded in kind and we shook hands. "My name is One Step and you are the guy who hung my bear bag when it was raining. That really saved my ass! Thanks," he stated. I smiled in relief. One Step was a kind, gentle man, luckily for the world, because he is large.

After breakfast, it was time to hit the trail. Socks was already on the trail ahead of me. I wanted to catch up but it was no big deal. Cargo was going to start later and catch up with me. That was the plan. After one last check of the map, I checked with Cargo, checked my water, then loaded up my pack and away I went.

My hike took me on the blue blazes of the Creeper Trail. This trail was an easy hike. The path slowly rises in elevation using an old railroad bed. Many people rent bicycles and ride up in a van, then coast back down to Damascus. The Creeper Trail was so easy to walk it was almost sinful. The trail was covered with cinders and was smooth. There were no roots, sticks, rocks, or other obstacles to trip over.

After a few miles, I came to a small town that had a deli. It was about lunchtime, so I stopped in for a bite to eat. There were three people, cyclists, sitting outside at a picnic table. After giving a warm greeting and receiving the cold shoulder, I went in to get lunch. The cool thing about this place was the old rock music and jazz constantly playing.

The lunch was pretty good. I was about ready to leave when Lotat showed up. I stuck around as he ate. We hiked together the rest of the day. Lotat was an awesome hiker. Hiking with the dude kicked my butt. He was fast.

Two days after my resupply in Damascus, Cargo and I were hiking together for the day. We stopped for lunch and I ate some spam. Then, I decided to eat one of the trail bars I got from him. Mmm, yummy! After I ate the bar, I looked at the brand name on the wrapper. Talk about reading the label too late; I was way too late. The wrapper read, "Fiber One." And I yelled "No!" People fifty miles away probably heard me.

One thing for certain, hikers don't usually need help getting enough fiber. We have no problem with bowel movements; quite the opposite is true. My wife Deb once bought Fiber One bars. They were great. I loved the flavor. The problem was, I didn't know what they were going to do to me. So, after eating four of them in one sitting, I was one surprised hurt puppy. But that was then and this is now. For lunch I had eaten Spam and a Fiber One bar. Pain was coming, there was no doubt!

After another three miles of hiking, I felt sawed in half by the fiber. Each time I ran to the woods, cursing at Cargo, who would only laugh. At one point I ran to the woods and did my business, only to find that one hundred yards farther down the trail was a public restroom at a road crossing. Looking at the restroom, I wondered if I should use it anyway. I made the unwise decision to go on without using the facility. That proved to be a big mistake.

We continued hiking up a hill that was a bald. On a bald there are no trees and you can see for miles. The fiber was at it again. Everyone for miles away was getting a glorious show. So, hey, if you are gonna give a show, you make it good, right? With each movement, I would give a loud cry, "Yahoo!" just in case someone wasn't looking. The lesson here is to never eat Spam and a Fiber One bar then walk on a bald. I hope no one had a video camera on me then.

I was losing weight just by hiking. A thru-hiker burns about six thousand calories a day. The lunch combination took another five to ten pounds off me. It really emptied me out. I had to sew the button on my pants again, as they were too loose. Cargo's mother had sent him the bars. He didn't know what they were. After seeing how well they had worked on me, I didn't see him eat any of them.

My pack was falling apart. To repair the pack, I hand stitched it with a large needle and dental floss. My shirt had been shredded, so Cargo had bought me a "new" one at the thrift store in Damascus. My food supply was holding up well. The new sleep pad was awesome! So, maybe I would finally be able to get some sleep. My legs were stronger; ten miles was nothing, fifteen miles was easy, twenty-plus miles were doable but still hurt. My feet were hurting more and more each day and at night they were keeping me awake. And, I missed Deb.

Ponies and Peeps

WE ARRIVED AT a shelter called Thomas Knob. This was a truly delightful experience. I had no idea what I was about to see. There wasn't anything I had read that mentioned seeing wild ponies, but here they were at Thomas Knob Shelter!

A father and son hiking team were in the shelter. They were doing a section hike. The team went by the names Chili and Pepper. Chili was the son, about twelve. He was fun to banter with, as he could give as well as he took.

Later that evening, Chili suggested a game called "Mine." You play by not saying, "Mine." If you say "Mine," you have to do ten pushups. Let the games begin! To my surprise, there were no attempts to get me to say, "This is mine" or "That is mine." Did Chili forget we were playing the game?

The night was cold, so most of us slept in the upper loft of the shelter. The ponies were noisy several times during the night. When necessary, finding the privy in the dark was a true feat in navigating. It was almost hidden. Cold winds cut through the trees and into the shelter. To get to sleep, I used the hot water bottle trick. It worked again, keeping me warm throughout the night.

Morning came, hikers stirred. Since my feet were getting cold, I drank the last of the warm water in my water bottle. I found my socks frozen stiff. Putting them on proved to be quite a chore. Then Chili pointed at a pair of hiking shoes, asking, "Whose shoes are these?" "They are mine," I answered. The shelter erupted with laughter. I was confused. Did I say something wrong?

It was quickly pointed out to me that the game was still on and I owed ten pushups. I completed them in good form. Chili got a good laugh making me say, "mine." He certainly had patience. Cargo and I gathered our gear and headed north. Chili and Pepper were headed back toward Damascus.

A pony and young foal came up to us wanting to be petted. They may have been looking for food, also, but we don't feed the wild animals. Thru-hikers need what they carry and do not feed any of the wild animals. Well, we do feed the mice, but not by choice!

Cargo had a rough day hiking. His shin splints were getting the better of him. I hiked ahead and found a sign offering trail magic. It consisted of hot food cooked at a campsite, pop, water, and beer. I also found Peeps. No one wanted the Peeps? I love the "marshmallow-sugar-coated-treats-from-heaven." There were three packages, each with three boxes of Peeps in the package. Not wanting to be a glutton, I ate only one package . . . in less than a minute!

The host was from Ohio, coming to support his nephew who was thru-hiking. They were super friendly and offered me all the food I could eat. Really! And after much coaxing, I relented and ate a second package of Peeps. They said, "Go ahead, eat the rest of the Peeps, no one else will." How could I refuse that kind of pressure? I am only human!

I packed the remaining Peeps to take with me. I had their permission, of course. The campground had a hot shower. Even though the air was freezing cold, the shower was steamy hot. I pressed the shower button and held it to keep the water flowing. If the pressure button was released the water stopped.

The water pressure was like a car wash, so using soap wasn't required.

All the scum and grime was being power washed off my body. The heat and pressure gave my muscles a much-needed message. This was indeed an unexpected and awesome surprise. I set up my tent with the host, his son, and his nephew. Four tents were allowed at each site.

The morning came and I was sad not to see Cargo. He did not make the trek from the trail for trail magic. It was understandable, his legs hurt. After a short explanation about Cargo, the host offered a couple of beers to take with me. I packed them along with the rest of the food he offered. Honey Buns are always a hit and there seemed to be a bunch of them that "needed" to be eaten.

As soon as I got back to the trail another hiker was sitting at the crossing. He explained that Cargo went ahead about an hour earlier. An hour head start is huge. But, this was to be my good deed for the day, so I ran. The trail was easy enough. I ran and ran. Four miles later I arrived at a shelter.

There sat Cargo in the shelter. "Hey, Mingo! Did you go for the trail magic?" "Yup, sure did!" I panted. "Tell me about it." Cargo asked. "No!" I refused to describe the magic. I opened my pack to share the magic instead. Cargo was pleased to get a beer at a shelter. A shelter beer is rare.

Other hikers stared with hungry eyes. They were demonstrating good Yogi skills. I offered the Honey Buns, which they gratefully took. I also gave up one box of Peeps from the package. Cargo and I had a beer together. We were happy hikers.

Thimble

CARGO TOLD ME about the shelter where we were headed, Partnership Shelter. There was a Ranger station close by with an outdoor phone. You could use the phone to order pizza, which they deliver to the shelter. Even better, there is a shower at the shelter. This was great! So, after our beers, we packed up our empties and headed to Partnership Shelter.

At Partnership Shelter we met a female hiker, Thimble. We three went to the ranger station to order our pizzas. An old, white-haired thin man sat on the curb staring at us. Cargo figured he wanted to order a pizza as well. The guy declined, saying the pizza shop would charge him extra for delivery. We told him delivery was free.

Then, Cargo guessed the ole buzzard wanted to mooch pizza from us. Well, we felt generous, so we offered to share. We asked him what he wanted on the pizza, expecting a normal answer. "Pineapple and onions!" he replied. We cried out in unison, "You're out!" There was no way we were going to defile our Meat Lovers Supreme. The hiker got mad and left without placing an order for himself.

Pizza, hot pizza! Oh, how delicious it was. We ate till we could eat no more and split the leftovers to pack away for breakfast. We each drank two liters of Mountain Dew. It helped fill us up, plus those calories were badly needed. Later that night we sat around a fire, talking quietly. Hiker's midnight had passed. Hiker's midnight is any time after 8 p.m.

I was telling my famous badass mouse joke in a quiet but animated fashion. A voice yelled out from the shelter, "Hey, Joker! Keep it down, we are sleeping in here!" Who was calling me a joker? My blood pressure went up. I was already being quiet. All the other hikers agreed that my voice was respectfully low. I was not pleased! Grumbling, I went to bed minutes later. My night was shot.

The next morning came, and I was ready to find the guy who had told me to "be quiet" when I was already being quiet. He had left earlier. It turned out the guy was the old man who wanted pineapple and onions on our pizza! He had a reputation of trying to tell everyone what to do. Intending to intimidate the other hikers, he would stand inside the shelters and do a "Tai Chi dance." Well, I was ready to Tai Chi his butt. Others confirmed he was a real jerk wad. Now, I was even angrier. This dude was trying to take advantage of the kindness of other hikers. His rudeness, apparently, was legendary. I would see him again, I promised myself.

Cargo, Thimble, and I hiked all day long. Cargo and I got ahead of Thimble. We came upon a cooler just across a creek. Trail Magic! We opened it with bated breath. In the cooler were homemade peanut butter and jelly sandwiches. The magic was still there! Also in the cooler were lunch cakes and generic Dr. Peppers. We stopped for lunch and to rehydrate. When Thimble arrived she was pleased to get the last of the trail magic. There were only two lunch cakes for the three of us, so Cargo cut each cake into thirds.

Thimble and Cargo talked about the upcoming Trail Days. Trail Days is an event for hikers in Damascus. The event lasts from three to five days. Hundreds of people attend every year. It could be described as an annual Hiker's Woodstock. Thimble had already arranged a ride at a later date farther up the trail. Cargo was planning to hitchhike back to Damascus.

It was a warm day and the bugs were thick. Cargo had a few short cigars. The smoke helps keep the bugs away. At least, that was our justification for smoking cigars. After stopping for the night, we started a small fire, sat down, had a cigar, and told stories. The night was uneventful, yet the kind of night most people would give anything to enjoy. It was pleasant and it was our night to relax.

If we had stress in our lives it didn't come into the camp with us.

We gazed at the stars, told stories, and sang songs. The night was as relaxed as could be. The mosquitoes even took a break and decided not to bite anymore, or maybe the cigars were working. Either way, our small fire was perfect and the company was excellent.  The site was what used to be a shelter but is now listed as a tent platform. The shelter has been taken down and the platform was left behind. The privy was still usable. Cargo and I slept on the tent platform. I set up my tent and he "cowboy camped." Thimble set her tent up a few yards away.

Bland, Virginia, with Deb

THE DISTANCE THIMBLE and Cargo needed to go to get a ride to Trail Days was getting shorter. I was going to leave them and continue on to Bland, Virginia, where Deb was coming to meet me. This was the first time I would see her since I had "hit the trail." If I left Cargo and Thimble I could make more miles, but my decision to hike on was dashed by an impending storm. We hiked together only ten miles before we made it to a shelter when the rains hit.

The rains came down really hard. So, we checked our maps, revised our plans, and called it a day. Other hikers arrived during the steady down pouring rain. Three dudes were having a lively discussion. They felt they had run out of things to talk about, so they invented new topics of, "What would you do if . . . ?" Or, "Where would you go if . . . ?" Today's question was: "Where would you go if you could turn into a monkey at will?" The most popular answer was church. I don't know why.

As we were going to bed, a few other hikers arrived, filling the shelter. The rain stopped and the woods were quiet and everyone was quietly trying to sleep. While lying there, more hikers arrived to an already full shelter. They had to set up their tents in the dark. They all complained about finding trail magic in a cooler a couple days earlier but the magic had been gone. That was the magic we enjoyed.

Later, everyone was sound asleep. All the hikers were too exhausted to hear any snoring, or were used to it by now. Each hiker rested comfortably, lost in his own dream world. The rain returned, gaining momentum. Bam! Bam! Two loud explosions went off echoing through the woods.

Hikers attempted to jump up but were prisoners in their own sleeping bags. We were bound up as if in straitjackets. I grabbed for my gun. It was gone. "Holy Shit!" slipped from my lips. I searched for a gun as my mind brought me back to the trail: I did not bring a gun. "Easy, Mingo!" called Cargo. Nervous laughs filled the shelter. Lightning had struck a tree only a few yards away. That was the first blast. Then the tree exploded from the force, and that was the second blast.

Gathering my wits back by counting the days and countries, as I used to do to gain my bearings and to remember where I was each morning when I was traveling throughout the Middle East, I realized more and more where I was. I was on the Appalachian Trail.

It would not have been pleasant to be the guys who had set up their tents in the woods near the lightning strike. Thimble asked, "Are we safe in the shelter?" I responded, "No, but not much we can do about it now. Good night." I smiled and went to sleep.

The next day Cargo and Thimble headed to Trail Days. I stopped at one more shelter that night before heading to Bland. The shelter was almost empty, as most hikers were headed to Trail Days. The privy was uphill from the shelter. It wasn't difficult to find, just difficult to believe. After following the side trail to the privy, I found a platform. On the platform was a plywood box. The box had a hole cut in it and a toilet seat covered the hole. This was the privy. So, if it doesn't have walls, how could it be called a privy? Thoughts like this keep me up at night.

Privies, better known as outhouses, vary along the trail. They are most often found near shelters. At the beginning of the trail, privies were "duff privies." Duff is the organic material found just below dead leaves on the forest floor. You throw in a hand full of duff after each use. Other privies may call for foliage or dead leaves.

Most privies have four walls, a door, a roof, and one seat, but I have seen privies with sky lights. I think it is so you can gaze at the stars while doing your business. Some privies have no door. Others have three walls. There were a couple of privies that had only two walls. If you think that is odd, there was one privy with only one wall and a few with no walls at all.

There are privies with twin seats. That's efficient! In the White Mountains of New Hampshire there is a campsite where you are asked to register in the privy. In Maine, signs on the privy warn hikers to close and lock the doors or porcupines will eat the privy. I don't want to be a porcupine!

Some hiking clubs get fancy and add solar power to aerate the privies. What is most disturbing is that most privies are uphill from the water sources. Shouldn't the water source be higher than the privies? Hikers tend to treat the privies well. Most are clean and usable. But all of them are BYOTP, bring your own toilet paper.

The hike into Bland was bittersweet. The trail was not difficult. The weather wasn't too harsh, the air was moist, making the ground slippery, and the temperature was rising. This was the warmest day so far. I hiked as fast as I could. *Deb is coming to meet me at Bland,* kept repeating in my mind. This was going to be my chance to get new shoes and to fix some of the gear that wasn't holding up well. Deb was bringing a good resupply.

I had hiked ten miles the day before and hiked twenty-one miles the next. There was no way I was going to wait longer than necessary before seeing Deb. I hiked faster than expected and thought Deb was supposed to be at Bland in about two or three hours. When I arrived at the road to Bland, though, there sat Deb's car! She had arrived early. Surprise! My heart jumped with joy at seeing her.

The best part of my day was meeting Deb, but that event was bittersweet as well. Of course seeing Deb was sweet. The bitter part was I had a terrible case of "monkey butt!" If you are not familiar with the term, let me enlighten you. Remember all the chaffing I had suffered from earlier? Well, monkey butt is chaffing between the cheeks, and you can't put tape there! Man, was I suffering! Monkey-butt chaffing had caused swelling and a redness that rivaled the brightness of a shiny red apple.

Deb was understanding of my plight. Monkey butt isn't too sexy. I felt bad, as she had come a long way to see me and I was a mess. Her first words to me were ordering me to put the car window down. I smelled! Another hiker and I jumped into the car for a ride to get food, a hotel room, and a shower. Oh, and beer! It had been some time since my last shower. Hikers will go for days with no shower. Hiking in the day's heat and moist air caused more sweat and stink than I had thought. Deb tried to drive with her head stuck out the window.

When we arrived at the hotel, I tried to walk normally but that hurt intensely. Deb went to get Epsom salts so I could soak. To my surprise, she had brought clean clothes for me to wear. It didn't take long for me to lose the thru-hiker look, but I still had some of the thru-hiker stink! Soak and shower as much as you desire, the stink remains on your body for a long, long time. Our time together had just begun.

Our first night at the hotel was quiet. The reunion was enjoyable, topped by full meals and looking for new shoes. The running shoes Deb had made me bring were thoroughly worn out. I felt every stick and stone on the trail. My feet ached and they would awaken me at night with sharp, stabbing pains.

We didn't buy shoes the first night, but Deb did bring a pair from home. While she was in Bland, I was going to slack pack. She would drive me forward down the trail and I would hike back. That was a great plan to make easy miles by slack packing.

In the morning, I laced up the new shoes brought from home. A small pack was loaded with food and drink. I checked the area map and planned a nineteen-mile slack pack. My monkey butt was still a problem, but it was healing. My feet hurt, but I had new shoes. Deb was there, but I was going to make easy miles. Admittedly, my priorities were a bit screwy.

Deb dropped me off and away I went. The air was moist and warm. Flying bugs were thick. Spring smells filled the air. Sunbeams stabbed through the woods, causing leaf buds to open on the trees. The day's hike was good. What a great plan, slack packing! However, I soon found a hot spot on my right ankle. I must have been two miles in the woods when the spot became a problem, but I only had seventeen miles to go. The hot spot formed a blister before mile three.

During lunch I rubbed the hot spot and soaked it in a creek. Lunch was good and I met several hikers I knew already. You tend to get to see who is close when they are headed northbound and you are hiking southbound. My slack pack was sobo, southbound. It dawned upon me, other hikers could be close and you never know it because they stay just ahead or behind you. Going sobo allowed me to see them.

My pace slowed as the hotspot continued getting larger. I tried stuffing tissue between my foot and shoe. That didn't work. I tried two socks on one foot and none on the other. That didn't work. Changing my gait, how I stepped, didn't work. Then, twelve miles away from the end of the day's hike, I could go no farther in those new shoes. I found what finally did work. Going barefoot was my only and final option.

Going barefoot seemed easy. The trail was soft and kinder to my feet than I had expected. The leaves on the trail hid sharp sticks, roots, and rocks. That was okay, as occasional stabbing on the bottom of my feet was tolerable. Then, the leaves became thicker and deeper. I stepped down onto a thick pile of leaves with my right foot, and the ground moved. I leaped high into the air as a five-foot black snake showed his displeasure of me stepping on him! After landing back on the trail, I leaped again . . . yelping. The snake slithered away with superiority like a monarch of the trail. I hiked on with trepidation.

Once safely away, I called Deb, asking what other shoes I had available. Sandals were my only other option. Using my map, I located a shelter that was between us. I would meet Deb there. It was two miles away from me and two miles away from her.

Deb arrived at the shelter shortly after I arrived. A rain cloud blew over, showering the area for a few minutes, then cleared. The short rain brought about masses of flies and other pestering bugs. I showed Deb around the shelter and told her how hikers prepared to spend the night. After a quick entry into the shelter journal, we headed back to the car. Deb's knee was hurting so we walked slowly.

We were no more than a half mile from the shelter when a hiker appeared. He was a white-haired, thin man. I recognized him as the man who called me "Joker" and intimidated other hikers. I stood to the side of the trail, as he had the right of way. The hiker going uphill has the right of way. I said, "Hey, I know you." He looked up at me. Without responding, he hiked toward me, then shouldered me. Yup, this jerk shoved me with his shoulder! That was the last straw.

I turned and yelled, "Stop, you son of a bitch!" He took several quick steps and stopped about fifteen feet away. He turned and started back, as if he wanted to fight. I was so happy to comply. "Do you want something?" he asked. "A piece of your ass!" I answered starting toward him. "Your Tai Chi isn't gonna save you here!" He quickly responded, "I don't know you!" I responded, "You're the one who called me 'Joker.'"

"I don't know you," he tried again. Seeing this response wasn't working, he tried, "You don't know me and what I can do." I responded with a smile, walking toward him, saying, "That's right. I have to assume you are the baddest person out here and take you out quickly." That got his attention. Fear covered his face. His intimidation techniques against other hikers were not working. Deb stepped between us to stop me.

I explained to the hiker that he should not be so rude to everyone. He could never know when he might meet someone alone in the woods. He saw Deb was protecting him, so he started again with a little more courage. "You don't want to try me," he said. My eyes saw red, "The hell I don't." He stepped back, "What do you want?" "I'm gonna teach you a lesson, and kick your ass!" I said. He grabbed his wristwatch, pulling it to his eyes, yelling, "That's it! I have it recorded." Then he ran off into the woods away from the trail.

Deb and I started back toward the car again. We hadn't gone two hundred yards when we met two young hikers. One of them was hiding his backpack in the woods. We had never met before, but we knew and liked some of the same hikers. Vegan was the hiker hiding his pack. He explained how he and the other hiker were on their way to a Subway when a rain cloud hit and he had put on his rain gear. While at the Subway the sun had come out. He had left his raincoat in the restaurant and needed to go back to retrieve it.

Wanting to do a good deed, I offered to help. Vegan and I ran back to Deb's car. She was okay walking back slowly to the parking area while I drove Vegan to the Subway. He retrieved his raincoat and we returned to the trailhead. Before heading out I gave Vegan a beer to replenish the calories he had burned up running to Deb's car.

Deb was ready to head back to the hotel. She had experienced enough excitement for the day. The camaraderie hikers share was more personal than she expected. Deb was feeling out of place. I explained to her there were different ways to connect with people on the trail without actually having to hike. We went to a Dollar Store and bought candy, water, Power Aide, and Honey Buns.

Deb and I returned to the trailhead and waited. As hikers came by she offered trail magic. This was her first experience being a trail angel. When hikers needed a ride to town, she took them. Hikers appreciate every bit of outside support. When the food magic started running short we went back to the hotel. Hikers now recognized Deb as "Mingo's-Wife-Deb" and thanked her for the trail magic.

Deb was now part of the trail. She was building a reputation as a trail angel. As other hikers came by with their tales of adventure Deb could share her tales of adventure as well. "I stopped Mingo from hurting that guy." That was a good story!

Socks and her dog, Doobie, were at the hotel with Socks' mother. Her mom had come from Ohio to visit. We sat together that evening, watching the sun go down, drinking a cold beer. A few other hikers from Ohio joined us. We were the last holdouts who hadn't gone to Trail Days.

I needed a different pair of new shoes, so off we went to buy some. I found a pair of hiking shoes that seemed to fit well. But with each new item purchased comes another lesson. The next day I set out for a twenty-four mile slack pack to try the new shoes. Never wear new shoes when hiking twenty-four miles! As if my feet didn't hurt enough.

The insoles of the shoes had a gel around the heel. The gel was exposed without any lining and was in a horseshoe shape. By the end of my slack pack, I had horseshoe-shaped blisters on each heel. The shoes were good, but the insoles were awful. Never buy shoes without buying new insoles to replace the ones that come with the shoes. Lesson learned! We bought replacement insoles.

Our third and last night together we had moved up the trail to Pearisburg. I had hiked that far. We found a hotel that served hikers. Deb met Alien, Freight Train, and other hikers. After short visits, we kept to ourselves. I repacked my new backpack. The first pack was worn out and falling apart.

Deb had brought me an old army "Alice pack." I took the waistband from the first pack and sewed it to the Alice pack making my own gear. It seemed to work okay. Of course, I hadn't tried it yet. I continued sewing and Deb helped some, too. I sent old maps home and packed my resupply. I had to get things right. Deb would be gone, leaving in the morning. That night rains came down hard. I was happy to be in a hotel staying dry.

With my gear packed, fresh food, new Hubba tent, a new sleeping air mattress, a new water filter, and a homemade backpack, I was ready. I was ready, except the pack was most uncomfortable! I wasn't going to say anything. I would make this work. My biggest concerns were the blisters on the heels of my feet. Plus, I really was going to miss Deb.

The next day, Deb took me and a few other hikers to the trailhead. The trail through town was somewhat confusing. I went the wrong way! Road construction had hidden some of the signs. But before long, I was back in the woods, taking on a fifteen-hundred foot climb. The rest of the day was easier, although the trail was mostly rocks. The woods had turned greener as leaves were popping out everywhere.

Food Run

AFTER TWENTY MILES, I stopped for the night at Pine Swamp Branch Shelter. The mosquitoes were thick and hungry. They swarmed like mad, hungry wolves. Having hiked twenty miles on wet rocks, I had often slipped, hurting my feet. My left foot had taken a severe beating. It started to swell and turn dark.

Freight Train was already at the shelter, as was Alien and a few other hikers. Two young kids, twelve and fifteen years old, were also at the shelter. They were thru-hiking. They called themselves the Runaways. The sister was the older of the two. She went by Goldie Locks and the young lad went by Forest.

Rains came that evening. I built a fire in the fireplace built inside the shelter. That helped dry everyone. We set up our individual sleeping spots for the night. I was grateful to be sleeping in the shelter. It was cold out, but the shelter had a nice, warm fire. Everyone quickly fell asleep. Around eleven that evening I was awakened by a hiker moving around. My snoring woke him up. He told me Freight Train got up and set up her tent outside to get away from my snoring. She no sooner had moved than rain started falling in a heavy downpour.

Before leaving the next morning, Freight Train wrote in the shelter journal about my legendary snoring. I wrote an answer of apology and a promise to never sleep in a shelter again if she were there. I packed my gear. The kids headed out, then Alien, and then I followed, heading north.

I hiked four miles and reached a shelter. Rains fell and then changed to hail. Chunks of hail pounded upon the ground. The winds kicked up fiercely. Alien was also taking cover in the shelter. We ate lunch. The weather never relented. We each decided this was far enough for today. I set out my sleep pad and bag, climbed in, and went to sleep. Four miles was good enough on a bad day.

The next day was much better. It was only eight miles to the next shelter. Hiking an average of fifteen to twenty plus miles a day would have been a better plan, but the rain forced me to accept much less. Stopping after eight miles at War Spur was prudent and necessary. I had to stop for the night. The pack I had reworked was less efficient than I expected. It caused some discomfort. My feet were still taking a beating. And the rain was absolutely relentless, never quitting.

Luckily the next day was warmer. I arose well refreshed and ready to go. Fast running streams, caused by the previous rainy days, provided a place to filter water. This promised to be a great day. I hiked with a little pep in my step. My feet hurt, but it was okay. My pack settled to a nice position for the first time. That was good. I would hike many miles that day in good time.

Lunchtime came along with the highest daily temperatures yet. The heat could have been considered sweltering. Sweat dripped into my eyes. The salt burned, blurring my vision. It was a good time to rest, anyway, so I kicked back, putting my bare feet in the air. Hunger pangs struck, so I dug into my pack for food.

There was no food! I had planned to be at Catawba before now, to obtain a resupply. The rains had prevented that distance and I had no contingency plans. I was totally out of food. Then it dawned on me—I could make it to the post office in Catawba tomorrow to retrieve my resupply. One day without food was no big deal. I lay back, resting well.

Sleep was coming as my mind wandered away. This was going to be a pleasant nap. No need to worry, just take my time and burn as few calories as possible. My eyes blinked frantically as I sat up all astir! *Crap! Today is Friday*. The post office would be closed by noon the next day. I needed to make miles now! Some post offices don't open on Saturdays at all. I needed to be in Catawba by four o'clock that day.

I saddled up my pack and I ran. Holding my map in front of me, I counted every mile, every incline, and every decline. There was no way I could get to Catawba on time. My mind rushed with fear as my feet blindly hit the trail, twisting my ankles time and again.

Then, I saw there was a way. I had to use the most direct route to Catawba. I had to make it by four or five o'clock, if that was when the post office closed, and I had to make it quickly. There was another path that was more level. It took all the inclines and declines out of the equation. I had to get off the trail and on a road to run. Hitchhiking would be cheating, but if I ran the entire distance it would still be me hiking from Georgia to Maine. This was my hike. *Why was I was screwing it up?*

I got to the road. My mind was made up; I ran. As the road had a slight incline, I ran slowly. As it slightly declined, I ran harder. One mile faded behind me. If I had wanted to hitchhike, it would not have done me any good. There wasn't any traffic on this back road. I ran as best I could. The farther I ran, the hotter the sun baked down on me.

I was not sure how many miles I had to go, but now I needed directions. I flagged down a pickup truck and asked how far it was to the post office. The gentleman said it was only a few miles, but I would not make it before they closed, not unless I rode there. I had no choice, so I took the ride. The gentleman stopped at a store for gas. We had gone only a couple of miles. I bought Snickers and a precooked pizza for a quick lunch. When the gentleman returned, he said he wasn't going to the post office! He wished me luck after pointing the way. I was back on the road, trying to make up time. I had nourishment, so I was ahead of this game. I hiked faster. Cars blew by without as much as a glance my way. No problem, I wasn't asking for a ride.

The road turned steeper. I trudged forward. Getting to the post office on time was a must. A car stopped. The lady asked where I was headed. I told her the post office. Like an angel in the nick of time she explained she was headed there also and if we didn't hurry we wouldn't make it on time. I jumped in and we sped off to the post office.

We arrived at the post office just as a lady was coming from behind the counter to lock the front door. It was about to close, but I got my resupply package! My mind and body were exhausted. I went behind the post office with my new supplies, intending to put them into my backpack. Eating was also high on my to-do list.

After an hour of rest, it was time to get back to the trail. This had been one tough day. I looked at the map. The trail was just over a mile away, but it was all uphill—a steep hill. I hiked to the trail. Not a single car offered a ride. At this point, I would have happily accepted a ride. My legs were developing shin splints from running on the road. Both legs started swelling. They hurt so badly, and I was dehydrated.

My plan was to get to Catawba Mountain Shelter and call it a day. When I reached the trailhead, Freight Train stepped out of the woods. She was shocked to see me there already. I explained how I got there and why. She needed to call her mother, but her phone did not get service. Verizon got the best service all the way up the trail. I had Verizon, so as a good deed I offered my phone to Freight Train. This gave me a chance to rest for another half hour as she talked to her mother on my phone.

Freight Train headed down to Catawba as I headed into the woods. The hike to the shelter was easy. Setting up my tent and sleeping area was routine. I was the only person at the shelter the entire night. I had a pleasant night's sleep, except for a few leg cramps.

A Break

AFTER STARTING OUT the next morning, I called a buddy, Ken, who lived close. I had met Ken in the army when we went through Special Forces training together. He and his wife Laura are good friends of mine— really, the absolute best. He was the friend I had met in Georgia the day I arrived to hike the AT.

Soon the trail led me to McAfee Knob. This is an overlook on a cliff's edge. The scenic view was spectacular. I looked over the edge and outward to the vast landscape of Virginia.

The wind was blowing but the air was dry and the sunshine warmed me. At one point, I was squeezed between the edge of the overlook and an evergreen tree. A branch from the tree pushed on my tent poles, which I kept in a long bag strapped to the top of my pack. The branch pushed the poles out from under their straps. The poles fell and started over the edge of the cliff. Quickly, I bent down to grab them. I felt as if I were going over the cliff as my backpack started sliding off my back over my head. Looking down, I saw certain death! I was off-balance; my weight was too far over the edge. The wind kicked up in a lucky, hard gust to help push me back. I was safe, but shaken.

Securing the poles back under their straps, I sat down and took a moment for reflection and rest. That had been close. Having escaped a dangerous fall to certain death, I went deeper into the woods, away from the cliffs. It would be a twenty-mile hike until I met Ken at a road crossing in Daleville.

At Daleville, we met a trail angel named Santa's Helper. He was an older man who had a van loaded with trail magic for hikers. Santa's Helper looked like Santa, but much thinner. He was a kind man.

Ken took me to his home for a long-needed rest. My clothes were cleaned, I had a bath, slept in a bed, and ate home cooked food. Being with friends was great. Ken wanted to hike some of the trail with me, but didn't get a chance, other than the short distance he had hiked in to meet me coming out of the woods. After two zeros and a long visit, I was taken back to Daleville. My adventure continued.

The Trail Days event was over and most of the hikers were returning to the trail. The hikers who had stayed on the trail were few and far between. Staying at shelters in solitude had been a relief. There was comfort in not waking another hiker because of my snoring. That made being alone even better. I stayed at Bobblets Gap alone. By being alone, I mean just me and a million mosquitoes.

Water sources started getting scarcer. Cove Mountain Shelter had no water. Once I arrived at Jennings Creek I met a few other hikers. This was a swimming hole. We all jumped in and enjoyed the refreshing, cold water. This was to be the first of many chances to swim while on the trail. It felt invigorating to swim in the cold water.

Bryant Ridge Shelter was three miles away. My clothes had dried by the time I arrived. Doc Boom and a few other guys were already there. The shelter was huge, the biggest shelter I had seen so far. I think it had three stories. That was more than enough room for the four of us.

We gathered wood and made a huge fire. We were like boys having fun in the woods. Doc Boom was a hyper sort of character. I heard later that his twin brother came out to hike some of the trail with him. Doc Boom gave his brother his trail name, Spare Parts. That's the kind of humor to expect from Doc Boom. He was an entertaining, funny guy.

From the moment I had started my hike on Springer Mountain, weight had been a concern. As I said before, thru-hikers carry only what is needed and try to cut out all excess weight. Toothbrush handles are cut in half. Cargo had gone as far as drilling holes in the buckles on his gear. He had drilled holes in the handle of his plastic comb to lighten the weight of his comb. Other creative ways of lightening the load have been found. Most thru-hikers will use a ziplock bag as a wallet. It is waterproof and light weight.

At most shelters, hikers lose pennies from their pockets. The fact is, hikers are sore and don't want to bend down to pick up pennies, and the pennies are added weight. So, the pennies are left on the ground. For some odd reason, I collected the pennies. I had no idea why, as I have never collected pennies before. The section of my pack that served as both pouch and cover flap, called the brain, was where I kept my penny collection.

The pennies kept getting heavier. I had no idea why I was carrying them, but it seemed to be the right thing to do. The next day, I hiked down to a spot called Matts Creek. The heat of the day caused me to sweat excessively. I bathed in the creek, alone. Being the only hiker at Matts Creek made bathing simpler. In the shelter journal I reported that I had skinny-dipped in the creek and the water was cold. I also washed my clothes. The mosquitoes were less offending after the cold water bath.

I called Cargo to see how he was doing. He told me he had a problem. His girlfriend, Julie, was coming to finish hiking the trail with him. She was driving from Oregon. He didn't know where she would be able to leave her car. At that time, she was somewhere around Kansas. That was easy to fix. The weekend coming up was a long weekend, Memorial Day. I told Cargo to call Julie and have her drive to Ohio. She could leave her car at my house and Deb would bring her down to his location. That way, Deb would be back on the trail with me. This was my best idea yet and another good deed done!

Dehydrated

THE NEXT DAY brought even warmer weather. I came to a long foot-bridge crossing a river. The bridge was called "Foot Bridge," named after Mr. and Mrs. Foot, who built the bridge. They were ex-thru-hikers who went by the trail name "Happy Feet."

A three-thousand-foot climb awaited me. The sun was shining brightly, raising the temperature. The weight of my pack felt heavier than ever. I passed a stream, thinking, *"There is always a stream to cross . . . there is a spring on top of the mountain at Salt Log Gap . . . why carry water to water . . . and I really don't want to carry water up this mountain!"* Good, reasonable thinking. Glad I listened—not!

The mountain was steeper than I expected. It was so hot that the lizards were scurrying across the sun-scorched rocks. These were real lizards, not moisture-loving skinks. I took pictures of the lizards. I felt as if I were in the desert. The spring water on top of  the mountain at Salt Log Gap would be gratefully received. Higher and higher I hiked up the trail. This three-thousand-foot incline was one of the hardest on the trail for me.

My legs were shaking, my head was spinning, but I made it to the top. A winding trail led me to a sign that read, "Salt Log Gap." Below the name, someone had written, "No H2O." If true, not a good sign! I had made a dumb, rookie mistake. Passing up a water source thinking there was water on top of a mountain was not wise. My map noted that there was water on the gap, but it was wrong. Never pass by water when hiking on a hot day. After a five-mile hike and a three-thousand-foot climb in eighty-eight degree weather, I found no water.

Maybe there was water downhill from the gap? The rock bed looked as if water had flowed over it. Maybe the spring was farther away from the trail? I went through the woods, wading through a field of chest high nettle weeds that stung my body. I searched the area downhill about a mile and still found no water. Hiking the mile back to the trail through the nettles proved painful. Trying to find water had been a mistake.

The heat was getting to me. I would have to hike another five miles to find water on the trail, including a hundred-foot decline followed by a thousand-foot climb uphill. The effects of the heat were showing me just what a bad mistake I had made. Dehydration was always a true fear. My steps were getting shorter as the sun was growing more intense. I had to get to the next shelter in hopes of finding a good water supply.

Prior to reaching the water supply, I crossed over Bluff Mountain. A small headstone sat along the trail. I paused to read the writing. A young four-year-old lad, Ottie Cline Powell, on November 9, 1891, went looking for firewood for his one-room school. Little Ottie never returned. He was found dead at this location. He had frozen to death.

Without thinking, I took off my pack and retrieved the pennies I had been collecting. Placing the pennies on his stone, I told Little Ottie he was a good boy. That thought struck me as odd, me thinking of him as a little boy. If he had lived he would be a hundred twenty-four years old. Instead, he would always be the cute little four-year-old whose bright eyes lit up every room he entered. I left Ottie's site with an admonishment for him to behave, then hiked on. My need for water seemed less tragic.

My hopes were to find a cold mountain spring. That would have been heavenly. But here on the trail, that would be too good to be true and most unlikely. I made it to the next shelter and found water. It was not what I had hoped for, but there was plenty of water: thousands of gallons of warm stagnant water in a scum-covered pond. Lucky me! After running the warm water through my filter, I drank about two liters. At one point, every muscle in my body was cramping up. My stomach convulsed, and I threw up the water. My feet were screaming in pain as muscles in my legs, arms, and stomach cramped. It was certainly time to take a break.

After a short rest and a slow rehydration period, I found a road and began walking to town. My map showed that the town was only nine miles away. I needed to recheck that map. It was wrong about water being available and the town was more than twenty-five miles away. After a short five-mile hike on the blistering hot road, I got a ride. The guy took me all the way to Buena Vista. Again, lessons learned!

I am not always the sharpest lightbulb in the box or the brightest tack on the wall . . . or something like that. Anyway, dehydration must be added to the perils to guard against. My bad! I should have known that already! Injuries are common on the trail. Twisting an ankle is a daily occurrence. Stubbing toes happens almost hourly. Getting stress fractures are common. Early on the trail, when people quit, it is because the arduous hike was not what they had expected. At this point, when someone quits, it is often because of an adventure-ending injury.

There are many perils to face when hiking the trail. The weather can get pretty rough at times. Early on the trail, ice-cold temperatures, high winds, and cold rain make hypothermia a true threat. I shivered for the first few days, soaking wet and cold. Another threat during that time was losing footing on the trail in the slippery mud and rocks, which could cause falls and injury.

Another hazard I never realized was the pounding on my poor feet. I never heard of planter fasciitis before hiking the trail. That is when the tendons on the bottom of the feet get so tight and inflamed it is almost crippling. That was the pain I was feeling now and each step was more painful than the last.

Lately, the weather had been getting hotter, bringing the bugs out in full force. I had removed several ticks already. Mosquitoes were biting at all hours and the flies were relentless. Those doggone horseflies were the worst ever! When they bite, you bleed. I discovered a cool way to kill them. When they start hovering overhead, stop. Turn your back to the sun. Look down at your shadow and you will see the shadow of the horseflies. You can then grab them based on where they are by their shadows. I killed twenty horseflies in an hour.

It is a daily occurrence on the trail to see several snakes. I hadn't come across a rattlesnake, yet, but many other hikers had. I had almost stepped on a copperhead a few days earlier. It was lying on the trail, and as I was about to put my foot down I noticed it. I leaped high into the air. The snake never moved. Now, that was fun; I had no idea I could jump so high. The spiders are hungry at night, so it is always expected to get a bite or two if you are sleeping in a shelter. Luckily, the bears had not been a problem for me, yet. Others had had their food stolen by bears, and one bear came into a shelter while several hikers were inside sleeping. That would have been interesting, to wake up with a bear on top of you, eating the food you had hanging up away from the mice. Oh yeah, the mice were a huge problem.

Injuries can be guarded against but cannot be avoided a hundred percent of the time. Once, as I was hiking on a ridgeline that was nothing but slanted rocks, I slid about thirty feet before I was able to stop. The slab was steep and it was slippery from rain. There was a lot farther to slide, maybe hundreds of feet. At least, that is what I saw. That experience tightened the old buttocks! I was lucky.

Those are a few dangers everyone faces while hiking the AT. Oh, I should also include the rushing currents in creeks after a hard rain and the lightning strikes that get up close and personal. I bet I am forgetting more than I remembered to note here.

So what about the hazards that aren't under foot? Let's see . . . during the high winds, which are about every day, falling branches are a threat. If I ever needed a job, I could get one as a "branch magnet." So many branches nearly hit me that I thought I would need to start naming them. And those were big branches, the kind that would be "Good night, Agnes," if you were hit by one. Other falling debris included whole trees. Yup, the complete tree! And the answer to the age-old question is "yes;" if a tree falls in the woods and no one is around it does make a sound. I looked and no one was around. The loudest noise was me, screaming like a little school girl. You would have thought a mouse had run up my shorts or a little bird flew between my legs.

After arriving at Buena Vista, I found a room at the Budget Inn. The room was hidden in the back of a hotel. The room was set-aside for hikers. It was well used but kept clean and had everything I needed. There was another hiker roomed next door. I didn't know who it was, yet.

Off I went to shop for food and drink. I was dehydrated and needed liquids fast. After getting plenty to drink and hitting the shower, I felt much better. So, I called Deb. Julie was with her in Ohio. They would leave the next day and head my way first. Now, it was time for dinner, but first, I needed to find out who was staying next door.

I held a beer in hand as I knocked on my neighbor's door. The door opened and there stood Alien. What a pleasant surprise to find him again. We drank our beer and left to eat dinner.

Buena Vista is a small town a long way from the trail. A hiker has to hitchhike into town. I was amazed how many hikers were there. The town had everything we needed. We found different places to eat, an ice cream stand, and lots of beer. The hot shower was a good thing. After a large Mexican dinner, I slept really well that night.

The next morning I checked out and went to breakfast. This was planned to be a great day. I was not going to hike. Deb was coming to my location first, to pick me up, then we were headed to Daleville to meet Cargo. Daleville was where my Army buddy Ken had picked me up for my break from the trail.

There wasn't much to do in town as I waited. I didn't want to carry my pack around all day, so I stashed the pack in a small patch of woods along some railroad tracks. Later, it started raining. This was going to be a long, slow day. Not wanting a soaked pack, I retrieved it and went to the local police station and asked if I could leave my pack with them. The police were cool about it and stowed my pack in a small out building.

The town's library was open, so I went there to send out an e-mail to friends and family. There was a line waiting to use the computers. Several hikers whom I had never met before were in that line. After using the computer, we all went to a restaurant and had snacks and more beers.

I anxiously waited for Deb to arrive. My patience was disappearing. So, I went back to the police station and got my pack. Deb was coming from the west so I started hiking west. My feet were hurting from the lack of hiking that day, so this made them feel better. I called periodically to get an update on her location. We met about seven miles outside of town. I needed the exercise.

Once I was loaded into the car, we drove south to meet Cargo. Meeting this way was great and I got to see Cargo again. He got to hike with Julie and I got to spend time with Deb. Family visits are a big plus. Hikers refer to them as conjugal visits. After being so dehydrated and run-down the day before, I felt things were going well now.

We went to Daleville to the Holiday Inn. Cargo had paid for our rooms. It was an awesome reunion. Deb was happy to be there with me. A group of hikers whom I had met previously during my hike was there also. They were really partying it up. We stood outside as Cargo led the hikers in song as a choir singing, "M-I-N-G-O and Mingo was his name, oh!" We all had a blast catching up and exchanging stories of our adventures.

Cargo and Julie were going to slack pack with Deb's help. They wanted to catch up to me but I was days ahead of them. I also wanted to take advantage of the chance to slack pack. Deb took me to the trail after dropping Cargo and Julie off at their spot. I hiked only twelve miles that day. That didn't sit well with Cargo, since he was trying to catch up. I was slack packing away from him.

Secretly, I did not want them to catch up—at least, not yet. I had "my hike" to do and I was doing it. My plan was to keep hiking at my pace and enjoy it alone. I fully expected Cargo to catch up with me by Pennsylvania. Then, Deb would come to us so we could slack pack the entire state together. That was when and where I wanted Cargo to catch up with me.

I thought it was a good plan. After we finished our day's individual hikes, Deb picked all of us up. Then, we headed out to find a hotel and a big dinner. We found a hotel centered between our locations on the trail.

The rooms were clean. A small restaurant was just downhill from the hotel. The food was superior. We ate, talked, laughed, and planned our future hikes. Cargo fitted Julie for a backpack.

Looking for a Real Hiker?

DEB HAD TWO more days with us. We continued slack packing. She dropped Cargo off by himself so he could travel far and fast. The man can hike! I decided on a sobo hike, southbound. Deb took me to the trailhead. Surprised, there at the trailhead sat the young brother and sister from Ohio, and The Cape Crusader was with them. They were making good time.

I headed out, planning to hike about twelve miles. The trail was easy and the weather cooperated. This was a good trail day. My feet were hurting, but the pain went away after I was on the trail. Occasionally, my feet would go numb. The trail wound uphill and downhill, but mostly downhill. Around noon I stopped at Brown Mountain Creek Shelter for lunch. There, I resupplied my water. The shelter wasn't much to write home about, especially since I was staying in a wonderful hotel room.

A group of boy scouts arrived. One of their scout leaders said, "Now, wait here guys and one might show up here. They usually stop here at the shelters." Hearing this, I asked if they were looking for a thru-hiker. He said they were.

I introduced myself as a thru-hiker. I figured I could talk about my hike and plans and about life on the trail. This is an interesting topic for young boys and I expected many questions. This was going to take some time away from my hike, but I could always run to make up the time lost.

The troop leader looked at me with dismay. He then looked at my small pack and said, "That's not a pack a thru-hiker would use, is it?" I explained

I was slack packing this day. "Oh, you have road support!" he sneered. "My wife is here, so she is meeting me along the trail, but . . . " I attempted to explain. He interrupted, "Well, we want to meet a 'real hiker!'"

Shocked by the comment, I walked away and back to the shelter. I picked up the journal and wrote about this guy. In the journal, I informed the other hikers how I was not a "real hiker." I had hiked only hundreds of miles. This guy was an ill-informed, know-it-all jerk. I wrote a more accurate description in the journal and signed it, "Mingo." One of the other troop leaders asked about the notebook. I explained how we use the shelter journals to pass information along to other hikers.

He read the shelter journal and read my entry. He looked up at me and smiled. Obviously, he agreed with my description of the jerk who was looking for a "real hiker." He called the jerk over and told him a thing or two. I told him he was an ass. At this point, I was not going to give a demonstration or talk about life on the trail. I was headed down the trail toward Deb.

Once back together with Deb she took me to the hospital. My left foot was swollen. A couple weeks earlier I had slipped into rocks and smashed it. It might have been broken. It had turned dark from bruising and was difficult to stand on. After walking a while, it would go numb. While sleeping, I would get the feeling back in my foot, waking me in pain. X-rays revealed nothing that was unexpected. The doctor said to stop hiking for a few weeks. That was not an option!

Cargo had a good laugh at my expense for not being a "real hiker!" It became a running joke that I was a magnet for jerks. To everyone's surprise, I didn't knock the "stuffing" out of the guy. He didn't need to be teaching or leading young men. That dude should stay home, eat Bonbon's, and watch soap operas.

On our final day together, Cargo and I packed up. Deb and I gave Julie our best wishes. Deb took Cargo and Julie out to the trail one last time. She then took me back to the trail where we had seen the Ohioans and The Cape Crusader at Hog Camp Gap. They were now a day ahead of me. Deb and I parted. I was on the trail and she was headed home. Hiking alone was a little more difficult, but she would be coming back when I reached Pennsylvania.

Bugs

THE DAY WAS hot and bugs were thick. The woods had become greener as the leaves were opening up fully. The scenic views were few as the leaves hid the vast hills. The trail was easy to hike, which was a plus. Still, I went only seven miles. Not having Deb there with me slowed my hiking pace.

I set up my tent at Seely-Woodworth Shelter. The bugs were absolute hell. I read the shelter journal, where other hikers complained about the mosquitoes as well. This was one of the worst locations for a shelter. For some reason, the mosquitoes are tremendously thick. Eating dinner outside was difficult. While getting water, I lost a quart of blood feeding the bugs. I ran back to my tent, jumped in, and started scratching. The rest of the night was spent scratching and the next morning was even worse. It was good to get out of the area. An hour later I stopped to eat.

No one else stopped at the shelter that night, and I can't blame them. This was another night alone at a shelter. Cargo texted me that he had made good time. Julie, now named Pony Express, had hiked nineteen miles. She was doing well.

Horseflies were making my hike difficult. The heat was sweltering. Time and again I had to stop for water. I hiked only seven miles and had to stop for the night. Cargo was trying to catch up. I half wanted to hike with him again, but my concern was that if he caught me I would not be able to keep up with him!

The Priest Shelter was empty. I set up my tent and fixed dinner. Phone service was good, so I called Deb. All was good on the home front. No one showed up at Priest Shelter, so I had another night alone. There hadn't been another person around now for two full days and nights. It was a rare pleasure to be alone in the woods. The night was quiet. My routines of unpacking, setting up, eating, sleeping, putting on smelly, wet clothes, and packing up again were repeated.

Five miles away from the Priest Shelter, I was at the Tye River. Before crossing the river, I tried to hitch to a store to get a cold drink. It was an extra hot day. No one stopped to offer a ride. It was a long hike to the store and proved to be a bad idea.

The store had the appearance of being on hold from the 1920s. A fan sat on a shelf blowing hot air around. I bought a Mountain Dew that was warm. The ice cream I bought had already melted. But, I needed the break. There I sat, wondering if my choice to come to the store was a bad one. It was. It was too far to go without getting a real refreshing drink.

One of the locals was taking a logging truck back past the trailhead and he offered me a ride. I loaded my gear in the truck's toolbox and hopped in. We talked as he drove to the trail. It was a good break to get a ride.

After hiking three miles uphill, I arrived at Harpers Creek Shelter. There was a fast moving stream by the shelter. A couple of people were there, but were headed out as I arrived. The area was clean and cooled by the stream. The sound of rushing water was relaxing. The bugs were not biting. I needed to wash my clothes in the creek.

Setting up at Harpers Creek was an easy decision. The shelter journal had many names I recognized. Sitting by the creek was so relaxing. The water was clear and refreshing. I washed off and hung my wet clothes on a line that I stretched between two trees. My entry in the journal stated I was alone again.

Nighttime fell; darkness encompassed the woods. Soon, someone or something made a noise just outside my tent. Taking quick peek outside, I saw Shenanigans. He was tired and panting. He was in a hurry, trying to get to Harpers Ferry, West Virginia. Fancy Pants was to meet him there. Shenanigans had taken too much time off, partying, and was behind schedule.

Shenanigans wrote in the journal an apology for showing up, breaking my record for the number of nights I had spent alone. *No apology needed!* We ate dinner together. Then, he was fast asleep in his tent. The next morning he was up and gone in a flash.

My map showed a side trail, the Mau-Har Trail. This trail started nearly a mile back from the shelter. It went by a waterfall and followed along a stream, then reconnected with the AT. Hiking in the heat had not been pleasant. Hiking along a stream would be about fifteen degrees cooler and draw fewer horseflies.

Without a second thought, I went back to the Mau-Har Trail. It was steep at some spots, but well worth the hike. The trail followed along a stream with swimming holes that were particularly refreshing. I swam in one spot and washed my clothes. While my clothes were drying on a flat rock, I ate lunch.

Farther up the trail was a larger swimming hole just below a small waterfall. That was a beautiful place to rest and to record a video. After the video, I decided to swim again. It was too tempting to pass up.

The Mau-Har Trail led directly to another shelter on the AT, the Maupin Field Shelter. Hikers there told me they did not enjoy the hike between there and Harpers Creek Shelter. There was nothing to see over Three Ridges and the horseflies were thick. After seeing my videos they were jealous of my decision to Blue Blaze. I had time for a second lunch with the other hikers and then we were back to hiking.

Two miles later another hiker and I came upon a cooler along the trail. Trail Magic! This was good. Was the magic gone? Slowly, we moved closer, as if approaching a bomb. Carefully, we lifted the lid. Then, as if the cooler had exploded, we threw the lid high into the air in celebration. The magic was there! Beers and ales filled the cooler along with sodas. This was a wonderful surprise.

We each sat down and slowly drank our beer of choice. Moments like this are almost indescribable. We spoke of the generosity of the trail angels who leave the magic. During these times, grown men and women find the same joy as a child opening a birthday present. Any type of food or water is an awesome gift. This is also a good time to listen to how another hiker has overcome an injury or a gear problem. They can give good advice with creative ways of handling difficult situations. We shared our stories and lessons learned.

Having downed our beers, we put on our packs and entered the Blue Ridge Parkway. The parkway started miles before this location, but this is where the trail and parkway merge and follow the same direction. As a matter of fact, the trail used to be the parkway until somebody came along and paved it!

Waynesboro

WE STOPPED AT the Paul C. Wolf Shelter and called it a night. The nightly routine began, again. Set up the tent, put down the sleep pad, and lay out the sleeping bag. Then, eat, drink, and rest for the night. More hikers were now showing up at shelters in this area. It wasn't as crowded as in the beginning, though. These hikers were more serious about finishing their hike.

Conversation in the shelter was about Waynesboro and "aqua blazing." To aqua blaze, you take a kayak down river from Waynesboro to as far as Harpers Ferry. That sounded interesting. It would really add to the adventure, but aqua blazing isn't hiking. I decided I would look into it when I got to Waynesboro and see if it was worth the effort and cost.

In the morning, I checked my food supply; it was nearly gone. A resupply was supposed to be waiting for me in Waynesboro. I planned on taking a zero there. The hike the day before hadn't been too difficult, but it had had its moments. It was a long day because I started late and took too many swim breaks. I had still hiked twenty-one miles, so I was happy. Chaffing was starting to come back because of the heat, though, and my knees were taking a beating. My feet still hurt; as a matter of fact, they hurt a lot.

The hike from the shelter to the road was an easy one. The weather grew much warmer. Water was becoming a big issue. Sweat poured out of me like a fast, leaky faucet. There were other hikers in the woods, mostly day hikers. The more day hikers I saw the better. Usually, I didn't relish seeing day hikers, but in this heat it was a sure sign I was close to town.

I passed a family with a mother, father, and two daughters. The gals were around three or four years old. One of the girls was as talkative as any kid I had ever met. She had never met a stranger. She had more questions than a prosecutor at a trial. She talked more than a preacher on Easter Sunday. Talk about being funny, the little gal had a future in the entertainment business. I would pay to listen to her. After a good laugh, they moved on deeper into the woods. They had enough water, but I still informed them where the next water point was located.

Just before reaching the road that led into Waynesboro, I passed an older man. He seemed nice enough, and said, "Hi." I returned the same as I hiked strongly uphill toward the road leading to good food and drink.

About three hundred yards later, I reached the road. A parking lot was across the roadway. That was where the hikers parked. It wasn't full. But then again, there were not too many hikers in the woods. The heat must be keeping them away.

A piece of paper was taped to the guardrail along the road. It was a list of trail angels in the area and their phone numbers. This was a hiker-friendly town. Awesome!

As I read the note, I started digging for my phone. "Hey, do you need a ride?" a voice came from behind me. It was the older hiker I had passed just a few hundred yards back. "Sure!" I smiled, relishing my good fortune. He was one of the trail angels listed on the note.

Now, it is one thing to be given a ride, which we appreciate, but this guy drove me all over the town of Waynesboro. He explained what was where and gave the hours of operation. The angel explained who had the best food and who had the all-you-can-eat deals. He gave every bit of information needed by a thru-hiker. After the tour and explanation, he asked, "Where do you want me to drop you off?"

Waynesboro is genuinely a hiker-friendly town. This trail angel was one of many who provided support for thru-hikers. The town might be friendly to hikers, but the layout of the town was difficult. It was spread out, wide and long. The distance to a store or restaurant was a far hike. The upside was that it had everything we needed.

Waynesboro seemed to be a small, sleepy town. Heck, it was probably a big city, but because it was so sprawled out it never had a chance to develop a big city attitude. The people in Waynesboro were the friendliest folks I have ever met. I stayed at one of the nicer hotels. It was a little more expensive, but worth the extra money. The trail angel went in first to see if a room was available and to ask for a good deal. I got a discount!

He helped carry my gear into the lobby then left with the satisfaction that he was helping a thru-hiker. Trail angels are the best, and there are no better angels than the ones in Waynesboro! While checking in at the hotel, the clerk handed me a large three-ring binder. "Here is the list of trail angels. Just don't call the first ones on the list as we like to use them all."

My room was comfortable. The tub was just right for soaking in Epsom salts. After a quick wash, I went out to eat. The world's best burger was just down the road, or so I was told. I needed to find out if that was true. If the world's best burger was here, I wanted it!

The restaurant was not close and I walked past it a couple of times before I finally found it. It was only an extra mile of walking. This was it, now I got to eat a great hamburger. The place was packed and there was not a hiker in sight. It appeared the locals had flocked to this joint; it must be good. Now, I needed to find a place to sit.

Navigating my way through the restaurant was easy enough. My destination was the back patio. I could eat there without offending anyone with my hiker aroma. There were no empty tables, but three guys who sat at one of the umbrella-covered, round tables offered the fourth seat to me. Happily, I accepted.

It isn't every day that people offer a stranger a seat at their table. Waynesboro certainly drew a good sort to their town. The people are so friendly it is eerie, like getting caught in a Stephen King novel. They are almost supernaturally friendly, but that is a good thing. I sat, ordered, and ate. The strangers who offered their seat also bought my beers. Man, this place was cool.

After returning to my room, I sat down and wrote a list of items to buy at the local outfitters. The outfitter was about three miles away, maybe two. The hike was long and all within town. I started off. The day grew hotter. The beers had made me slightly dehydrated and were giving me a headache.

As I crossed an intersection, a kid ran in front of me and started walking the same way. He was obviously a teenager. Not a small kid, the boy stood a couple inches taller than me. He could have been an athlete, but his posture was sloppy. To make matters more interesting, the kid adjusted his pants, gangster style! This little dude just "dropped trowel," showing his ass. Granted, he had his undies on, but why?

Not wanting to see this kid's butt, I made an on-the-spot correction. Politely, I said, "Get your damn pants up! I don't want to see your panties. What the hell is wrong with you? Do that again and I will spank your ass." I do not know why I responded so passionately, but, my response worked. The kid pulled his pants up and said, "Yes, sir!" Smart kid!

I had been planning to take a zero in Waynesboro; the friendliness of the town's people made it an easy decision to keep. At the outfitters, I became a little disappointed, though. The prices left a lot to be desired. I needed a hat, but was not willing to pay twenty bucks for it. The DEET that I needed was more costly here than anywhere else. I needed the DEET, so I paid for it.

While in town, I called to find out about "aqua blazing." There were not any services that went more than fifty miles and then you had to find your own way back to the trail. I was not interested in this; the logistics were too much. Then, I went online and found a kayak for sale on eBay. It was only two hundred dollars. My thought was I could get it, paddle to Harpers Ferry, and then have Deb come pick it up. The plan was okay, but was too spur of the moment and it was not hiking.

I opted to not aqua blaze, but stay on the trail instead. Waynesboro certainly was good to me, but my hike needed to continue. One zero was enough to recharge my spirit, and now I had DEET to deal with the bugs, which were going to get thicker as the days got warmer.

Breakfast was good and checking out of the hotel was easy. With pack in hand, I stood outside the hotel. There was another guy standing at the corner with an Ohio flag on his pack. The hiker was named Full Time and was working on his thru-hike as well. His friend was coming to hike part of the trail with him that morning.

Full Time offered me a ride to the trail if his friend had room in his vehicle. I waited with him. There was room, so I rode to the trailhead, back to the large parking lot. There we donned our gear and headed out, looking for the check-in station for Shenandoah National Park.

We found the check-in station along the trail. It was nothing more than a big map and sign. I almost missed it. That could have cost me a few dollars if I hadn't checked in. Full Time called me back to register.

Once we completed our registration form and properly attached it to the outside of our packs, we were off. Keeping up with Full Time and his friend was easy. They asked about my hike. I told Full Time about hiking the Mau-Har Trail, the blue blaze. "I only hike where I see a white blaze. I have to see every white blaze with a pack on my back. I don't want to do any hiking if it doesn't count." Full Time disparaged.

That made me feel belittled and I bitterly responded, "What the hell counts? Who is counting? I am hiking my hike. I am hiking from Georgia to Maine. I am not taking a ride to Maine!" This was a good example of how thru-hikers can demonstrate their maturity and ability to part ways. If you don't care to be around someone, you have a couple of choices. One, you may hike faster, long and hard to create a distance between you and the other hiker. Or, you may let them hike long and hard, allowing you take it easy, slowing down to separate you and the other hiker.

I needed a slow day, so this was an easy decision to make. I stopped for lunch along the trail. I really didn't dislike Full Time; he had a strong opinion that he expressed in a way that just rubbed me wrong. If a hiker wants to be a purist it is his own business, but he shouldn't proclaim it is the only way to hike. You shouldn't look down your nose at others. Blue blazers have their reasons and are still hiking the AT. Yellow blazers are hitchhiking or renting a car. Now, that isn't hiking. That is cheating!

Not wanting to get into an argument with Full Time after he gave me a ride to the trail, I opted to enjoy a slow, easy day. It wasn't long before I found a group of tractor seats in a semicircle, cemented into the ground.

All the seats had a beautiful view into a valley. I sat down for a long lunch and a long reflection. Today was to be an easy day! It was swelteringly hot outside, too hot for a long hike. Two miles later I was calling it a night at Calf Mountain Shelter.

Bears

I HAVE EXPERIENCED a few heart stopping events. Once, as I was hiking along the trail, I saw a bear "hiking" the trail. He was going the same direction as me, so it was cool. The bear stayed about thirty feet ahead of me. When I stopped to get my camera, he turned around, looked at me, and then shuffled into the woods. That must have been one camera-shy bear . . . who would have thought?

Immediately, I called Deb to report my bear sighting. It was pretty exciting, or so I thought! Later that evening, a couple of cubs scurried up a tree with momma bear standing by, watching me. She must have thought I was a bad dude and she didn't care for me at all. I could tell by the scowl on her face. I continued walking, enjoying the scenery. The trail was smooth dirt. The leaves were full on the trees. Breezes made the trees dance in a slow sway. Streams trickled, glistening water. It was a beautiful sight.

The temperature grew hotter outside. The woods within the Shenandoah Mountains were growing thicker with day hikers and section hikers. The woods were also teeming with new life. I stopped near an old logging road for a short break. Out of the corner of my eye I noticed movement in the weeds. There lay a fawn. The little guy could not have been a full day or two old. His big brown eyes stared into the world, wondering why momma left him there. Hoping momma would be coming back, the fawn lay perfectly still.

Knowing not to disturb the weeds or to expose the fawn in any way,

I left him alone. Other hikers, day hikers, came by. I said "Hi," they said "Hi." They didn't ask about the fawn, so I didn't share his location with them. Some things are best left alone. A baby deer is on top of my list of things to leave alone. In about two hundred yards I would reach the top of a hill. There was a spring on this hill and I needed the water. The heat was causing me to use more water than usual. It was okay; there was a spring just on top of the hill!

As I was approaching the hilltop with the good spring—a much-needed spring—I found the world's dumbest section hiker. She was thin and well dressed in all the latest REI wear. She stood in the woods just ten to fifteen feet from the trail. Standing still, as if hoping no one would see her, she had a long line extending from her hand. As I approached, a sour feeling reached my gut. The line was a strap and a dog was on the end of it.

The hiker stood there with her cocker spaniel lying in the spring—the spring I needed to stay alive! She had contaminated the drinking water! This person thought it was a good idea to come to the woods on a hot day and let her dog lay in the middle of the water source needed by thru-hikers. At least the dog could have laid in the stream downhill from the spring without contaminating the water we needed. But that's not the worst of it; no, she had to top even that stupid move.

I asked her which way she was traveling. She informed me she was headed southbound. So, I asked her, when she got past the fire road down the trail, to please keep her dog on a short leash. "Oh! Why? Is there a bear down there?" she asked. "No," I replied. "There is a small fawn lying in the weeds right next to the trail." Her next response floored me. "Oh! That deer won't hurt my dog." My thoughts . . . well you know me, my thoughts were unkind. "Lady, I could eat your dog! Do not let it bother the fawn."

I stopped at Pine Field Hut. There wasn't much to do but to get water. I sat back and listened to the other hikers, section hikers, day hikers, and thru-hikers. They shared information that was helpful. In the Shenandoah Mountains it is not necessary to carry food. There are wayside park areas located frequently within the park. At each of the waysides you will find food, water, beer, and laundry facilities. Since day and section hikers are on the trail, we might as well take advantage of being in their territory.

A quick stop in Lewis Mountain Wayside proved to be convenient. The beer was cheap and cold. The food and camp stores were well stocked. I wished I had not received a resupply already. While at the camp store, I didn't see any other thru-hikers. I wondered where Cargo was at this time.

There were signs that Bearfence Hut was closed due to a bear attack on a hiker. During the night, a bear had come into the hut area and attacked the tent of a sleeping hiker. Imagine waking up to a hungry bear. I heard the hiker left foodstuffs in his tent. Too bad for the bear! He was captured and probably taken away, though I don't know.

Once I got to Bearfence Hut there was a sign that it was open again. The bear had been taken away. It was nearly dark when I arrived. A doe was hanging around the hut. She acted like a dog wanting to be petted. However, she was a wild animal, and petting her would not do her any good. Respecting her distance would be best for her. She stood still for pictures. Nice doe!

In the shelter was a section hiker, Rat. Rat had thru-hiked before, so as far as section hikers go, he was the "bomb." Midnight, a ridge runner, was staying in a tent near the shelter. They were the only other people at the shelter. That made for a quiet night. But, best of all, there was a spring that had fresh, fast-flowing, cold water. Meeting Rat and Midnight was a pleasure.

The trail is scenic and easily hiked in the Shenandoah Mountains. Miles can be made without too much effort. But great distances should be guarded against, as this is a good place to relax and take your time. A steady pace in the Shenandoah Mountains is easy to keep because there are no great climbs or rough rocks to traverse. These are enjoyable, easy miles.

In Big Meadows Campground, I took a shower and washed my clothes. The restaurant was elegant but the deli was even better. A friend of mine comes from Ohio every year to camp here. Her and her family wouldn't be at the campground for another few weeks, and I would be in Pennsylvania by then, I hoped. After having my shower and washing my clothes, I sat down to eat before leaving.

After a short visit with Midnight and an Animal Planet film crew, who were tracking a bear and her cubs for filming, I was off to Rock Spring Hut. That night, my stay was again at one of the shelters, another three-sided building. I pitched my tent again. There was no one there, just a doe hanging around the shelter. This was another night camping alone . . . pretty cool. Then, while in my tent, I heard a commotion—the rustling of leaves and branches. My thoughts were, "Hey, someone is putting a tent next to mine." I quickly opened the tent door and popped up like a jack-in-the-box. I was going to have whomever it was move farther away; they were right on top of my tent. They had even made my tent move by bumping into it. I stood up and turned to face them. Wrong!

It was two cubs and one pissed off momma bear. She was less than pleased to see me pop out of the tent like bread in a toaster. She lunged forward, luckily in a mock charge. The "fight or flight" response took me. Uncontrollably, I yelled, "No!" Thoughts of punching the bear in the nose flashed through my mind. She was within reach. My heart pounded in my ears.

Hearing my voice and fearing momma, the little ones bravely ran away. I stood frozen to the ground. My eyes were locked onto the momma bear's eyes. I have heard you are not to stare at a wild animal, but, we were locked into a staring contest. She had pretty eyes. The way the situation was evolving, I believed showing any weakness would cause the bear to attack. The safest action, so I thought, was to keep a stalemate with the bear. With her cubs safely away, the bear walked off, but kept looking back at me as if saying something hideous under her breath. That was a close call!

Once I had presumed all was well, that momma and cubs were safely away, the tables turned. The mother bear turned around and headed back toward me. She walked diagonally to my position, coming closer and closer. From time to time she would look up at me during her approach. She was coming back!

My immediate response was to grab my camera and take photos. The pics are of her getting closer and closer. Then, I changed the camera setting from still pics to movie. She continued her approach. As the bear got into charging range, I became unsettled and my response changed. I called to her, and started throwing sticks and rocks around my area, but not at her! I thrashed saplings around like a silverback gorilla. I jumped up and down, making monkey noises, and swung my arms over my head. The bear turned slowly and walked back to her cubs.

It was hard to tell what the bear thought of me, and here, I thought the place was safe. All I saw at the shelter when I arrived was the doe. The doe was cool. The bear was bad news. But wait! What's worse than a bear? A mad momma bear! So what is worse than a mad momma bear? A skunk! And the following morning, a skunk came up to me while I was talking to Deb on the cell. It gets better. What is worse than a skunk? Think about it. How about a rabid skunk? As I was filming the skunk it was staggering and fell over on level ground; it was shaking all over. The poor thing was sick. Of course, I informed a ranger within the hour and she alerted animal control.

Later, I heard another hiker had killed the diseased critter. Most of the other hikers following thought I did it. I did not. The credit goes to someone else.

Hiker's Midnight

MY RIGHT KNEE was giving out. Taking Motrin helped some, but not totally. The knee was swollen and was extremely painful. The pains were taking control of my hike. Enjoying the Shenandoah Mountains was not happening. I remember little about the next two days except the pain, and trying to hike when hiking was the last thing I should do.

Traveling through the Shenandoah Mountains was on an easy trail, even though my right knee was swollen. The leaves were full and green. The trail was well tended and there was never any debris laying across the trail. It was more of a pleasant path in the woods than an actual hiking trail. Water was easy to find, as long as someone didn't let her dog lounge in it.

Zig Zag, Ranger Bob, and Full Time were at a shelter. They were talking about slack packing using Zig Zag's car. Zig Zag was going home for her husband's birthday, and when she returned they would all slack pack. Strangely, they didn't offer to take me along for the slack pack. I didn't ask; they didn't offer. They bragged about what they were going to do. I was the only other thru-hiker there. Oh well!

The best parts of the Shenandoah Mountains are found at the waysides. The waysides have picnic areas, campgrounds, stores, and delis— and best of all, cheap beer. I bought beer for seventy-five cents. That is a great deal. The people didn't bother the hikers; everyone was friendly. I was never there during the busy times, so I lucked out in that regard.

Rusty Bumper, a hiker from Cleveland, Ohio, was setting up his tent in the wood-line. He was one of the steadiest hikers I had ever met. He stood with a thin-framed body. His white hair was long and curly; his long, white beard perfectly matched his hair. A smile always shined through his thick beard. Rusty Bumper never got excited and was always soft-spoken and calm. The man was well disciplined in the woods. He always got up at the same time, hiked the same number of miles, and stopped to camp the same time every evening. He averaged around seventeen or eighteen miles a day. The man could hike!

At the end of the Shenandoah Mountains was a hostel, Terrapin Station. The hostel was set up in the walk-out basement of a home. It was a pretty smart setup. The host had a washer and dryer and shower for hikers to use. There was entertainment by way of a TV, and there was plenty of food to buy or you could fix your own. A ride to town was available daily. I was comfortable there.

While at Terrapin Station, I got to slack pack ahead by about twenty miles. It was an excellent way to make many miles without burning out. By the end of my slack pack, though, I certainly was ready for some rest. A section hiker, Flute, showed up at the hostel. Flute carried a flute and was always ready to play for any audience he could find.

That night, after ten o'clock, more than two hours after hiker's midnight, I was sound asleep. Hiker's midnight is usually eight in the evening. Just after ten o'clock, I was awakened by beeps, bloops, and bings. The noises were from a video game being played on a cell phone. There was another room for games and TV, but these noises were from another bunk. Someone was playing video games while we were trying to sleep. The least they could do was put the game on silent mode.

Annoyed thoroughly by the disruption in my sleep, I sat up and asked who had the game on. Flute responded that it was him. I asked him to turn it off or turn off the sound. He said he was almost done. I had asked nicely, really, I did. The noises continued. My anger grew at the arrogance and rudeness of some people.

I have a three-step plan: first, ask nicely. I did that. Second, tell them exactly what you want from them so there is no mistake. I sat up a second time, "Dude, turn the sound off now. We are sleeping, turn it off or go to the other room." Those were both fair options. I thought they were fair and easy. "I am still playing. I will be done in a minute." Flute responded. The beeps and bongs continued.

The third step of my three-step plan is to take action. Not being a violent man, I was not going to hit Flute. That would be inconsiderate. I only wanted the noises to stop. So, my plan was to get up, take the phone, and smash it against the wall. Then, I would quietly go back to bed. That was a simple solution to resolve the issue at hand. Announcing my displeasure, I said "That's it!" I got up, but Flute quickly took the battery off his phone, ending the noises immediately. I lay back down without having to smash the phone and quietly went to sleep.

Dragon and a Banjo

THE NEXT DAY I was back on the trail with a full pack and headed north again. I had received and sent e-mails from the hostel. In one e-mail I was asked, "How do you keep going month after month, week after week, day after day, hour after hour, mile after mile, hill after hill, knowing there is so much more to go?"

You have to keep your mind occupied. That day I was hiking deep in the woods, knowing the weather report included thundershowers around three in the afternoon. At 3:15 p.m., I heard a low rumble in the sky. The storm was rapidly approaching. Without turning completely around, I saw the sky had darkened behind me. My pace increased. Getting to the shelter before this storm overtook me was a priority.

My mind raced, and I likened the storm to a big dragon chasing after me in the woods. Each thunderclap was the dragon's roar. I walked faster, and each step was chosen carefully so I would not twist an ankle or sprain a knee. The dragon roared again. The air smelled of impending rain and became heavy with humidity. The trail twisted through the trees. Luckily, the trail was smooth, flat, and had few rocks, I thought. Then, that thought was dashed by plenty of rocks. Rain began falling—the dragon's breath. I walked faster to get ahead of the rain. The dragon's breath was behind me now. Quickly, the trail fell down to swampy, low ground. If the shelter was close it would mean bugs, and lots of them.

The trail continued winding, twisting farther and farther. When you want a shelter it just always seems to be farther than expected. The sound of thunder was just ahead—wait, but the dragon was behind me. I looked up as two jets flew past. I winked, and thought, "Baby dragons can bark, too." Still trying to beat the dragon to the shelter, I hurried through the woods. Damn, my ankles ached. The tendons were as tight as banjo strings. I imagined a tune was being played as I walked. So, to try to get into a rhythm, I tried to hike to the tune of "Dixie." I was imagining each step as strumming or picking the banjo. If you could have heard my tendons, I bet I had a good tune going.

I continue hiking, "racing the dragon," to the beat of "Dixie." There, just ahead, was the shelter. Rain began to fall much harder. The dragon and I tied getting to the shelter. It was okay. I was out of the rain and my ankles could rest. Racing the dragon to the tune of "Dixie" got me through the last four miles. When I hiked, my mind would wander to various visions to keep me going.

While at the shelter, a strange character came in. He was an odd sort, of the "hillbilly" variety. His pack was way oversized. His tent was a four-person tent. When he spoke, he was as loud as he could possibly be. It startled me when he first started talking. Involuntarily, I jumped back and yelled, "What the hell!" I was shocked at his loud manner. Talk about setting you back a couple feet, he really pushed people away by how loudly he spoke. Not being able to understand most of his dialect and definitely not appreciating his noisy invasion of nature, I chose to move on.

The dragon had passed by, and so had the storm. Before leaving, I noticed the other hiker's mustache had grown over his lip and into his mouth. Oh my God! It was like looking into a mirror, as I felt my upper lip covered and my mustache in my mouth. My mustache was so getting trimmed!

The Roller Coaster to
Brazil Nut and Lady Pants

SINCE THE "DRAGON storm" has passed, leaving the shelter was an easy choice. I walked about three miles and came upon a sign, "Warning All Hikers!" The sign explained I was about to hike the Roller Coaster. This thirteen-mile stretch is a series of five hundred foot elevation increases followed by five hundred foot elevation decreases again and again and again. At the end of the sign I notice the small print "See you on the other side, if you survive." Hmm? I started up the first hill, and in true fashion, at each hill's apex, I raised my hands high in the air and exclaimed loudly, "Whee!" Hey, this is the roller coaster, right?

After a few hills, I heard gunshots coming from my left. I paused; the shots were close, but it sounded as if the gun was aimed the other way. No problem. I continued down a slope on the roller coaster. I took a deep breath and exhaled slowly. Goose bumps ran down my spine. Now, this was different. Something was wrong. The first thing I do when something feels wrong and I don't know what it might be is to take inventory and do a quick assessment of the situation.

My surroundings provided a perfect ambush location. My mind went back to the sign: "If you survive." Then, I heard in my mind Johnny Cash, singing, "I shot a man in Reno, just to watch him die." Great! That's all I need, to come across somebody with a gun who wants to get away with murder just to see what it would feel like. This would be the perfect spot. I made a quick reaction plan. If threatened with a gun, I would pull my chest strap off, loosen my shoulder straps, pop my waistband, drop my pack, and then dive to the right into a steep ravine. Next, I would throw a rock downhill, as a decoy, then run uphill to flank the threat. I had a good plan if ambushed. Okay, granted, my mind was working overtime!

A footbridge spanned a small stream just ahead, at the bottom of the hill. I crossed over the bridge, dropped my pack, and then crossed back with my water bottles and filter. But, it was not time to get water yet. I was drinking the water left in the nalgene bottle when I saw movement. Something or someone was coming up the hill my way. Then, I saw two guys headed up the hill toward me. They reached a thick brushy area, losing any sight of me. I hurried to get back to my pack. Quickly and quietly I put my pack on and stepped behind two large boulders. The boulders were a good vantage point.

The two guys walked past me. Standing still, I was able to observe them without them noticing me. Never give away your position with movement. One guy was heavy set and the other, thinner guy looked as if he were following his larger friend. The larger guy had what looked like a 4-10 shotgun, possibly. The other guy was unarmed, as far as I could tell. It wasn't hunting season. Hopefully, these guys were out shooting for fun and just enjoying the woods. Nice guys, I am sure, but I chose not to make contact. After they passed by, I continued up the next hill of the "roller coaster." Once on top, I exclaimed, "Whee!" in a softer voice. The roller coaster continued.

That night, I stayed in my tent at a shelter near a stream. The following morning I hiked three miles to the Bears Den Hostel. Bears Den is a building that looks like a castle. Hikers stay in the lower level, where they have everything they need: a bunk, washer and dryer, a shower, TV and videos, and a computer with Internet connection. Upstairs is the kitchen and food.

While we—several other hikers and I—were watching a movie in the lounge room of the hostel, a storm came by with a vengeance. Clouds darkened the sky and rain plummeted the ground in anger. Thunder cracked loud enough to shake the earth around us. Then lightning hit close—well, it hit us. Lightning hit the building and sparks flew through the screened window across the room. Electrical sparks flew out of each outlet. The sparks that came through the window jumped from person to person. The electric arc started to my left, crossing the knees of Erin, a young hiker. From Erin, the sparks crossed my knees to the next hiker, Shark, then to another hiker.

One of the hikers asked, "Did you see that?" We all laughed at what had just happened. It was a nervous laugh. We continued watching the movie on the DVD player, trying to ignore the lightning. Thunder clapped again, shaking the earth again. The storm was growing even stronger.

A second lightning strike came with the same results as the first. The sparks raised the hairs on my legs. This time, we quickly unplugged the computer and cell phones. The TV we left on. We didn't want to be too bored, and we were enjoying the movie. Shortly after unplugging the electrical equipment and protecting the computer, the power went out. It stayed out for several hours, so we didn't get to finish watching our movie.

The rain increased to what seemed as impenetrable as a force field. When the rains were falling the hardest, a small face peered through the window. A dark-haired gal with a thin face and dark features looked soaked and exhausted. She asked if someone would open the door to let her in. She could not figure out the lock code on the door. I went to the door to let her in.

The new hiker was a Brazilian gal. She had a strong Portuguese accent and spoke in a highly animated manner. She wore shorts that highlighted her long brown legs. On her left thigh was a tattoo of a swirl. Her hair was jet black and a bit more than shoulder length. Coming out of the rain she looked like a soaking wet puppy. She had a way about her that relaxed the other hikers and could get everyone laughing. Her tale of hiking in the weather, trying to beat the rains to the hostel, was funny. It was funny because it happened to her and not to us. She was totally soaked to the bone. Fittingly, her name was Brazil Nut.

The storm passed as quickly as it had arrived. Brazil Nut decided she was going no farther. Her plan was to dry off and spend the night. I had already planned on staying overnight. The other guys all pushed on north. They were excited about getting to Harpers Ferry, West Virginia, as soon as possible so off they went.

Another hiker arrived. She was a younger gal with a round face, bubbly mannerism, and an odd style that fit her well. Her hair was cut short in Tomboy fashion but she hiked in a sundress in a girly-girl style. This hiker's name was Lady Pants. Funny name for a gal in a dress! She was lots of fun. The three of us—Brazil Nut, Lady Pants, and I—took a short tour of the building. The upper section of the hostel had a kitchen for hiker use and a large dining area.

The next morning I searched for coffee. There was some made and it hit the spot. Then, I went downstairs. Lady Pants was already up. Brazil Nut was still sawing logs, snoring like a trooper. I started packing my gear, preparing for my hike. The hostel's hostess came down to announce that her camera was working and she wanted pictures of the hikers who had spent the night. Without missing a beat, I leaped onto the bed where Lady Pants was sitting to have my picture taken with her.

The camera failed. I hugged Lady Pants for a close-up picture. The camera failed again. So, I wrapped tighter around Lady Pants, who was now growing uncomfortable with me. The camera failed again. Lady Pants groaned, and I gave up waiting for the camera to take a picture.

Like a kid looking for an Easter egg, I was looking for trouble. I found trouble still sleeping. Brazil Nut was snoring lightly. I grabbed her leg and started pulling her out of bed. She groaned, "No, Mingo, I sleeping." Pestering Brazil Nut to get up, I continued pulling on her leg, "Get up!" I ordered. "But, Bingo Mingo I paid my ten dollars so I can sleep." cried Brazil Nut softly. "Get up!" I demanded.

Lady Pants went upstairs for a cup of Joe. Brazil Nut relented and sat up to talk with me for a bit. How did you sleep? When did you get up? What are your plans today? She made small talk asking that kind of stuff. We decided we were hungry. I called for a vote. "All in favor of Lady Pants making our breakfast say, 'Aye!'" Brazil Nut and I both called out, "Aye!" Being there were no objections, I ran upstairs to tell Lady Pants the good news: she won the election to make our breakfast. Funny thing, she didn't see it as good news. But as a good sport, Lady Pants began making pancakes and bossing me around. A large bowl was shoved at me, "Mingo, go get mulberries for our pancakes." As an obedient servant, I went outside.

The ground was wet with heavy dew, and it was cold. Mulberry trees lined the yard and they were heavy with fruit. I filled the bowl quickly.

Returning with my bowl full and a smile I asked, "Mingo do good?" I gave the berries to Lady Pants and waited for a pat on the head, which never came. I deserved at least a "That-a-boy." Not hearing any praises, I asked again if I did okay. Finally, Lady Pants said I got good berries, but there should have been more. With the empty bowl in hand, I returned to the trees to pick more. I picked more berries than before, gave them to Lady Pants, and left her to make breakfast. Humbled in spirit, I turned to coffee to drown my sorrows. With a fresh cup, I went back down stairs to Brazil Nut.

Lady Pants was stirring the pancake mix when another couple came in. One was hiking and the other was driving their car. Lady Pants worked out a deal for a slack pack to Harpers Ferry, but to do the slack pack we needed to send our packs to a hotel. Lady Pants called and made reservations for our packs as well.

Returning for more coffee and to check on the progress of our breakfast, Lady Pants asked if I would be interested in splitting a room with her and Brazil Nut. "Well, heck yeah!" Sharing a room with other hikers is no big deal. Lady Pants set everything up for us. Brazil Nut didn't slack pack, but was staying in Harpers with us. She didn't need to slack; she was a speed demon. The gal could hike faster than anyone I ever met. Next to her I felt like a turtle.

Breakfast was great. Lady Pants did a good job cooking. I repacked my gear and took what I needed for the day of slack packing. This was going to be a good day. Off I went, first on the trail of our pack of three, Brazil Nut, Lady Pants, and me.

Harpers Ferry

WELL INTO THE day I saw the sign for the one thousandth mile. Exhilarated that I had reached the one-thousand-mile mark, I grabbed my camera to video the occasion. This was a great milestone in my hike. I had completed 1,000 miles and only had 1,181 miles to go. I would have stayed around the sign longer, but swarms of mosquitoes were enjoying the sign as well!

With a little more pep in my step, I hiked as if I were Dorothy going to see the wizard. Skipping along the trail, happy as a June bug, I met three volunteers working to maintain the trail. They were pulling weeds that were an invasive species. We talked a bit then I offered some of my food. Shocked that a thru-hiker offered food in the first place, they declined. But seeing my generosity, they asked if I would carry a lunch to one of their crew, who was farther north. That's the way I was headed, so it was no problem. Another good deed!

Off I went with a lunch for Hardy. His wife, Laurel, short for Mountain Laurel and shorter for Laurel and Hardy, had packed him a bagel. Hardy was running a grass trimmer to clear overgrowth away from the trail. This was important because it helped keep snakes away from the hikers' ankles.

Hardy was farther away than I expected, but he was on the trail, which was not out of my way. I stopped to give him his lunch. While Hardy ate his lunch, I joined him. Having an extra candy bar, I offer it to Hardy. No big deal! The candy bar was added weight as far as I was concerned.

Reluctantly, Hardy accepted the candy. Truth be told, the guy was working hard and deserved the extra calories and energy.

Having done my good deed for the day, I was back on my way. The trail was still easy to hike. The hills were not steep. The day grew warmer. The sun shined brightly through the trees. A path to a shelter led away from the trail to the right. Since water can be found at shelters, I headed down the path.

The shelter journal read that water could be found a half mile down a steep path. Damn! Oh well, off I went with my filter in hand and both water bottles. Reaching the water source wasn't as easy as I had expected. Hiking to the water source was actually more difficult than the day's hike. The ground was uneven and weeds covered the path. The water source I found was a mere trickle!

Luckily, I had brought two water bottles. I filled the first bottle and drank it dry. After refilling that bottle and the other, I drank half that bottle. Again, I refilled it, so I had two full bottles. With my stomach full of water, I headed up the hill and back to the shelter. There was a swing at the shelter. I sat there, enjoying the view and giving my feet a rest from wearing shoes. This was a relaxing day.

Lady Pants showed up at the shelter. She had made good time. Knowing the water source was far away I gave her a bottle of water. Lady Pants asked why I had taken the extra water bottle in the first place. She was reluctant, but took the water after hearing how far it was and that I had deliberately got the extra bottle for her. We were only a few miles from Harpers Ferry, twelve at the most.

Off I went, headed north. I left Lady Pants at the shelter sitting on the swing. The loud hillbilly was there, but I figured she would be okay. Lady Pants was a tough, capable gal. Besides, that guy wouldn't bother her. He was a strange sort of fellow but all in all he wasn't a bad person.

There was no sign marking the West Virginia state line. That was disappointing. The hill down to Harpers Ferry was quite steep. I arrived at a bridge around 4:30 p.m. After crossing the long bridge, I headed into town. I was to meet Brazil Nut and Lady Pants later on.

I had reached the one-thousand-mile marker, then, after that, I had reached West Virginia. Hurray for another state! That was good. Reaching another state was awesome. Everyone had been getting the Virginia Blues. I was tired of being in Virginia, tired of the same old scenes. Now, Virginia offered some great hikes and had been the best state so far, but I was glad to be finished with it.

In West Virginia, I was happy to be at Harpers Ferry. Cool town. It is the home of the Appalachian Trail Conservancy and I had to visit it. Arriving in Harpers Ferry just after five in the afternoon, I made a discovery. The Conservancy was closed. The restaurants were all closed after five o'clock. The only pizza shop was closed for renovations. There were no pubs open, and no stores available to buy beer, food, or beer. You can't even get a beer after five. That made the thrill of being in Harpers Ferry less exciting!

Brazil Nut was having a beer on the patio of a pub with other hikers in town. The pub was closed and not allowing new customers to come inside. I jumped the fence to join them. The fence had a sign that said, "Do not jump the fence." Oops! The waitress was slow bringing beer, but I got one. Lady Pants showed up minutes later. We made a plan. They would get the room reserved earlier and I would go looking for food.

Bark Like a Dog

THEY LEFT TO get the room as I headed off to hitchhike out of town to get beer and food. It didn't take long before three women stopped to pick me up. They were schoolteachers! They drove thirty miles to the nearest 7-Eleven store. My first purchase was—no, not beer—a Snickers, then beer. The teachers, one from Chicago and two from St. Louis, took me to Burger King. "Six double cheese burgers and three large fries please!" My friends were vegetarians, so they were going get a large fry each and the rest was for me.

The teachers took me back to my hotel with my food. I was so hungry and so happy! There was food and beer for all, not to mention I had eaten my Snickers already. No sooner did I exit the van then those crazy ladies drove away. I had my food and my beer, but they had my backpack. My pack was in the back of the van as it coasted down the steep road through Harpers Ferry, late in the evening. The van threatened to vanish into the night on the dimly lit streets.

My mind flashed messages of what to do next. Do I keep my food and beer? The fries were hot and the grease was still melting. My six double cheeseburgers were just waiting for me to devour them. Would they be safe if I dropped them off on the street? Where were my friends? I had to decide quickly. I sat the beer and food down just off the sidewalk and ran after the van.

I sprinted down the hill in the dark of the night, chasing this van with three women. Like a dog chasing a car, I ran as fast as I could after them. A reenactment show was being performed along the street as I ran by. Tourists turned their heads away from the era-clad performer to wonder at me as my feet slapped the pavement with each out-of-control lunge downhill on the road. Realizing how similar to a dog chasing a car I must have seemed, and knowing tourists were watching me as I ran by, I barked. Yes, I gave those tourists something more to talk about. I must have bow-wowed at least two blocks while running full steam downhill.

I never did catch the teachers, but, being a good listener, I knew where they were staying. After a couple of phone calls, we arranged an early morning meeting. They wanted to take me to breakfast. Oh, the cost of my backpack was getting high. I agreed! The next morning came, but the pack never showed. Hmm?

Get this: there isn't any place to eat breakfast in Harpers Ferry. That was bad. But there were a couple of beers left, so that was good. While I was at the Appalachian Trail Conservancy, the teachers arrived. I was happy to see them and to get my pack back. They seemed happy to see me. Nice ladies!

With pack in hand, I ran back to the hotel to drop it off. Then, it was off to eat lunch with a hiking friend. Guess who arrived at lunch—the teachers! You would think I was wearing a sign or something that said, "Follow me!" Maybe they put a GPS device on me somehow. They were nice ladies, and Harpers Ferry is just a small town. Everywhere I went, there they were. Each time we talked, I mentioned my wife, Deb. With each mentioning of my wife, I somehow heard Deb's words in my head, "Good answer, buddy."

After a zero in Harpers Ferry, I headed north. Soon, I was in Maryland. Yahoo! Another state! Another momentous occasion! To top everything off, Deb was coming to visit. Life couldn't get much better. Brazil Nut and Lady Pants wanted to stay for a second zero in Harper's Ferry but that would have been too much for me. I had to escape the "vortex." A "vortex" is a town that sucks in a hiker and will not let go. It can be tough to pull away from a fun place, but the hike must go on.

Seductive Poses

ONCE IN MARYLAND, Deb and I talked on the phone, coordinating her plan to pick me up at US Route 40 Alternate in Maryland. An elegant restaurant was there at the trailhead. The restaurant was painted white with large bay windows all around. It had the appearance of a southern glassed-in gazebo. This was certainly a place with class. White cloth covered each table and the flatware was large, gleaming chunks of silver. Crystal flutes and glasses were strategically placed around white porcelain plates and bowls. Why, I bet Cinderella and Snow White would dine here.

I had been warned that the appetizers could cost as much as twenty-five dollars. A meal, I surmised, would be well over one hundred to two hundred dollars. A sign out front read, "Food for Everybody." What a tease! My stomach growled as I saw the people inside eating in a dainty fashion. The flavors from the kitchen wafted by my nose, only to taunt my hunger. The smells were most appetizing.

Deb was getting closer. I moved to sit in the yard of this fancy place. There I sat, a dirty little hiker. Smelly and sweaty, I sat with bugs flying all around me like Pig Pen on Peanuts. I had a fog of gnats and flies around me. My shoulders hung low and wet. The sweat poured through my clothes where my pack had been. This reminded me of the sweat and frothing on our horses when we take the saddles off after a good, long ride. Dirt was dripping from my brow through the bandanna that was rotting from salt and sun damage. I was not what a restaurant would want in front . . . or, so I thought.

A lady came out from the restaurant. I was certain this was it; she was going to scold me for being here and demand I leave. They must want me to crawl back into the woods from whence I came. I just hoped that if they threw water on me, like an unwanted dog, they didn't heat it first. The lady got within speaking distance, and to my surprise, asked if she could take my picture. Oh my God! I must have been a sight. "Sure, I don't mind." I lamented. She took a couple photos and promptly turned and walked away.

A couple minutes later, the lady returned. "Can I take more pictures of you?" "Why yes, yes you may," I replied, feeling much better. Here was another admirer of Appalachian Trail thru-hikers. This time, she was taking photos from the front, side, and all around. Being the typical camera hog and silly jackass that I am, I began to pose for her. I lay in the grass, sat up, leaned back, twisted, smiled, scowled, and gave my seductive poses. Hey, everyone loves a seductive pose. She really put her camera to work. Then, to my surprise, she asked what I was doing with a backpack. I explained how I was hiking the Appalachian Trail. Then it dawned upon me: she did not know I was a thru-hiker! Why the heck was she taking pictures of me? Cool! She thought I was homeless or a hobo or a gypsy or something!

I explained how I was hiking the AT and how far I had traveled. She was fixated on every word. After a few moments of questions and answers, she began to walk away. Before going too far, she built up more courage and quickly turned back around and asked directly, "Can I buy you dinner, Honey?" My mind flashed with a big, "Oops!" My poses were too seductive; that's my curse. I bear that curse well. Deb was on her way and this lady was offering to buy my dinner—an expensive dinner. Was I to be dessert? Would I be posing on a white bearskin rug before the night's end? A quick answer flew from my mouth, "My wife is on the way right now and she hasn't eaten yet, either." I was hoping the Good Samaritan would extend the offer to her as well. She spun around, turning away; like the comic book super hero, The Flash, the lady was in her car and gone. She left me all alone, sitting on the curb like a dog that was dropped off by bad owners. I whimpered.

Deb showed up after following a few wrong directions. She was on Route 40 and I was on Route 40a. That was an easy mistake, but we got together okay. I was safe. We headed to a hotel. I showered and showered. Then, after a long shower trying to get the hiker scum and "stank" away, I emerged from the bathroom. Deb had brought clean clothes for me to wear. I felt like a shiny new penny, all nice and clean. But if I were a penny, then it would be a penny that was laid on a railroad track for a train to come by and run over it. My body felt smashed, beaten down from hikes and carrying my pack.

Deb asked if I wanted dinner. She was hungry from her road trip. Of course, we went to eat dinner. Deb wanted to buy me dinner. Man, I must have been one good-looking guy, women wanting to buy me dinner? Denny's was the lucky restaurant to serve us that night. I ordered three separate meals! By this time, I was down to one hundred sixty-five pounds. I started at a whopping two hundred five pounds. Deb had once brought me pants that used to be too small. I had to re-sew the button to make them tighter, and then had to double up a seam. Now, the same pants were loose again.

The next day, Deb and I went back to highway 40a. There, we picked up my buddy, Cargo, the dude who slipped me the Fiber One Bar, and his gal, Pony Express. As Cargo came from the woods he began singing, "Ballad of the Green Berets" by Barry Sadler. He often did that as he approached wherever I would be found. I would sing a cadence back to Cargo about Army Rangers.

We went for breakfast a little late, so we had to eat lunch. After eating, we went to a campsite, which I had called to reserve a spot for us. When we arrived, the office was closed; the owner was out to lunch. It started raining, so we went on in to set up and figured we would pay later for the campsite. I did call first, so I figured it would not be a problem.

We noticed the place had the appearance of a dump. Ratty old trailers littered the place and looked as if they could each be operating meth labs. I should have looked for ether bottles or lithium battery shells.

The place really stunk of a foul odor, but we were determined to make the best of it. After setting up far away from everyone else, we began having another lunch. We ate a lot. During lunch, an employee of the campground arrived and was polite. We explained no one was around when we arrived so we had set up and would come back up to pay for the campsite. All was okay.

Pennsylvania

CARGO, WHO IS the mellowest of souls—I call him my Zen— went to pay for the campsite. He returned and explained he was most unsuccessful. Cargo said the owner was screaming at him, upset we didn't wait for him to come back to the office. In his mind, we were supposed to sit in the rain and wait. Cargo never did pay for the site and he wanted me, of all people, to go talk with this lunatic. Cool! I relish meeting lunatics.

I approached the guy slowly. Giving the guy all the time he needed to compose himself, I paused to tie my shoe . . . as if. Upon reaching the thin, shaking, older man—he was about forty but looked fifty-five or more—he grabbed a cigarette and tried to light it. His hands were shaking from the adrenaline dump he was having and he couldn't hold his lighter still. The guy was scared and had rehearsed telling us off and wasn't going to give us a chance to be nice. He yelled, he screamed, he called us liars about the rain. He didn't want to hear anything reasonable. He was my kind of guy. So, I politely informed him he needed to stop his rant, step back, take a deep breath, and "shut the hell up." Then, as nicely as possible—and I was nice—I told him we were packing up and headed out. He wanted to say something else, but I was quickly within reach of his throat and he dared not speak. Hmm? Maybe he was smarter than he was acting.

That ended our chance to sleep in a trash-filled meth hole. We were so disappointed . . . not! Everyone was happier for the decision. After packing up, we headed out. Not long after heading down the highway, we saw a

KOA, Kampgrounds Of America, sign. Quickly, we pulled in and snagged a site. The KOA was awesome. We had showers and laundry and toilets and even ice cream. It was the best ever. Thank you, KOA!

We set up our site and made ourselves at home. The KOA suited our needs well, but I did miss the dump and dummy. The next day we were back on the trail. On the first hike, Cargo and I hiked thirty miles and made it into Pennsylvania. The next day, we did fifteen miles close to our camp-site. We were tired and our feet hurt.

On the third day, we changed our routine a bit. We had Deb meet us along the way. She had water and food in the truck. Deb was waiting at every road crossing. This was a great idea. We had never eaten so much on the trail before. I think we hiked only about twenty-five to twenty-seven miles on the third day, but we surely did eat a lot.

The fourth day brought a new adventure; it was an exciting day of hik-ing. We were pumped for the big hurdles of that day! This was it . . . the good stuff . . . many changes. First, we hit the halfway point: 1,090 miles! Cool! It was a cold, rainy day as we hiked. The cold rain hindered our progress as we got to a park, Pine Furnace, where there is the "half-gallon challenge!"

The "half-gallon challenge" is a challenge for thru-hikers to buy a half gallon of ice cream and eat it in one sitting. Yummy! We watched as friends and fellow hikers sat down to meet their challenges. Lady Pants and Red Moose were there. Both started their half-gallon challenge quick-ly. Lady Pants got up and went to her pack to retrieve her sleeping bag. Lady Pants was freezing cold from the wind and rain and ice cream. She slipped into her sleeping bag while sitting at the picnic table to eat her half gallon of ice cream. Next, Red Moose put on his sleeping bag as he ate his ice cream challenge. They were both shivering out of control. Red Moose finished his challenge in forty-six minutes. Good show!

I was cold and not sure if I would try something as "cool" as that. So, while waiting, to add a little courage, I bought a cold root beer and chugged it. Okay, I decided I was ready. I went into the store and bought a half gallon of chocolate swirl. The root beer had not been a good idea. My stomach was half full already. But, I am the guy who shot himself in the knee with a nail gun before starting on the trail so . . . ?

I started eating the ice cream and soon needed hot coffee to go with it. I swell up in the cold and break out in a rash, so the cold was one of my difficulties with hiking the Appalachian Trail. Each bite became a struggle, more difficult as time went on. The cold ice cream was swelling my throat closed. The coffee helped some. Again, I say, drinking root beer is not a good idea to start an ice cream challenge. It makes your tummy hurt. It makes you almost have to go poo. The forces that worked within my stomach were tremendous. The gurgling sounds from within me were some of the most unnatural sounds ever heard. But, this challenge was going to be met, mistakes or not. I continued eating. The more I ate the less progress I seemed to be making. This "challenge" was getting frustrating. Damn root beer!

There was an end to it, almost. I finished the half gallon in forty-three minutes. If you finish the challenge you get a little wooden spoon announcing your success. But that wasn't the end of my day. I still needed to hike another twelve miles! Oh, the pain! My hiking pace was much slower. Somehow, and I am not sure how, I did manage to keep the ice cream down. My stomach was not happy. Each step seemed to add more pressure, making me ready to explode as the root beer and ice cream mixed. It is a small wonder I didn't eat a couple of Alka-Seltzers before doing the half-gallon challenge.

The next day we picked up Lady Pants to slack pack her. Red Moose wouldn't slack pack, but he was a strong hiker and kept up with us. Kept up? Heck, he out-hiked us most times. Deb was at every road crossing with food and there were a lot of road crossings on this stretch of the trail. She gave trail magic to any who showed up hiking the trail. She gave hot food, cold food, water, Gatorade, beer, and candy bars. Red Moose met Deb at every crossing and was glad to see her. I think he felt guilty for eating so much, but that was why it was there.

Pennsylvania was the first state to have blueberries. They were every-where along the trail. I loved eating the blueberries. After a long hike, a short stop, and a moment of picking, I had handfuls of food. Free food! That was the best kind.

Red Moose laughed about how Pennsylvania was where he got the most trail magic and it was all from Deb. That was true for most hikers who were hiking around the area at the same time. Zig Zag and Ranger Bob showed up. Ranger Bob asked if we could slack pack them. I put the brakes on that idea. They were not offering to help with fuel, but Cargo was. They didn't offer to let me slack pack with them back in Virginia, so they were getting the same courtesy back that they gave me. I was fond of them, but I repay kindness the same as I receive it.

Pony Express took a day off as Cargo and I planned to hike thirty-three miles. That was a big day. As a matter of fact, it was "Hike Naked Day." "Hike Naked Day" is on the first day of summer. Wanting to do a good deed a day, I did a great deed that day: I kept my clothes on as I hiked! We met Brazil Nut, who was sun bathing by a river. We stopped for lunch.

We stayed by the river and soaked our feet in the cool water. Other hikers came and went. We stayed for a long break and a good lunch. Brazil Nut led the way after lunch. This was the first time I had actually hiked with her. She had a strong, fast pace. Her stride was almost unnatural. She appeared as if she were gliding on cross-country skis. Her hiking poles were long and she used them with each stride. We could barely keep up. I tried to stay close as we were talking as we walked. Cargo stayed close behind me. We didn't slack off at all. Then, the trail reached the base of a hill—a steep hill.

Brazil Nut continued her long, smooth stride without slowing her pace. The hill meant nothing to her. She had the same pace uphill, down-hill, or on level ground. It was awesome to watch. But, it was painful to try to keep up. We maintained pace with her, trying desperately not to pant or pass out. There was no way we were going to show any weakness.

Then, as we reached the crest of the hill, there was a sign. The sign was a true lifesaver. There was a shelter along the trail to the right. "Hey! A shelter! I gotta use the privy!" I called out. "Me too," added Cargo. "Okay, Bingo Mingo, I will see you later," answered Brazil Nut. She was gone in an instant. We hiked slower to the shelter. There was no way I would let her see she was hiking my ass into the dirt. At the shelter we rested and laughed. We were amazed at Brazil Nut's ability to hike. She was a class athlete. We ate a snack and rehydrated, then headed out. The last eight miles were extremely rough. The trail turned rocky, and rocks are not nice.

We had a good plan to hike thirty-three miles that day, but at mile thirty-one we came across a bar called "Doyle's." After a quick stop for a beer, the last two miles didn't seem worth getting off the bar stool for us to just finish. Deb came to Doyle's to pick us up. Brazil Nut was there and I introduce her to Deb. Another hiker, Doc, was a there also. Doc had served in the army as a Ranger. We sat at the bar, had a beer, and talked a while. Doc and his son, Do-What, were hiking the AT together. I had been reading messages in the shelter journals from Doc and Do-What for a long time, almost from the beginning of the trail. It was a fun time to finally meet them.

A Dead Smurf

PENNSYLVANIA HAS CRAZY rules about beer. No store may sell beer. You may not get a six-pack at a gas station. Now, that was strange. Beer can be bought at pizza shops, beer distributors, and BBQ shops. Most restaurants won't or can't sell beer, but they do allow a BYOB, bring your own bottle. Try that in Ohio!

I had no injuries, but I had no feeling in my left foot. It hurt whenever I did get feeling back to it. Whenever I hiked, I would try to run on it or slap my foot on rocks repeatedly to make it numb again. A couple leg cramps haunted my nights, a few bad fly bites irritated my skin, but all in all I was doing great. Deb was in Pennsylvania with me, so it was a good time. I was definitely as happy as a beet in soup.

Cargo, Pony Express, and I hiked together on most days. At the end of our hikes, Deb would pick us up and take us back to the KOA. There we would shower and pack for the next day. Deb fixed dinners for us and did a great job. We ate well. Using the KOA as a base camp was a perfect idea. Pennsylvania went by quickly. On one occasion, we were finishing a hike into Port Clinton. The path down was the steepest path I had seen on the Appalachian Trail that was not made of sharp rocks. The way down looked fun to me. I pressed my feet together then leaped into the air. My feet landed about five feet downhill. Next, as if I were skiing moguls, I hopped and turned. The entire descent from the top of the ridge to the bottom was done in mogul fashion. My knees were hurting! This was not one of my better ideas.

Cargo and Pony Express came down carefully, taking their time, walking. Deb was waiting at the bottom of the hill. We each had our own hiking style and speed. The days hiking with Cargo and Pony Express were good days. But, before Pennsylvania was completed, Cargo and Pony Express parted ways from us. They wanted to give Deb and me time away alone. That was kind for them to do that.

One day, when I was hiking alone, about to finish my hike with a big, open-faced climb and five more miles to finish, I parted from Deb by the road. I was crossing a bridge at Lehigh Gap. Traffic was routed one-way on the bridge for construction, but no work was going on this day. Halfway across the busy bridge was a Porta John. It was sitting smack dab in the middle of the bridge and next to the moving lane of traffic. Well, when you gotta go, you gotta go. I jumped the short dividing wall, went to the Porta John, waved at the oncoming traffic, and jumped into the Porta John.

It was an odd, eerie feeling when large trucks drove by on the bridge. I could feel the bridge move with each passing, speeding vehicle. Then, a thought dawned on me—man, I was gonna get hit by a vehicle while taking a dump on the road! Being covered in poop wasn't the worse thought. It washes off. But the purple-stained fluid would make me look like a dead Smurf. And knowing Deb, she would have an open casket, so everyone would see me and have a good laugh. That worried me.

I texted her about what I was doing, using the Porta John in the middle of a bridge with heavy traffic in the other lane. She was busy picking up Doc, Do-What, and Erin, and was taking them to McDonald's. It was the first time they had been to a McDonald's since they had started on the trail. After a quick relief, I got out of the Porta John and waved at the traffic again. Talk about surprising folks. The look in the eyes of passing motorists was priceless.

Time to Go!

IT WAS GREAT having Deb with me during that time. Each day cooked food, fresh fruits, and veggies were waiting for me. Yuck, veggies! Deb and I stayed at a hotel in Wind Gap. The place was under new management. The new owners were less than hiker friendly. The room stunk, slime was on the walls, there appeared to be a large amount of blood on the floor, and electric wires were exposed, hanging from the ceiling. Alien showed up at the hotel. He was tired and hungry. We gave him a beer and let him go get situated in his dilapidated room.

When dinnertime arrived, Deb and I went to Delaware Water Gap to eat. At Delaware Water Gap, we met with Brazil Nut for dinner. She had already started eating. Pizza was the meal of choice, and it was a good choice. After dinner, I bought socks, new hiking poles, and two water bottles. The socks were the "Darn Tough" brand. Great socks, but the guy at the store recommended I wear a size too small. That proved to be a bad idea that cost me four toenails. Never wear Darn Tough socks that are too small.

While walking around Delaware Water Gap with Brazil Nut, we met Comfortably Numb. He was headed to a different restaurant to have dinner with Shenanigans, the Run Aways, Ompah, and Buckeye. Buckeye had changed his name to Flowers. Meeting them all again was super cool. This was a great reunion. We exchanged stories, shared laughs, and had a few drinks. Then, they told me about some guy, a section hiker named Power Strip, at the local hostel.

This section hiker seemed to have moved into the hostel. He started with the name Whisper, but that got changed when others saw he was carrying an electrical power strip. The staying limit at the hostel was two days. He had been there much longer than two days. The other hikers asked me to come and "take care of him." Deb refused to let me. She is the wiser one of the two of us. Besides, he couldn't be as bad as everyone claimed. But, most importantly, this was my last night with Deb, as she was headed home in the morning.

On the first day without Deb for support the hike seemed a bit boring. My feet stayed steady on the trail. There wasn't much to see. After a while, I reached Delaware Water Gap along with another hiker. We went to the hostel. It was run by a local church. It is a decent place for hikers and they ask for only donations. The hostel was a welcome sight. I was hoping the section hiker, Power Strip, had already left without any intervention required by me.

Brazil Nut decided to stay another day to make repairs to her equipment. Ompah was still there, but Flowers, Shenanigans, and the kids had all moved on. To my displeasure, the section hiker was there as well. This guy annoyed everyone. While I was sitting outside talking to a couple of friends, he walked up and started singing, "O Canada!" at the top of his lungs. The dude was literally screaming the song. He was terribly annoying.

After his absurd singing of "O Canada," he stated he knew the George Carlin version of the National Anthem. I asked him not to sing it. This nut job then responded, "Why, are you some kind of patriot or something?" My answer was a quick glance at him, changing into a long stare. He started to speak again. After a growl formed in my throat, he stopped, turned, and walked away. That was the smartest thing he had done so far.

The time had come for this dude to leave. My hands were no longer tied. Deb was home and I was free to politely make a change in the scenery at the Delaware Water Gap Hostel. Now, I needed to figure out the best and most efficient way to handle this freeloader. There were several key factors involved. First, I must respect the church and all they have done and do for hikers. Also, the guy might be a bit touched in the head, so I didn't want to embarrass him. But, ultimately, he had to go! There were no ifs, ands, or buts about that!

Later in the day I invited the other hikers to a local bar and grill. To get the hikers to the bar, I announced the first round was on me. Lucky for me, it was happy hour. Ompah, Red Moose, and another hiker joined me. Everyone got his drink while I quickly downed my beer and headed back to the hostel. The dude was alone. That took care of not embarrassing him. Next, I would not approach him; he had to come to me. That way it wasn't me attacking him.

I sat quietly and alone. Before long, the dude came up to me to ask if I smoked. Prior information led me to believe he bummed from all the other hikers. It was also believed, but not a proven fact, that he was allegedly taking money from the donation box as well. My response to his attempt to bum from me was plain and simple. I didn't have smokes. I jumped up quickly and got just inches away from him. I am five feet eight inches tall and he was around six feet one inch. We looked mismatched but that actually made things easier for me.

The height difference was no problem. I saw his eyes showing concern and weakness by my rapid approach. Taking my cue from his facial expression, I exclaimed, "It is time for you to go!" I aggressively stepped toward him and he stepped back as if looking to escape. "You have to leave. Get out!" I said. He questioned, "Why?" That was to be his last question. I had to be the one asking questions to keep his mind on track to leave.

When asked how long he had been there, he said only a day or two. Knowing that answer was false, I stepped forward again in a drill-sergeant-manner and barked, "Do not lie to me!" Shocked at my tone, he stepped back again and stuttered, "Six days or more." It was obvious he wanted me as far away from him as possible. That was my leverage.

With each question I asked, he answered as a child would a father, hoping to not get disciplined. He soon agreed, "it was time to leave." While packing his gear, he slowed down and started to change his mind. Seeing this, I focused on his using two bunks, blocking other hikers from using the space for their comfort. Then he admitted he had his gear on two bunks, but he was sleeping on the couch and had a hammock up in the shelter in the back. Any arguments to stay were eliminated by that fact. He had been unduly selfish and had worn out any welcome by other hikers.

After packing, the section hiker came to me, reaching out his hand. "Thank you, Mingo, for telling me what I needed to hear." My answer was one of concern, "You better hurry to the trail so you can find a site to set up your tent. Go on!" And then he was gone. This guy claimed he had hiked ninety-one miles in thirty days. He would do better now. That night, the other hikers were happy to find Power Strip was gone.

Jack and Jill Came Down the Hill

THE NEXT DAY I headed into a wilderness called New Jersey. My buddy, Jim, who lives in New Jersey, was coming to hike with me, but I wanted to get through the rocks first. I wasn't two miles inside New Jersey before I saw two bears. The bears are huge in New Jersey, and these guys aren't afraid of anything. They stand there just looking at you, wondering if you taste good or not. Thru-hikers call these Jersey bears, "Guido-bears."

I stayed at a campsite for the night, Mohican Outdoor Center. It was a clean campground with tent sites strategically located all around. The next morning, Jim called and said he was coming, ready for a hike. What an adventure that was.

We paid a local to take us up the trail so we could hike back to Jim's car parked at the Mohican Outdoor Center. The hike was perfect, except we were going southbound and I was meeting many friends along the way. Of course, I had to stop to talk with them all. Jim got a little tired of stopping and talking with all the hikers. I understood. We would have never made it back had he not said something.

The day was perfect; there were no bugs, and it was slightly warm and sunny with a light breeze. We were headed back to Mohican Outdoor

Center. That was our goal. I was reading the map and was looking at Mohican Mountain on the map. The mountain was about three miles past the campgrounds. Okay, I should have put on my glasses to read the map better.

Well, we crossed a road with our butts dragging and started up a hill. A young couple was headed down the hill. The guy asked, "Do you know how far it is to Mohican Camp Grounds?" I replied, "I thought it was this way," pointing up the hill. "No, we haven't passed it yet," he replied. "It is at the next road." "No," I said, "That road is Camp Road." Well, guess what I found out: Camp Road is where Mohican Outdoor Center was located. Duh!

So, I asked the guy their names. He replied with the short answer, "My name is Jack." Not hearing any more information, "Okay, Jack. What is her name?" I pointed with my hiking poles toward the young lady. Not wanting to reply, he quipped, "She's my wife." I persisted, and asked again, informing him I didn't ask if they were married, "What is her name?" After some delay, he replied, "Jill." Jim laughed and said, "Jack and Jill came down the hill and saved our stupid asses." Man, was he ever right? We were tired and wanted to get back to his car.

When we got back to the car, I had to go potty. Upon returning from the outhouse, we had a couple beers and snacked on candy and an old sub sandwich Jim had left in his car. Time to go! Jim typed into his GPS "find food." Burgers and fries were what we needed. The GPS took us to a house. The house had been converted into a store downstairs. Jim asked the young man behind the counter where we could find a burger and fries. He said he could make them for us, so we stayed.

In the house, the living room walls were lined with coolers for drinks and snacks. The young man began making the burgers in the kitchen. A counter separated us from the kitchen. There was one small table with four chairs in the middle of the living room floor. That's all we needed.

We sat and reminisced about the day. While having a good laugh at meeting Jack and Jill, we were surprised by the gigantic burgers brought to us. What a great place! We ate our fill. A lady appeared, the mom, and I asked if they had a restroom I could use. She replied, "No, we don't have a bathroom, but you can go out back and use the dumpster." My mind raced, "Wow, how cool will that be?" So, off I went to the dumpster. I climbed in for privacy. The dumpster was half full so I stood over the top edge and could be easily seen. *Was it number one or number two? I will leave that to your imagination. I will say I used the dumpster.*

We went back to Brink Road, where we started our hike that day. I needed to pick up the trail there so I didn't miss any of the AT. Once we made it to Brink Road and I was putting on my pack, I found I had forgotten my hundred-dollar poles at Mohican Outdoor Center campsite. Jim graciously drove me back to recover my poles. Then he drove us back to Brink Road again. Jim and I reached the road entrance at eleven o'clock. We were both exhausted.

The night was dark, darker than most. I had a half-mile hike uphill on an overgrown logging road to the trail crossing. One mile northbound on the AT, I needed to find the side trail to the shelter. I found the AT and headed north. I hiked and hiked, tripped and cursed. Startled at the sound of every breaking branch, I thought, "Stupid Pooh Bear!" Midnight came and I realized I had missed the shelter! In the dark I set up my tent for the night.

To not be eaten by bears, I decided to hang my food bag in a tree. But, typically for me, I had sent home my string for hanging bear bags. Maybe a tall, thin tree would work as a good alternative. Looking for a tall, thin tree, I found one and started climbing. Reaching high with my hands, grabbing the narrow trunk, I pulled my legs up and wrapped them around the tree. Navigating around thin limbs took me ever higher. Once I was high up in the tree, it began bending down. Thoughts of the tree breaking in half filled my mind. Quickly and calculatedly, I let go with my feet and let them hang downward.

While hanging onto the top of the tree, my feet finally landed softly on the ground. My arms were stretched overhead, like trying to do pull ups. My hands gripped the tree tightly. The tree didn't break and was bent over in a great arch. Reaching for my food bag with one hand and hanging onto the tree with the other, my arms were stretched out far apart.

The food bag was too far away. The strength of the tree was too much for me to hold with one hand. My fingers barely touched the food bag on the ground when I lost my grip on the tree. The tree snapped back up. Damn! I had to climb the tree again!

During my second climb up the tree, sweat poured into my eyes. Using a different strategy, I kept the food bag in one hand. Once again, I was high in the tree and it began bending. I held onto my food bag with one hand, held the tree with the other, and kept my legs wrapped around the tree. The tree had weakened; I hit the ground much harder than before, landing on my back. Hitting the ground knocked the wind out of me and caused me to let go. The tree snapped back up, again!

Undaunted, I tried climbing the tree a third time, promising it would be the last time. To keep both hands free, I slid the loops of the drawstring on the food bag over my arm. I climbed slower. If bears were watching me they would have thought I had lost my mind. The tree began to bend. My feet hung down to feel for the ground and I held on with both hands. Once on the ground I secured the food bag to the tree and let it go. The force of the tree recoiling back up made me fear it had worked like a catapult. My food may have been launched through the woods.

The food bag was safely up a tree, or so I hoped. It was too dark to see if it was still there. Hopefully, it was safe away from bears. Of course, it dawned upon me as I looked up the tree: I was hungry.

I went to my tent to sleep without a snack. My back ached from landing on it while trying to hang the bear bag. There had to be a better way to do this. Oh yes! Don't send the string home!

I awoke at five in the morning, as I usually did. Still tired and sore, I decided to sleep in for a while. Five hours of sleep was not gonna suit me. A couple hours later I heard movement just outside my tent. I popped out of the tent and saw the largest bear I have ever seen, just ten feet away. I had set up in a blueberry patch and this guy was having breakfast. He was huge. I quickly dove back into my tent to retrieve my camera and take some video of the bear. He was walking away, but I got great footage of him as he left.

Being visited by a bear was enough to motivate me to get my butt up. I packed as quickly as possible. Once packed, I was ready to head out. My pack seemed to be a little light. I felt good and was making good time hiking at a fast pace. After a half hour of hiking away from my campsite,

I realized I needed to go back, climb the tree, and retrieve my food bag.

Even with the slow start, it felt good to be hiking. There were no major elevation changes, so the miles flew by. It wasn't long before I was passing a third shelter. I spied a beaver pond and dams close to the trail. This was the perfect dinner spot. I decided to eat and look for beavers.

God's Gift

I HAD ALREADY hiked seventeen miles that day and was feeling good. What really put pep-in-my-step was the fact that I had only eight hundred fifty miles left to finish the AT. Comfortably Numb hiked by and informed me that seven miles ahead was a place called the Murray Property. I set out to make it there to spend the night. This would be an easy hike. The trail was well kept and gentle on the feet.

Toward the end of the day's hike the sky became thick with storm clouds. Flashes of lightning lit the sky. I hurried to get to the Murray Property before dark and before the storm hit. Well, that was my hope. To make time pass, I made up a quick song or chant to keep track of how far I had to go. "Road, a road, a pond, a road." I repeated this until the first road was crossed then it was, "A road, a pond, a road. A road, a pond, a road." Then came "Pond, a road. Pond, a road." I chanted these over and over again to keep track of landmarks. My final chant became "Gotta go, gotta go, gotta go to the road." These chants helped save time by not having to repeatedly look at the map.

Reaching the last road was not as easy as expected. With thick clouds overhead, night came on fast and it was too dark to see. Making my way through the woods became difficult. Time and again I stepped into deep mud and water. The closer I got to the road the more mud was on the trail. The road had no signs indicating which way to go to the Murray Property. This was going to be a shot in the dark—no pun intended.

This twenty-four mile hike was more exhausting than I thought it would be. Tired and hungry, I sat down to eat a snack. My hope was a car or truck would come by and I could get a ride or at least directions. Nobody came. My water supply was finished. Humidity drained sweat from every pore of my body.

The night was warm and the mosquitoes were swarming and hungry. Choosing to go left, I hiked in hopes of finding my way to the Murray Property, and soon. Bears were thick in these woods and I didn't want to meet any after dark. Staying on the road was easy enough, but twisting an ankle in the dark was a concern. The road was covered with loose rocks, making that both possible and probable.

The farther I hiked, the more the woods parted away from the road. It was almost impossible to see in the dark. Ahead, I saw a flashlight shining toward me. The light flashed three times, then it lit again. "Who is there?" a voice called from the night. "It's me, Mingo!" The voice answered, "We are over here. This is Doc." He was still hiking the AT with his son Do-What. Luckily, I had made it to the Murray Property.

Doc explained the setup at the property. Water was available from a yard hydrant. The water pressure was extraordinarily high. It would blast a water bottle out of your hand. An outdoor shower was up the hill on the side of a building. There was no hot water, but the pressure felt great. Washing the sweat off was a tremendous relief. The cold water eased the itching from the multiple mosquito bites. A one-room building was empty and I could put my air mattress inside. The building had electricity, so cell phones could be recharged. The hike to the Murray Property was well worth the effort.

It rained all night long. The next morning, the rain was coming down hard so I went back to bed. All of the hikers who had set up their tents had packed up and moved on. Around noon I awoke to sun shining brightly through the window. It was time to go. I put on my pack and headed out.

About a mile down the trail was a town. Hot food would be a good change of pace, so I headed in for a bite. Eureka, a pizza shop! Sitting in the pizza shop was Alien. We chatted a bit and ordered lunch. When I saw the rains had come back, I quickly headed out the door to get our packs and put them on the porch to keep them dry.

Returning, I told Alien I didn't have any rain gear. The door of the shop instantly opened and there stood a young lady looking me straight in the eye. "God told me to bring you this umbrella," she said as she handed me a new umbrella. "Thank You!" was all I could say in my shocked state. Alien, being an atheist, was shocked by the coincidence and timing. He muttered the f-word. The young lady turned, went out, and was gone.

We ate, talked about our hikes, and later, went to a general store for supplies and coffee. The umbrella kept me dry. We sat on rocking chairs on the porch of the general store, had our coffee, and watched the rain. The rain fell as hard and heavy as any before. This was going to make the trail wet and soggy.

Our coffee cups ran dry but the sky didn't. We headed out, walking in the rain; no other way around that. I used the umbrella for a while, but then lightning started flashing. This lightning was the kind that hits the ground. Looking at the umbrella, I realized it was metal. Could God have sent me a lightning rod? Was He planning on taking me away? Would being struck by lightning be God's gift? I didn't want to tempt fate, so I put the metal umbrella away and decided getting wet in the rain was better than getting hit by lightning, again.

That evening I arrived at a road where another hiker and I hitchhiked to a town that had a church hostel. We got a ride from a young man. We stashed our gear in the trunk of his car then were off to town. We couldn't find the hostel! We got out of his car at a major intersection and retrieved our equipment. One of my new collapsible water bottles fell out of my pack into his trunk and was lost forever.

Comfortably Numb was walking by, carrying a pizza and a two-liter bottle of Mountain Dew. We followed him to the hostel. It was located in a church that allowed hikers to stay in the walkout basement. They had a laundry and showers. The town had a large grocery store and fast food places. This was good. The next day I would be in New York and needed to shop for food.

Hiking gear was scattered all around on chairs and tables to dry. The hikers each sought out a spot on the floor to bed down for the night. Some section hikers stopped in and stayed as well. They tended to dominate the conversations and were a bit annoying.

4TH of July

MY JOURNEY THROUGH New York started out as a fun day. Well, the day was fun for me, as Lady Luck seemed to be smiling on me the entire day. That is the same Lady Luck you know and not the trail name of another hiker. This was going to be a Fourth of July to remember. I had something special planned and wanted a pic to prove it. Yup, there was going to be digital proof that my plan had come together. This was going to be really, really big.

I had just learned that I would be able to see the New York City skyline this evening, from the Appalachian Trail, on the Fourth of July! I thought long and hard and came up with the perfect way to celebrate the occasion. This was to be my best plan ever. I was so proud. I hiked with a little more pep and vigor. Walking tall never felt so good. Man, people are gonna be jealous, I thought. The plan was that good.

I met another hiker, Mike D. from Florida. He was also known as Florida Mike, but usually we called him Mike D. from Florida. We were that clever. A cool kid, he was twenty years old and already had life by the reins. Mike had contracted Lyme disease, as so many other hikers had. One foot was still swollen from the disease. Despite that, Mike was a strong hiker. I could barely keep up with him.

We stopped the morning of the Fourth of July and chatted with a couple southbound section hikers. They told us about the best creamery in the world. We decided we would find the creamery and get some most excellent ice cream. The plan was beginning.

Arriving at Lakes Road, where the creamery should have been, we tried to find any sign for it. There were no signs for the creamery. We found signs for hotdogs, but no creamery. No problem, we decided to hitchhike. We no sooner had our thumbs out than a guy in a pickup truck stopped to give us a ride. This was the first time a pickup truck stopped for me and this was also the quickest hitch ever.

We explained we had no idea how far the creamery was, but wanted to go there for ice cream. We loaded our packs through the broken-out side windows of the camper shell sitting on the bed of his beat up, rusted old pickup truck. After piling in, off we went. We rounded the first curve and there was the creamery. We yelled, "Stop!"

The guy spent more time waiting for us to load and unload our gear than he did driving us to the creamery. The place was literally less than a couple hundred yards away. If we had listened really hard we might have heard kids licking their ice cream cones. That was the shortest hitched ride ever.

Having been in the woods during July when the heat index was in the triple digits, we smelled. We were two hikers reeking of human sweat and foul body odors. That was us, all right, just two more stinky hikers. Mike wasn't wearing a shirt; I think he wanted to show off his tattoos. That was okay; it was too hot to wear too many clothes anyway. Besides, our clothes really stunk.

We jumped in the long line for service. Mostly old folks were in line for ice cream, along with a few younger couples. But the over-sixty-five-year-old crowd dominated the scene. Poor ole Mike was getting some pretty mean stares. I don't think the grannies cared for his young, shirtless body in their line for ice cream. We didn't care.

Mike said to me, "I hope they take plastic because that's all I use. I don't carry cash." Well, I was certain a place this busy would take plastic. Every place takes plastic this day and age. A place that would be cash only just wouldn't get enough customers. So I thought . . . and I thought wrong.

There on the counter was a small sign that read, "Cash Only. No Plastic!" We were shocked. We had been waiting in line for twenty minutes before we saw the sign. Mike was disappointed and ready to leave. Cool! I saw an opportunity to show a fellow hiker a special courtesy. As Mingo, I was trying to do a good deed a day and this was perfect timing.

I quickly gave Mike five dollars with instructions to get whatever he wanted. Then I saw a sign for banana splits for six dollars. Without a second thought, I tossed another dollar to Mike so he could get the banana split.

The line seemed to crawl. But after waiting a short eternity, I was at the front counter across from a young female. She looked like a college prep making money at a summer job. She was not enthusiastic about her job. After asking for a banana split, which would have made the wait and the snide comments about our odorous bodies worthwhile, I was informed sharply there were no more bananas. This was not something I was prepared for and my mind went blank.

The young, ice-cream-dispensing, snooty princess rolled her eyes and asked, "What else do you want?" Besides a little respect and a chance to spank her for being rude, both of which I did not voice aloud, I asked for several scoops of ice cream, naming the flavors. Without saying a word, she turned around and walked to the back of the store out of sight. I waited and waited. Finally, this overpaid and over privileged "preppy" came back, scooped my flavors into a paper bowl, and handed it to me. I should have asked for full scoops, as mine were less than half full.

At least the ice cream was okay. There was a water spigot on the outside of the building, so we gathered our bottles and filled them for the trail. We then splashed water on ourselves as a makeshift bath. The other customers didn't seem to mind. But, oddly, no one was sitting near our picnic table. Everyone was crowded together at the other side of the creamery's lot. Maybe we stunk worse than I thought. After the ice cream and bath, we walked back to the trail.

Shortly after entering the woods, we saw a small wooden bridge. Mike was hiking just ahead of me when he stopped on the bridge and bent over to pick up a note. Hikers leave notes this way that often provide good information. Mike slowly read aloud, "Warning, there is a live bee nest under the—Ouch! Ouch! Ouch! Son of a bitch!" Mike screamed. Like rapid gunfire, I yelled, "Run, run, run!" This was my battle cry. Mike took off in a blaze of speed and I was fast on his heels.

He had been stung on the ankle that wasn't affected by Lyme disease, and on his legs. Okay, now this day was starting to suck. But, I still had a plan to make this Fourth of July special. We hiked farther into the woods, closing in on the New York City skyline view. My big plan was going to be cool. Heck, this was going to be epic.

The trail went over Fitzgerald Falls. There were four day hikers, two guys and two gals, enjoying the cold water below the falls. They had beer, so Mike and I attempted a Yogi for a beer. We stopped, chatted, and listened to their lame stories, as if we were really interested. I took a couple of pictures of the falls with one of the gals in the picture. One of the guys, a chubby, drunken, jackass whom the girls were obviously not into, tried to jump into the picture. Sorry, dude, you have been cropped out! No Yogi beers were offered, not even for a bee-stung, Lyme-disease-stricken thru-hiker. Disappointed, we limped away.

As we got closer to the site where we could see the New York City skyline, we met three other thru-hikers. Goldie, Whisp, and Red Moose had set up a campsite. They were celebrating the Fourth of July with small bottles of liquor. They didn't have any to share with us, but that's the way it goes. We explained that it was possible to see the New York City skyline and the Fourth of July fireworks. They decided not to go any farther, but asked if we would come back to get them if we found a site with a view.

The final ascent to the top of Mombasha High Point was an easy, gradual climb. There were no signs indicating we had reached our destination. We carefully surveyed the area and figured there were no other places higher than the spot upon which we stood. We were on the high point, Mombasha High Point.

Excited about arriving at the high point, we looked for places to set up our camp. The point was small and rocky. I found a crevice in which to set up my tent. Mike opted to cowboy camp on the rocks. As we began setting up, Mike and I took turns looking for New York City.

The smog, fog, or mist in the air hid New York City from us. At one point, I saw odd, sharply edged mountains in the distance. I had to stand on the pointed edge of a protruding rock to peer above the trees to see the shadowed formations. There are no sharp mountains such as these in this part of the country. I had found New York City! We celebrated with traditional high fives and continued setting up camp and having dinner.

Now was the time for my big surprise. I recorded the event with my camera. After digging in my nearly empty backpack, I plucked out a big, bright red apple. In anticipation of being in New York State during the Fourth of July, I had brought a big, red apple to commemorate the moment. Proud of the symbolism and thinking out of the box, I stood tall with my apple in hand, showing it to Mike. It was a good apple!

Mike dug into his backpack and withdrew a fifth of Jack Daniels. Stupid apple! So, there I was, a forty-nine-year-old Special Forces veteran, and a retired police sergeant with multiple other qualifications and experiences, and I had brought an apple to New York to celebrate the Fourth of July. Mike, a twenty-year-old kid from Florida, had brought a fifth of whiskey. Old dogs can learn new tricks. Mike graciously explained how my unselfishly giving him money for ice cream was cool. So, he was sharing his whiskey with me. That was awesome! Stupid apple!

The evening arrived and so did the mosquitoes. They swarmed us with a fury. Slapping the bloodsuckers was futile. Kill one and five would take its place. We slapped and swatted till our arms were tired. The sun was about to set. I feared I would miss the sunset because I was going to hide in my tent. But we had whiskey. Mike, being frustrated at the growing swarms of mosquitoes, said, "I wish I had some DEET to keep these bugs away!" Then my memory sparked like a third hit in the head with a sledgehammer, "Hey! I have DEET!"

Smeared with DEET, we watched the sun set in the west. I had to give New York City one more gander. Like an explorer discovering a new world, my eyes grew wide as I discovered cool air had lifted the smog and mist. The sun reflected sharply off the windows, steel, and concrete. New York City was clearly visible! We were going to see the New York City Fourth of July fireworks! We had DEET, we had whiskey, we ate well, and I had forgotten the apple I had eaten just minutes earlier. All was good on the Appalachian Trail. There wasn't room for other tent sites or stealth camping. Too bad for the others; we opted not to call them. They should have come with us.

The fireworks were spectacular. Other cities in the area had their fireworks that night as well. We saw splashes of light across the ridges all around us. We had the best spot on the Appalachian Trail for the Fourth of July. The shows went on longer than I could stand. Mike began falling down from our excessive drinking. We called it a night when the last swig of whiskey was finished and Mike couldn't stay on his feet for more than a minute at a time. I slept well.

Ten Days of Hell

THE NEXT MORNING, as I headed out, I asked the trail aloud, "What adventure do you have for me next?" I had no idea how I was tempting fate. As I hiked, I felt great and didn't have a care in the world. Ten days of hell was about to begin, but I was oblivious and unprepared. My resolve to finish the trail was going to be tested to its limits. I just didn't know trouble was coming that day, and I had no clue it was going to be so freaking bad. Do not take this account as me whining. I asked to be on the trail so I earned all that I got. These next days show how the best prepared can even find themselves facing terrible odds.

Day one

Day one was the day of my asking, "What adventure do you have for me next?" and I tempted fate. While hiking up a ravine between rocks and the hillside, the ground on both my left and right was at eye level. I saw something flying at my face from the right. Something was coming from the ground fast; it was pink with vertical dark stripes and seemed to be shooting for my eyes. My reflex was to jump back and fall down the hill onto the rocks below. Then, I heard a loud buzzing. A large yellow and black rattlesnake had just struck at my face, narrowly missing me.

The snake missed me by less than an inch. I had faced death and his eyes were yellow. The snake was a Timber Rattlesnake, about three feet long or more. It was one angry snake. Carefully, I took out my camera and took video and pictures of it. My heart started beating rapidly. With shaking hands from an adrenaline dump, I called Deb to report that I was okay.

Well, no, I wasn't okay. My mind was restless. I was jumping at the sight and sound of every little

mouse and bird in the dry leaves of the forest floor. Hiking wasn't much fun that day. I couldn't relax or just enjoy the hike. I am not one to be afraid of a little snake, but that guy almost got me in the face. To be honest, it shook me up. Later that night I didn't sleep well either.

Day two

Day two was to be a better day—at least, that was my personal goal. I woke early and began packing before others in the area got up. The section hikers had been a bit loud the night before and had kept me from sleeping well. No problem, I would get water from the spring then head out before they got a chance to piss me off again.

There was a spring close. The spring was a small hole in the ground. The water didn't run but seemed to rise and lower like an ocean tide. When I was there, the water was high—not too high, but good enough to fill my water bottles. I dropped the siphon end of my water filter into the spring. The water looked fresh and cold. Working the pump, drawing the water through the filter and into the water bottle, was an easy task. Then, I saw a clump of toilet paper floating from the bottom of the spring. The clump of paper rolled over and revealed it had been used. Someone had taken a crap in the spring, contaminating the water that I needed.

Angry, I threw my water filter aside and sat there thinking. It was obvious I could not use this water, the water filter, or the water bottle. As soon as possible, the equipment had to be decontaminated. I loaded my gear and headed out, stomping mad. The sun seemed to take full advantage of my lack of water. Mile after mile, I passed old streams that were now dry. I made it over Bear Mountain into Bear Mountain Park. There, I bought an ice cream sandwich from a vending machine.

My mind was not clear. I walked in the heat with my mind in a fog. While walking through the park I heard, "Mingo! Hey Mingo! Hooker!" It was Comfortably Numb, yelling to get my attention. He was waiting for the concession stands to open. Comfortably Numb explained we could get good hot food and cold beers. This was to be a huge improvement. The stand opened and we were the first in line. Actually, there were no other customers.

I ordered nachos with cheese and a beer. The beer was opened and poured from the can into a cup by the server. She poured the beer so fast I swear half the beer was still in the can when it was thrown away. The cheese was still cold and tasted foul. But I am a true thru-hiker so I ate the crappy food and drank my shorted beer. Hey, Bear Mountain Staff, clean up your act; hire someone who knows how to heat cheese. I know, that is a real brain stopper!

After eating, we headed out to continue our hike. The Appalachian Trail goes through the zoo at Bear Mountain Park. Comfortably Numb wanted to make a short detour to see the reptiles. I followed and he walked straight to the rattlesnake display. There behind the glass lay a yellow rat-tlesnake. It was smaller than the one that had struck at my face, but it was the same color. Not cool! Shaken from the memory of the snake, the bad food, and the poo in the spring, I started to walk out of the zoo.

The walkway had a slight incline and I had a hard time walking up. Worry filled my mind. Everything was in a fog, and I couldn't walk up a slight incline? What the heck was going on? Comfortably Numb had hiked the trail before and knew right away what was happening. I was dehydrated. My body and mind were shutting down in a bad way. The heat was getting to me after not drinking water all day. The beer and nachos didn't help.

Comfortably Numb was a fast, strong hiker. He could leave me in the dust. Now, he seemed to be holding back to make certain I was okay. After crossing the Hudson River, we were five miles away from the Monastery.

The Monastery allows hikers to camp out on their fields. They have Porta Johns around the fields and an outdoor shower and water. There, I would rehydrate and clean my gear if possible.

Before reaching the Monastery, I came to a store, the Appalachian Store. This was a hiker-friendly convenience store. To end my dehydration, I downed a liter bottle of Power Aid. Then, I filled the bottle with water three separate times and drank it. This helped, but I still felt dehydrated. It would take time for the fluids to reach my blood stream to make me feel better.

The next day would prove to be somewhat better—or, so I hoped. My water filter needed to be replaced and the water bottle and hoses needed to be decontaminated. For now, I would just drink straight from the streams. I didn't try to wash the filter at the Monastery.

Day three

On day three of hell, I stopped at the RPH Shelter and called for a pizza to be delivered. Things were looking up, but sometimes it isn't all about the trail. Bad news came from home. My wife's favorite pet cat, Scratch, had died. He had kitty leukemia. He was a sissy cat, but unique in many ways. Scratch was aptly named, as you would know if you ever tried to pick him up. Every time he was walking around I could call his name and he would meow back. This would go on repeatedly.

We got Scratch from a neighbor's barn. We were looking for a good mouser. You need a good mouser if you have horses. Mice can cause damage and get out of control. A good mouser is a good control method. Well, Scratch wasn't much of a mouser. That sissy kitty would catch only grasshoppers and butterflies.

We called Scratch our ambassador cat. There was a feral cat that came around and would eat from our cat bowl on the porch. Scratch made friends with him quickly. When a skunk came up to eat from the cat's bowl, Scratch made friends with him too. We were not too pleased about the skunk coming around.

Scratch would sleep with his front legs extended straight out, like Superman in flight. The poor little guy had it rough, though. Our new puppy

was exceptionally rambunctious and thought Scratch was a soft pillow to sleep upon. Scratch would lay there squashed by the pup, unable to escape. Deb loved that little cat. I felt horrible I wasn't there for her when he died.

Thoughts of leaving the trail stayed with me all day. I felt I should have been there for Deb during her loss. Her words to me on the phone still ring in my mind, "I loved that damn cat!" It hurt her to lose the little guy, and it slowed my hike; it took the wind from my sails. Motivation was not flowing into my legs. I ate my pizza and called it a night. Tomorrow would be or could be better. I had nearly been bitten in the face by a rattlesnake, got dehydrated by having my water filter contaminated, and now, I was dealing with heartache. Tomorrow would be better, I promised myself.

Day four

The next day, my fourth day of hell, started with a torrential down pour and cold winds piercing through to the bone. I hiked in the rain. It rained all day and well into the evening. I was soaking wet, cold, and tired. My pack increased in weight as it became more and more water logged. If it weren't for carrying a pack and trying to make miles, I would have frozen. The rain caused me to be chilled. As I hiked I felt my body uncontrollably shiver.

After making it to a railroad crossing, I knew a motel was close; it was just a couple miles down the road. Cold and soaked, I turned left to hike the two miles to the motel. A warm, dry place to sleep was really needed after this long difficult day. I didn't finish many miles as the weather hampered my hike greatly. So, nearly snake bit, dehydrated, heartbroken, and now drenched and freezing, I needed a day off.

The motel parking lot was empty; there was not a car in sight. This was good. I would get a hot shower and a dry place to sleep. Hey, I was looking forward to finding a place to get laundry done as well. My luck had been bad, but now, it was looking up. I stood in front of the motel with passing thoughts of being thankful. That night, I would be dry and warm.

A lady came out to ask what I needed. "A room," was all I could muster to say as I shivered. To my chagrin, the motel was empty, and it was going to stay that way. The lady turned me away. I was not welcomed there. She claimed a hunting party had rented all the rooms. However, it wasn't hunting season! She certainly didn't want my kind in her motel, not some wet hiker.

I found myself standing in the rain, facing the motel by the side of the road again. My body shivered and shook. I was thankful I still shivered. If I were to stop shivering, I would be in trouble. I tried to cheer up.

Okay, next plan! I needed to go to Pawling, New York. The next day, I was due to get a resupply at the post office. I'd had a package sent there. Pawling was farther away, in the other direction from the trail. I should have taken a right and not wasted my time coming here. I decided then to go on to Pawling, get a hotel room, dry off, pick up my resupply the next day, and take a day off. Things had to get better tomorrow!

From the empty motel I hiked to Pawling, New York. A young man stopped and picked me up. I was frankly surprised, because the rain was still pounding down relentlessly. His car seat was instantly soaked the moment I sat down on it. Pawling was a little out of his way but he offered to take me there. He listened as I explained the situation of needing a place to sleep. There was reportedly a bed and breakfast in Pawling; at least, there was one listed in the book I had.

The young man took me to Pawling, as promised. I offered him some cash for his help. Surprisingly, he offered me cash as well! Now, that was true kindness. We parted. My finding a place to sleep was not his responsibility. The rain continued into the night. It was late. Looking for the bed-and-breakfast I walked a mile out of town, only to find it was closed. The place was boarded up and shut down.

"This is okay, it will get better!" I repeated as a mantra to myself. The rain remained steady. The mile back into town seemed longer than before.

My feet were soaked and now ached. My knees were swollen and did not want to bend. The pack on my back helped retain my body heat. That was my saving grace and the only positive thing I could think of at the moment.

Wet and walking in the night rain, I made it back to the central part of Pawling. I flagged down a deputy, thinking he would know where I could find a hotel. The deputy explained there were no beds for rent in Pawling. The nearest place was a motel closer to the trail. That was the motel that had refused me! Understanding that wasn't an option, the deputy explained that most hikers stay at a park where they are allowed to set up tents. The deputy offered me a ride to Memorial Park, seven miles south along the trail. That was seven miles I had already hiked!

Seven miles is big setback. Not only had I already hiked the seven miles, but I had hiked an extra four miles looking for a place to sleep, a wasted effort, as well. The cold rain running down my back was causing it to tighten and begin to ache. Would this day ever end? Oh well, I thanked the deputy for the ride. It was kind of him to assist me. He explained the park rules and pointed me in the right direction.

Over the crest of a small hill I found a cabana where I could get out of the rain. My tent would protect me from the winds, I hoped. The floor of the cabana was concrete and would be way too hard and cold for me lay upon to sleep. If the rains continued, the water could flood over the floor and make things worse. That wasn't going to happen this night. I set up my tent on a picnic table. The elevated position should provide a little extra comfort from the cold, hard, damp concrete.

Now, to get things rolling in my favor, I began a quick recon of what was available. My food supply was nearly gone, but that wasn't a problem. I was getting a full resupply at the post office the next day. There was a fireplace on the only wall of the cabana. I quickly went to the two trash cans and dumped their contents onto the floor. I searched the piles for all the burnable trash and then I cleaned up the mess.

The floor of the cabana was cluttered with bits of wood carried in from previous flooding. I stacked the paper in the fireplace with wood on top of the paper. It took me several tries to light the fire. My hands shivered as the wind worked its best to prevent the fire from starting. I won, the fire lit! The wind seemed to become an angry loser as it blew cold and howled.

My efforts to warm up were only partially successful as the wind forced colder air through the cabana. Luckily, I found there was electricity at the cabana. My phone needed to be recharged. The cold had drained its energy, just as it was draining my energy. Too bad the electricity couldn't get me recharged as well.

The phone was on the charger. The fire was nearly out. The wind was still whipping around wildly. The rain was pouring down with a deafening roar on the roof. I made my way to the tent to sleep, but I thought for a moment before entering the tent. The snake had nearly got me. I had ended up dehydrated, causing me pain. Scratch had died and my wife was sad. I had been turned away from a motel. I was still cold and wet! Once I got into my sleeping bag, it would be wet! I would need a place tomorrow night to dry out, no matter what!

Quickly, I stripped and hung my clothes around the cabana to dry. After getting in my tent, I snuggled into my sleeping bag and hoped for a quiet night. I soon had a sinking feeling. My air mattress was not as full as when I last filled it. Wasn't that just wonderful? To make the night complete, my air mattress had a hole in it. Sleep was not to be a partner in my tent that night.

Day five

The next morning finally came. This had to be the day ending my troubles. Things had to get better! I made a must-do list. I must get my air mattress fixed. Without fail, I must find a warm place to rest and sleep. Those seven miles back into town seemed much longer. Vehicle after vehicle passed me; not one stopped to offer a ride back to Pawling. Seven additional miles were tacked on to my already-planned long day.

A small store in Pawling offered cooked food. I ate breakfast and had coffee while waiting for the post office to open. As the post office opened I was instantly filled with dread. Would they have my package? There was only a small chance it would be there. Deb had mailed the package just a couple days earlier. Being stuck in Pawling would not be good. I slowly approached the counter and extended my driver's license. My heart skipped a beat as the lady stepped away and returned carrying a box. "Is that mine?" I smiled ear to ear. I picked up my resupply, sent by Deb. Life was good again and I was grateful.

Next, I needed to find an outfitter to fix my air mattress. I also needed to find a hot shower and dry bed. Doing laundry would be a luxury, but I could dream. All these items on my must-do list were possible, but I would have to hike another twenty miles to Kent, Connecticut. There is a hotel there called the Fife and Drum and an outfitter was also in town. All that and only twenty miles away! Granted, I had already hiked seven miles, so that would make my day total twenty-seven miles. "Those are big miles, but I will have to do it," I said aloud to myself.

My feet hit the trail late in the day. My steps were deliberate. I pounded away, mile after mile. The pack was extra heavy due to my resupply. The ground was still wet and the rocks on the trail were slippery from the rain the day before. Bugs were swarming in the air. The wind whipped through the treetops, but at least it wasn't raining now. I counted my blessings. One: it wasn't raining! The count ended at one.

The day was quickly slipping by. The miles seemed to stretch out as I tried harder to hike faster. Time was critical. I needed to get to Kent to get a room. I promised myself: this night I will be dry! This night I will be warm! The trail went up and down the hills as it always does. The trail went around every tree, twisting and turning. My steps grew faster and more reckless.

The road to Kent was close, only another three to five miles to go. The trail was steep, but it was downhill. Life was good, I could do this! I hiked faster without running. Suddenly, the earth shifted sharply and started spinning as I lost my balance. Before I could realize what was happening, I was looking at the earth from a sideways view. A sharp pain struck through my back like a lightning strike. I had stepped on a small stick under my right foot. The stick rolled downhill. My feet and hips went to the left and my upper torso went to the right. I hit the ground hard.

When I hit the ground I heard a loud snap from my back. The sound would make a grown man's knees weak. Pains shot from my ears all the way down to the heels of my feet. This pain was like no other I had ever felt before. Believe me, I have been hurt before. Something different happened here, and I didn't know what it was, but I was certain it was bad. My mind raced and filled with bad thoughts.

Methodically, I began taking an inventory of my body. Left foot moves . . . right foot moves but hurts . . . hands move. I started to straighten my body; pain shot down my right leg. I would yell, but no one would hear me. Before sitting up, I released the straps on my backpack and let it fall away to the side.

Now came the hard part: sitting up. My feet were still aimed up hill. I would have to spin around. I dragged my right leg around till I could sit up. I found myself sweating and my heart was pounding in my ears. The sweat was from the pain and not the hike. Three to five miles to Kent now seemed like a thousand miles away. As each minute passed by, precious time was being lost. Pain flooded my mind. My body felt broken.

My feet were sore, my knees were still swollen from the cold rains, my back ached from sleeping the night before on the picnic table, and now my back was injured. This injury worried me. Shock was setting in and my mouth went dry. Pains shot through my back like a hot nail driven through my spine. Slowly, I stood. My breath was taken away as I tried to reach down for my pack. There was no way I could bend down.

Using the steepness of the hill, I went downhill from my pack to retrieve it. As I lifted the pack its weight caused more pain than before and I instantly vomited. I put the pack on with great care. Strapping it tightly to my back was difficult, but I hoped it would serve as a splint. I started walking, slowly. My left foot went forward, my first step. My right foot dragged and would not go in front of the left foot. Pain—too much pain— racked through my body. I was hurt.

Making it to the road took a long time, even though it was only three miles away from my fall. The hitchhike to Kent proved to be a chore. Vehicle after vehicle passed me by. I tried standing without the pack, but that hurt my back. Standing with the pack hurt as well. Kent was to the right. My left foot led the way as my right foot dragged behind, moving slowly toward Kent. A pickup truck stopped. I crawled into the bed of the truck, trying not to scratch it as I could barely get over the tailgate.

The driver was helpful. He took me to the Fife and Drum. The passenger in the truck went inside to see if there was a room for me. There was nothing available. The Fife and Drum was full. There could be no other option this night. I must get a hotel room! My air mattress was flat and my back was hurt. The folks at the Fife and Drum pointed down the road to a bed-and-breakfast. I walked slowly, dragging my right foot to the B and B.

The bed-and-breakfast was quiet. It didn't seem as if anyone was around. Time after time, I rang the doorbell and knocked on the door. The sign in front said there was a room. There was a phone number on the sign, so I called it. As the guy answered the phone, a man stepped out the front door with a phone to his ear, answering my call. The man on the phone and the man at the door were the same person.

Oh! To my surprise, there was no room available for me. Apparently, they were also booked up. No beds available there. I asked if any place would have a bed. Reluctantly, he gave me a number for another bed-and-breakfast. I called, they answered. The lady said they did have a bed. My luck had finally changed, I had found a place with a bed. The cost for the bed was three hundred sixty dollars per night! That price was just too high. My luck changed again.

Undeterred, I searched for hotels in the next town. One was listed in my hiker's book. The Hitching Post was nine miles away; that was nine miles farther up the trail. Having hiked twenty-seven miles and injured myself from a fall, there was no way I could go another nine miles. I called the Hitching Post. There was a room available for sixty-five dollars a night. Relief came over me in a huge rush. The gentleman on the phone offered to come get me for a small price, but I had to meet him at the Fife and Drum. My left leg led the way again, as my right leg dragged behind.

The Hitching Post had small rooms, but they were clean and warm. The mattress gave my back good, firm support. After a long, hot shower, I ordered food. The night went by without too much pain. The hotel was exactly what I needed. But I had missed nine miles on the trail and would need to make them up. And, now, priority one was getting my air mattress fixed. That would happen tomorrow; tonight, I would enjoy sleeping in a bed in a warm, dry hotel room!

Day six

Sunday morning arrived. I had another hot shower and then called the outfitter. I was ready for a good day. The outfitter had a shuttle service that would come get me and then return me to the hotel. My air mattress was going to be fixed. With renewed hope, I set off for the outfitter in Kent. It was a strange place. They didn't have air mattresses, tents, hiking gear, or camping equipment. What gear they had was not the kind of gear used by thru-hikers. They did have ladies apparel, hotdogs, and ice cream.

The owner gave me a cup of soap and a brush so I could find the hole in the mattress. The plan was to find the hole and then patch it. After brushing the mattress and using three cups of soap, the hole was never found. The next course of action had the owner filling an ice cream cooler with water and then we would dip the mattress into the water finding the hole. Good plan!

The ice cream cooler and water hose were on the other side of the building. Off I went with my air mattress to the sunny side of the building. The mattress wasn't in the sun five minutes before "pop, pop, pop!" Three rapid and loud pops were heard. Jumping to my feet, I looked around. What the heck was that? Then I saw it. The baffles in my air mattress had broken loose. Baffles are what give the mattress ridges. Now, there was just a large bubble in the middle of the mattress.

The owner came out, happy to see the damaged mattress. He thought it would be better to get a new air mattress and not repair the old one. My thoughts were to repair the mattress; I wanted to get back on the trail. At least we had found the hole, but that didn't do me a lot of good.

Being Sunday, as my luck would have it, the manufacturer of the sleeping pad was closed for the weekend. So, I headed off to the library, where I could send an update of all that had happened the past few days.

The walk to the library wasn't too long, but with the pain in my back it seemed to take forever. I found the library was closed. They were having a book sale. This was grand indeed. Where was my good day?

On the way back to the outfitters I decided to stop for lunch. A small burger shop was located near the library. Before passing the threshold of the front door, I was stopped and asked to sit outside. Hikers were not welcomed. The owners prefer we did not come inside their place. We could sit outside and eat, but they didn't want us inside. This is the town that asked three hundred sixty dollars a night for a bed at a B and B. Wow!

My money was good enough for them, but my "class" was too low. They must have figured that out because I did not shave and my clothes were worn out. Yup, I was not good enough for these folks. After getting my burger and fries, I wanted ketchup. The table next to mine had a bottle, so I asked the young couple politely if I could borrow it. To my surprise, they answered snippily, "Get your own!"

Now this was getting personal, and was starting to get to me. The snake nearly got me. Someone took a crap in the spring and contaminated the water and my equipment, thus making me quite ill and dehydrated. Scratch died. The rain never stopped for a day and I had been turned away from a motel for being wet. I had fallen, hurting my back. My air mattress had a leak then blew up, and now these people want to keep the ketchup for themselves! I was pissed off; I was not a happy camper.

I ate my meal and had a beer. The waitress finally returned to get paid. She took my cash and I waited for my change. While waiting, the female half of the young, stingy couple came over to get the saltshaker from my table, without asking. Leaning forward, I stopped her, and then she asked for the salt. I smiled and softly replied, "Kiss my ass." I wished her "man" would have come over so I could take all of my frustrations out on him. I sat there with a smile, daring him to respond.

It took three requests for the waitress to finally bring back my change. Knowing the couple wanted the salt, I dropped my salt shaker in the glass of water left on my table. Sometimes, enough is enough. Then, realizing my water filter needed to be changed, I headed back to the outfitter and bought a new filter. I asked for my return ride back to the hotel as promised. The owner of the outfitters informed me that the return trip cost extra.

Day seven

Monday morning started normally; if normal could exist for me. The Hitching Post Hotel was comfortable. All I needed to do today was call to order a new air mattress and have it shipped to me. Nothing could go wrong with that. This was to be an easy, pleasant day. After a short walk to breakfast, I returned to the hotel and made my calls.

The company that makes the air mattress was easy to work with, and I had a new air mattress on the way. All I had to do was pay for the overnight shipping. I made a quick call to Deb to let her know my good fortune and that I would be on the trail again the next day.

While on the phone, Deb informed me that my jeep had stopped working. That wasn't a big deal, as we still had her car and my truck. I could fix the jeep when I get home. Then came the really bad news. FEMA had reclassified a property we owned. The property was now in a flood zone. The bank demanded that we buy flood insurance immediately. Get this, we had to pay the first year in full; the second year was to be escrowed. We paid out two thousand seven hundred dollars.

Now was the time for me to decide if staying on the trail was the correct thing to do or not. I rehashed the past few days: the snake attack had really shaken me up; being dehydrated hurt mentally and was still causing pain physically; Scratch had died and I was sad; I had been rejected from a motel for being wet and bedraggled; my air mattress couldn't be fixed; my back had been severely injured in a fall; my right leg would not go past my left leg when trying to walk; I was treated like a second class citizen because of my appearance; the jeep stopped working; and FEMA required us to pay two thousand seven hundred dollars without a blink of an eye. This is our government looking out for its citizens during hard times!

My decision was to wait and see if more happened before I decided to quit. Things could only get better. That was my hope. That night, I walked to a park to meet with some friends: Shenanigans, the Run Aways, and

Flowers. We had dinner and some beer and caught up on our adventures. Seeing them made the night pleasant. A pleasant night was certainly long overdue.

Day eight

My thoughts were not positive when Tuesday morning arrived. I had stopped being Mr. Sunshine days ago. However, this mood or doomsday attitude did not suit me well. But that was my true feeling, not hopeful. I paid the hotel bill in full, packed for the trail, and sat on the curb waiting for delivery of my air mattress. The day dragged on slowly, especially when the owners of the hotel kept asking me when I was leaving.

Any minute the delivery truck should arrive and I would then be on my way. It came! The driver asked for my name and ID. I told him who I was and gave him my ID. He handed me a tablet to sign electronically and then handed me my box. He left! I was happy! My air mattress was here! All was good in Mingo's world. I would hike many miles this day. Here I come trail, get ready for Mingo!

Quickly, like a kid on Christmas morning, I tore into the box. Pulling and twisting the paper and tape, the contents were finally revealed. My heart sank like a hot rock on a soft snowdrift. The box held a purse! The purse was for one of the cleaning ladies at the hotel. Why did the driver even ask for my name and ID?

Hitting a new low, I called Deb for help. It would probably be best if she talked to delivery service about not sending my air mattress overnight. If I spoke to them I could go to jail! Knowing my own limitations and knowing the hell I had gone through the past few days, it was best to have Deb handle things tactfully.

Deb determined that the delivery service had failed to get my package on the plane on time and it was now in Memphis. It would be another day before I could get back on the trail. Distraught by all the setbacks, I called Deb and announced, "I quit!" That's right, I'd had more challenges than most could conquer. The past week was too daunting. I had to decide if it were fiscally responsible for me to remain on the trail. No, I decided, it wasn't!

Without skipping a beat, Deb required me to state four good reasons to leave the AT. I thought of a dozen, but instead of replying to Deb's question, I responded with a new plan. I would stay on the trail for seven more days, and if I made it to Vermont by then I would complete my hike. That decision made Deb happy.

Since I did not get my air mattress, I checked back into the hotel. The owner offered to wash my clothes for five dollars. That seemed reasonable. Maybe things would start looking up for me now, I thought. All the events of the past days had been a great challenge, but each event needed to be viewed as another hill to climb, one day at a time.

My water filter was cleaned and disinfected. The air mattress would arrive the next day. The jeep could wait to be fixed after my hike was finished. Payment for flood insurance was done and settled, water under the bridge. My back still hurt, but the pain had lessened. The hills were being climbed, obstacles were being overcome, and I would conquer my hike and finish this trail.

Day nine

I had my pack ready when Wednesday morning arrived. Breakfast was less than filling, but I was ready for the trail. The delivery service promised my package would arrive before 10:30 that morning. The time was 10:28 a.m. when the truck pulled into the driveway at the hotel. My air mattress was finally in my possession. I packed it away. The hotel owner's wife offered me a ride to the trailhead.

Getting back on the trail was like returning to visit an old friend. Even though my spirits were still low, I began my hike anticipating a good, easy day. At exactly eleven o'clock my day on the trail began. The hills were not steep. Only a couple nonvenomous snakes crossed my path and none tried to bite me. The temperature was warm but not extremely hot. Each time I stopped to rest swarms of mosquitoes attacked. I used DEET at one hundred percent strength, but no one told these guys they weren't supposed to bite through this protective shield. I got to a road that the trail followed for a good ways.

As soon as I was in the open the rain began falling. Of course it did! Ten minutes later, safe in the woods, the rain stopped. The sun came out, stabbing rays of light through the trees, bringing life to all mosquitoes that ever existed. Swarm upon swarm found me. My blood was being drained by those tiny vampires of the insect world. There must have been a sign written in mosquito language "Eat At Mingo's." I had gone only a few miles, but at this rate I was losing at least a pint or two of blood to those damn bloodsuckers!

Trying to escape the mosquitoes' assault upon my skin, I ran. That hurt. The running hurt, the bites hurt, my legs hurt, my back hurt, my head was pounding, and I itched! My skin was constantly being covered by the insect swarms. Something unnatural drew them to feast on me. I looked back and could see a thick cloud of mosquitoes chasing me. Then, the pain hit. Pain like no other pain vibrated all over my body, all at once.

The heat of the day coupled with humidity from the rain, opened all the pores on my skin. Running in the heat had caused sweat to pour down my body. My skin was moist— actually, it was totally wet. Pain struck sharply, reverberating through my body like a chord being struck on a tight piano string. It hit and reverberated across my body. The feeling resembled taking an acid-rain shower. Somewhere, a switch was flipped, and I was totally in shock.

I felt burning all over. My mind went to survival mode; I stripped all of my clothes off as quickly as possible. I ran naked to lie down in a creek. My skin gleamed an unnatural bright red. Then, a light brown film formed on the red, burnt areas. The changing colors were the different layers of skin peeling off my body. Layers of skin were peeling off where clothes had rubbed my body. The creek was both soothing and burning at the same time.

My mind rushed to figure out what had just happened. If I could have reached my phone I would have called 911. A day hiker and his female friend walked by the creek where I lay in pain. He made a comment about my being nude. His comment let me know they would be no help. Unable to speak or to call for help, I was able to raise one hand and give a one-finger salute. They hiked on, never asking if I was okay or not. How could they not see I was hurt?

Every spot on my body covered by clothes was chemically singed.

My body had had a bad reaction to the detergent used to wash my clothes. The moist air and open pores must have made the reaction even more severe. Rinsing-off was the only course of action available. Now, when I say every spot on my body, think about every place on you covered by clothing. Yes, even there. My concern now was how deep the skin layers were peeling.

After a long soak in the stream, I thoroughly rinsed my already wet clothes, enough at least to be bearable. Shortly after dressing and replacing my pack, I continued hiking slowly. Socks had covered my feet and now they were burning. Chaffing never hurt this much! The weight of the pack and it's constant rubbing on my shoulders cause it to dig deeply into my flesh. I needed to escape the woods, not just for comfort, but because my situation might be getting serious.

Soon, I found myself at a State Store in Falls Village. Ahhh! But wait, this was Connecticut, a New England state, and I'm not sure how these folks feel about hikers. An old guy met me at the door of the wooden building used as a State Store. He was the kinda guy you would call a favorite uncle or grandpa, a nice guy you have to be partial to, the moment you meet him. He explained much about the area. "Go to the Toymaker's. Camp there; it is a café. Set up in the back," he explained as we talked. "Okay, you sell beer in singles?" "Sure do, keep 'em on ice for ya. It'll be a buck. And if you're hungry, there is a phone there for you hikers. The number to the pizza shop is on the wall. They will deliver to the Toymaker's."

I went off with my cold one, knowing the closing time of the store and pizza shop. Walking through the town I observed and said aloud, "Nice town." You feel comfortable and welcome in Falls Village. Really nice folks live in that town.

At the Toymaker's, I set up camp by the barn out back. A lady who was mowing the yard said it was the best spot. She explained how to get water at the spigot. She then showed me the outlet on the barn wall for charging phones and gave directions to "help yourself." I set up the tent, opened my cold beer, and called Deb. Life was good again. It became better by having a three-minute chat with Deb. Then, I focused on my beer as I lay in my tent, resting. A heavy rain began to fall. The rain came without any warning. No problem, I was dry. No bugs were in my tent. My skin did not burn as badly. The pains were less once I stopped moving.

The rain lasted only a few minutes. The swarms of mosquitoes lasted a bit longer. I waited till the mosquitoes gave up trying to bore their way, unsuccessfully, into my tent. I didn't get one bite, what a great moment. I was happy.

As the sun dried the town, more hikers showed up and set up their tents next to the barn. Soon, we had stacked four tents in that small spot. The other hikers had heard of me but I had not heard of them. That meant they were catching up to me, or I was slowing down.

I was at an all-time low and mentally depressed. But things seemed to be really looking up. I wouldn't ask, "What adventure will the trail bring me today," ever again. I would ask the trail to be gentle with me. I took the setbacks as I would another hill, climbing one step at a time, and remembering there are always two sides to a hill. I pushed on each time, my spirits recovering eventually. *Things will get better I promise, things will get better.*

Later that evening I returned to the State Store. After a quick phone call to order a pizza, I had to check out the liquor selection. To my pleasant surprise there were half-pint, plastic bottles of liquor. These were perfect for hikers. My purchase was made with great deliberation and forethought. The old guy bet me that a half-pint would never make it to Vermont. The bet was on!

More hikers moved in and set up their tents. Thru-hikers are considerate and observe hiker's midnight. That means voices are kept low after eight o'clock. It didn't take long for me to fall asleep. Then, laughter and banging woke me. "What the hell?"

From the sound, I guessed that three section hikers had come in after eleven o'clock. They had wild stories to tell. Someone's small dog was barking at them. They were barking back and teasing the dog. The late arrivals were loud and wanted everyone in camp to know they were there. They laughed and joked with each other, ignoring the hikers who were trying to sleep.

After giving the young hikers some time to settle down, I called out from my tent, reminding them it was after hiker's midnight. They said sorry and lowered their voices. The lowered voices grew louder as time went on. Then, the mocking began, "Hey, its hiker's midnight, ha ha ha!" They taunted and mocked me as I lay in my tent.

After several minutes, I finally realized these guys were not going to shut up. My best guess was they knew it was three of them against one of me. No one in their right mind would challenge a group of guys alone. They were counting on their numbers for intimidation, but I don't get intimidated easily.

While lying in my tent I made a plan. I would get up and confront them. They would probably kick my butt and hurt me. That would be okay. After my ass-kicking, I would drag myself back to my tent and wait. After a couple hours had passed, while they were sleeping, I would get their ringleader and get him good!

I exited my tent, searching for the mocking voices. While standing over two noisy tents, I identified my first target to attack. I then announced, "Enough is enough!" My eyes landed with shock; the voices belonged to two thru-hikers, Erin and Do-What!

These two youngsters were making enough noise to make me think there were three of them. That didn't sit well with me. I announced, "Hey, I came over here to kick your ass to make you guys shut up. But, now that I know who you are, I am still going to kick your ass!" Erin and Do-What both seemed surprised to see me. "Oh, it's you, Mingo, sorry. We didn't know it was you." They each extended a hand of apology and spoke in softer voices, promising to be quiet. After shaking their out reached hands, I returned to my tent for a quiet night. I slept well, although a good fight would have been better.

Day ten

The morning came and the sky was clear. This was going to be a new day, a good day. Breakfast at the Toymaker's was five-star service and quality at a good low rate. It was exactly what I needed. While eating, I met Dash and Shuffle. I think they had met on the trail and were a couple. Well, I know they were a couple. Dash was a strong, fast hiker. He was a young man in his twenties. Shuffle was a strong hiker as well, but not as fast as Dash.

Shuffle carried a rubber chicken on her pack. She had named the chicken Sheng Wei. Shuffle had carried Sheng Wei from the beginning of the trail at Springer Mountain, Georgia. Her plan was to carry the chicken to the top of Mount Katahdin, Maine.

After breakfast, they took off quickly. I hiked at a slower pace, hoping to stay safe and give myself time to recover. Before lunch, I arrived at a waterfall. High up on a ledge stood Dash. Shuffle looked worried while standing on some rocks with a camera. Dash was going to jump into the water below. It was a long jump. It wasn't something I was willing to do, especially after my last nine days, that's for sure.

I took out my camera and set it to video. Dash leaped from the ledge into the air, committed to the water waiting for him below. The fall took a long time. Dash gained speed as he fell feet first into the river. Bubbles churned in the surface of the water. Then, after a long wait, Dash popped up out of the depths. He was okay.

Dash took only one jump. Then, he and Shuffle put on their packs and headed off on their hike. I called Deb to talk with her and to send pictures of the waterfalls. She loved them.

While speaking with Deb, she explained that the central air at our home had gone off. It was going to cost three thousand dollars to replace the unit. If our insurance helped with the replacement, as it should, it would be only a thousand dollars out-of-pocket. Hmm, only a thousand? That sucked!

We talked about my quitting the trail, again. Was it worth continuing? Was I being fiscally responsible by staying on the trail? Was this trip going to be possible to finish? These questions haunted my mind with each step.

I recalled the snake striking at my face, the water hole that had been used as a toilet. After I had become dehydrated, Deb's beloved pet Scratch had died. The next day it had rained all day. While drenched, I had been turned away from the motel. I had to retrace seven miles. My air mattress went flat. If that wasn't enough, I had hurt my back the following evening. At the outfitters, my air mattress baffles blew up. While waiting to order a new mattress, FEMA reclassified our property, which cost us two thousand seven hundred dollars for flood insurance. The following day my air mattress didn't get delivered. On day nine I suffered a chemical burn resulting from a reaction to the detergent used in my clothes. And now, our central air had broken and it would cost us a minimum of one thousand dollars to replace it. Why was I still hiking?

Mirrored Life

WE, DEB AND I, decided I would continue to hike. The plan was that if I made it to Vermont in seven days or less, I would keep hiking. Deb would come to help with slack packs and give me the motivation to finish. I hiked on. Thoughts of the trail, memories of earlier days, slowly played through my mind as I walked.

I viewed the hike as having its own life. There are trials and tribulations in life as there are on the trail. I started the trail in a poor condition, hell-bent on making my way to the end, much like my life. I had started poor and disadvantaged, but was hell-bent on making it through life. There were obstacles along the trail. My life, just as anyone else's, has had its share of obstacles. I grew stronger midway through the trail. Most of my hike had been highlighted by overcoming the difficulties, mirroring my life experiences.

Finishing the trail was becoming more difficult. Growing older has its challenges as well. Granted, I am only forty-nine years old, but I have gone through a great deal. Equally, I had finished only three quarters of the trail, but I had seen my share of trouble. One thing I have learned in life as well as on the trail: "The future only looks as good as the moment it is viewed from." In other words, when things are rough now, the future looks rough. If things are going good now, the future looks good. I would put that lesson to use! I would wait until I reached another state and could feel good about it, and then I would decide if I should keep going.

My mind questioned finishing the trail. If hiking the AT is like life, how would I want to finish both? I wouldn't want to go to my end sadly. Finishing or quitting prematurely would be a permanent solution to a temporary problem, and that is always a bad idea. I had once read a sign that claimed sliding sideways to the Pearly Gates and saying, "That was fun. What's next?" would be a good way to finish. I wanted to figure out how I would or should finish my hike.

Ending the hike in a sad state would be neither glorious nor fulfilling. Finishing overconfident with vigor just didn't seem possible. The only way I could hope to finish was with dignity. That was my goal. Finishing the hike with a good name and having helped others sounded plausible. To do that, I needed to hike strong and hang on. My finish wasn't going to shatter records in the hiking world, but I would finish and be known for the good I had done. That is the plan!

I caught up with Shuffle. Shuffle was excellent at hiking. Dash flew on forward. He was another hiker who could put great distances under his feet quickly. Oh, to be twenty years younger! I passed them, but just for a short time. A large stone sat jutting upward all alone in the woods. The trail goes right by the stone. The stone is called "Giant's Thumb." Dash showed up, as did Shuffle. We took pictures of the stone and they were off again.

We headed down to the next road. I caught up with Shuffle in Salisbury. We didn't see Dash. We later found out he went into town to get some food. Salisbury is said to be hiker friendly, but ritzy. The hike out of town was easy. A harder climb was ahead at Lion's Head. It was a bit steeper than expected. By the time I had arrived at Riga Lean-to, other hikers had already setup.

Things were looking up. I was three miles from Massachusetts. It was another state, a true landmark. My spirits were picking up. I was going to make it to Vermont in the seven days, as planned. Morning came; I got up, and started off. For some reason I felt drained. It felt as if my clothes were still eating through my skin. Now my stomach was twisted up. Hiking caused me to feel dizzy. I was not well.

Massachusetts

THE PRIOR DAY I had felt good and hopeful that I would make it to Vermont. This day I felt like crap! The Massachusetts state line finally came, but it was a long three miles. Despite the feeling terrible I hiked harder and harder. The woods spread away from the trail, leaving an easy path to follow. The climbs should have been easier for me but weren't. In my drained condition I was lucky the climbs were not too difficult to complete.

The more I hiked the weaker my body grew. A calorie deficiency was playing a heavy toll on my ability to maintain a strong pace. My burned skin had not yet healed and I needed to get my clothes off. My pack's shoulder straps kept sliding around the makeshift pads I had taped to the straps and were cutting into my shoulders. Comfort was not something I would experience this day.

The miles finally fell away under my feet and I found myself standing alongside a road, US Route 7. The pages from my hiking book listed a place to buy resupply provisions. The place was called the Dollhouse. Getting some refreshments sounded good to me. I headed in search of the Dollhouse. After going more than a mile, I stopped at a car sales lot and asked where the Dollhouse was located. I had passed it!

Headed back, I finally found the place. It was easy to miss. The Dollhouse sold toys and dollhouses. Inside the store was a cooler set-aside for hikers and other customers. Within the cooler were Gatorades and candy bars. Crackers and other small foods were for sale as well. I grabbed handfuls of snacks then went to the register. The lady who ran the place was friendly and thoughtful. She explained how to get free water and how I could go get a shower in a back room. This courtesy did not go unnoticed.

After eating, I took a short shower. There was no way I could force myself back to the trail. The bugs were too fierce and the heat excessively oppressive. My hike for the day was finished. The store owner gave me permission to set up a tent in the front yard. As appealing as that idea was, I needed a bed for the night. I hitchhiked to Great Barrington.

A young lady stopped to give me a ride. She took me to a hotel that had decent rates. I offered her a few dollars for gas as she was on empty. She declined the money and seemed pleased to be able to help with the ride. Only one room was left. The hotel was booked-up. That meant the price of the room had to be full price. That was fine, I needed the bed.

A CVS pharmacy was next to the hotel. I bought Epsom salts and bandages for the chaffing that had started again. A few other aides could help case my pains, so I bought them also, including Motrin. Once I was in my room I ordered pizza and two liters of Mountain Dew. It was time to hit the bath, where I waited for the pizza delivery.

A night sleeping in a bed was needed, probably more than I knew. Before hitting the sack, I washed all of my gear and clothes in the tub. I rinsed everything over and over. Then, in true thru-hiker fashion, my gear and clothes were hung over the railing outside of my room. Deb was happy to hear I was safe in a hotel for the night. While on the phone with her I tried to sound as if I were doing well. She wasn't buying it.

To get an idea of what to expect the next day, I studied my maps before going to sleep. That didn't bring a vote of confidence to my mind. Each mile looked to be an obstacle and not something to look forward to completing. My mind still wondered why I was doing this hike. I could never figure out why I was doing it. With a low sense of motivation and an aching body, I needed to dig deeper in my soul to find the strength to continue.

The next morning I was offered a ride back to the trail by yet another lady. While riding in the pickup, I read my map. Fifteen miles later it became obvious that I was being taken away from the trail. The lady pulled to the side of the road and let me out. I now had fifteen miles to get back to town, then seven more miles just to get to the trail. This didn't start my day out right!

While trying to hitchhike back to town, a police cruiser stopped me. The officer turned on his beacons. Was I was going to get a ticket for hitchhiking? Once at the cruiser, the officer asked my name and where I was headed. After a quick explanation that I had been taken in the wrong direction and was trying to get back to the Appalachian Trail, the officer told me to get in the backseat. Was he going to arrest me?

During my ride in the back of the cruiser the officer asked about my past. I quickly offered information about being a veteran and retired police sergeant. He was more interested in my hike thus far. I loved sharing my adventures on the trail. The cruiser continued through town. We passed the police station; it was close to the hotel. It then dawned on me that the officer was giving me a ride to the trail. He asked if I knew another hiker. He had given the hiker a ride to the trail a week before. I didn't know him.

The Gang

MY FEELINGS ABOUT hiking improved once I was back on the trail. That day I saw few other hikers. I was feeling pretty darn good. The bed, bath, and food had really done me good, emotionally and physically. When the trail went down gentle slopes my feet seemed to be fond of running. With strong trail legs, I moved rapidly. It was a good day for hiking. I stopped at shelters to sign in and leave notes stating I was still on the trail and feeling good.

Upper Goose Pond Cabin was ahead. That was my goal. A twenty-seven mile hike was big, but I was feeling good. There were no big obstacles to overcome today. Nothing too steep stood in my pathway. Sweat poured from every pore. Lunchtime came and I ate big. A breeze coming through the woods made hiking a pleasure. The breeze kept biting insects away, even when I stopped for an occasional hydration break.

Huffing and puffing, slamming my poles into the ground, I arrived to Upper Goose Pond Cabin. A caretaker stayed at this shelter. It was a two-story building with lots of space. When I arrived, it was nearly full. I dropped my pack off at a bunk and headed to the pond for a swim. Soon, every bunk was taken. The water was cold but refreshing. After a quick swim, I lay on the dock taking in the last of the sun's rays. The sun went down and the air grew cool.

The caretaker had ice cream delivered for the hikers. We each had large scoops. The ice cream was an excellent gift. The next morning the caretaker made pancakes. We ate the pancakes as quickly as they were made. Then, some of us went back for seconds. I got two more pancakes. Another hiker asked for seconds but he was refused. The caretaker snapped, "You already had enough!" He had actually gotten less than me. I offered my pancakes to him, but he turned them down. Embarrassed at how this hiker had been treated, I felt angry. I still ate my pancakes, but wasn't pleased at the treatment of this other hiker. I ate, packed, and then left.

Dalton was only twenty miles away. A resupply package was waiting for me in Dalton, so I needed to get there. During my hike I received a text on my phone, "Mingo, where are you?" The text was from Goldie Locks of the Runaways. "I am coming to Dalton today. Where are you?" "We are in Dalton." Then another text, this one from Shenanigans, "Mingo, we will get a pint at the pub. I have a room saved for you guys at the Shamrock when you get here."

I hurried to get to Dalton. This was the best news yet. I was actually catching up with Shenanigans and the Runaways. It would be a nice change to hike with friends again. Only one short five-hundred-foot incline stood in my path. This was the easiest part of the trail in weeks. I ran most of the time.

Once in Dalton, the trail winds through town. A hostel was beside the road. "Hey, Mingo!" yelled Comfortably Numb from the porch of the hostel. Other hikers ran to the windows and called out, "Hey, Mingo! Where are you headed?" "I'm staying at the Shamrock with Shenanigans!" I answered without stopping.

The Shamrock was easy to find. Stepping into the office, I was asked, "Name?" "It's Mingo!" A key was tossed my way in exchange for a credit card. They knew the name, Mingo. After settling into the room, Shenanigans came over. "Hey Shay Shay, you said you were holding the room for you guys?" I asked, "Who are the, 'you guys'?" "Alien is coming in tonight. Is it okay if you share a room?" Shenanigans asked. That was even better news. I enjoyed hiking with Alien. My future hike was looking up.

Having a shower was a welcomed bonus. Getting the pond scum from

Upper Goose Pond off my body felt great. Time to get food and beer! The Runaways joined us at the pub. They ate lunch and drank water or soda as we ordered food and beers. We ate and talked, sharing adventures. Shenanigans and the Runaways had done several days slack packing. They had also stopped to tour cities and went to a brewery and a theme park. They were certainly on a holiday while I had been roughing it.

Alien arrived and settled into the room quickly. He didn't get a chance to check in as we took him straight to the pub for food and beer. The next day's weather report warned of heavy rain coming. We all decided to take a zero. The Runaways were torn between a zero and moving on. They had been off the trail long enough and wanted to get back. But the rains were a deterrent. I got my resupply at the post office and was ready, but not in the rain.

The rains came; it poured. The skies let go of masses of water. It was almost impossible to see fifty feet away in the heavy rain. Ten minutes later the rain was gone and it didn't rain again the rest of the day. It was a perfect zero day. We went out together for breakfast, lunch, second lunch, and dinner. We had beer enough to drown a drunken polar bear, but our rapid metabolisms kept us clear of mind.

Alien was as happy as I was to be together with Shenanigans and the Runaways. We were all pleased with the change of events. While at dinner I announced Deb was coming to Vermont to meet us and would slack pack us as long as she could. That news made the prospect of hiking together that much sweeter.

Vermont

AWAY WE WENT, like a line of ducks walking through the woods. The next town was Cheshire. The trail goes through the town and we arrived in time for lunch. The first order of business, after reaching Cheshire, was to find a pizza shop. Lunch! We dutifully stacked our packs outside the shop. Inside, we found two booths so we could all sit together and "have a feed." First, we asked for large glasses of water. We always drank an abundance of water at every chance.

After a good meal, our packs were secured and away we headed for a tough 2,500-foot climb up Mt. Greylock. It was a tough hike, but we were in high spirits and enjoyed the day. Mt. Greylock has a tower at its peak. A lodge sits off to the side where food is sold. The cost of food and a bed were extremely high. We ate our own food in a room with picnic tables setup throughout the area. While there we had a good, long rest. Other hikers were there doing the same thing.

We were hungry for something different. We looked around and found ice cream bars and cookies for sale. The cookies were homemade and cost the least. We all stood in line to buy a cookie. The cookies were okay, but not exactly fresh. It was the end of the day, so a discount would have been in order. If we hadn't bought the cookies they would have thrown them out. No such luck for us! We paid full price. Our Yogi skills were not effective!

The day had almost finished and was being replaced by dusk. The next shelter was four miles away. That would be over an hour and a half to get there. We opted to find a place to remote camp. I led the way, hoping to find a flat spot anywhere along the trail. Remote camping in the area was reportedly illegal. We needed a place where we would not be discovered. I found a place, but it was vetoed because it was too close to the trail.

The night sky took hold. All of the stars were out. The moonlight offered little help. The rays of the moon were shielded by the trees. The trail continued along a steep path, offering no place to set up for the night. Finally, I reached a spot where the trail curved around a flat soggy spot. The location was back into woods that had never been cleared. The place was barely large enough for four tents.

We voted on staying and decided to spend the night. The Runaways set up their tent closest to the trail and on the clearest spot. Shenanigans set his tent up next to them. He watched over them and protected them well. They enjoyed having him around and he seemed to enjoy them. Alien took the spot I had been eyeing; I was too slow setting up. A few branches covered the area left to me, so I cleared them away and setup my tent. It was time for sleep.

The next morning, I headed deeper into the woods to dig a hole. A large creature broke branches as it ran away. Was it a bear? Was Big Foot stalking me? I figured that whatever it was, it was scared of me. It ran away. Hopefully it would't run back. Finishing my business and burying it, I returned to my tent to continue sleeping. It was still dark out. This crew of hikers was fond of sleeping in late.

A bright morning broke through the trees. We all arose and started eating. A plan was outlined for the day. We had a goal. A town was located below Mt. Greylock where we would find a place to eat lunch then head on to reach Vermont. Vermont! I was going to get there in less than the seven days! Deb was coming to Vermont!

Once we were off Mt. Greylock and in town, a small ice cream stand sat beside the road. We each got a soft serve and went outside to eat at the picnic table. Some young guys were at the table, but after seeing us they took off on their bicycles. The ice cream cones were delicious as was the other food we bought there.

Packs on, away we went like a gypsy clan hiking through town. After another fifteen-hundred-foot climb, we would be in Vermont; it was only four more miles. During the climb we heard a ruckus coming up fast behind us. We stopped to see what was causing so much noise. Soon, three hikers showed up. I recognized one of the hikers. Shenanigans recognized one other. The third was new to us all.

The hiker we all knew was Doc Boom. The other hiker whom Shenanigans knew was a young guy who comically looked like Radar on MASH. I think his name was Toad or Frog, something like that. He was a quiet sort of character. The third guy was less quiet. He was laughing and clowning around as if he were hiking his first hours on the trail.

Trashcan was the name of the new hiker. We had never heard of him before. Doc Boom laughed at that fact and said, "Ask him when he started his hike from Springer." We did. "May first," Trashcan answered. This cat had flown up the trail. He was out running his own name. No wonder we hadn't heard of him. He was fast. If focused, he could probably set a record. I was delighted seeing Doc Boom again. I figured I would never have seen him again, as fast as he hikes. He had taken some time off to visit family. Then, his brother, Spare Parts, had come out to hike with him somewhere along the trail.

Minutes later, we all reached the sign for the Vermont state line and the beginning of the Long Trail. The Long Trail goes through Vermont. It shares the same path with the AT through half the state. We took photos to commemorate reaching Vermont. Alien stood over me to my side. I stood next to the sign, showing sweat through my pants and shirt. Goldie Locks stood on the other side of the sign making a cutesy face, as Ruckus reached high to hang his arm across Shenanigans' shoulder.

When we headed out, Trashcan took off in a flash, running full steam through the woods. He wasn't on the trail; he was in the woods, breaking branches and parting underbrush he ran as if nothing were in his way. Laughing as he went he started passing us, then "whoosh," he disappeared. Leaves and dirt flew into the air where he used to be. He had tripped and fell face first, clearing a path in the woods using his face.

Laughing even harder, Trashcan came back to the path. He didn't hike as fast as he had before. He was a real jokester, and I mean that in a good way. It was fun hiking with our ever-growing clan. We were all happy at our good fortune—being with great friends on the trail. Oh, and Deb was going to be waiting for us at the end of the day. She called and had arrived in Bennington thirteen miles away.

Talisman

FROM THE BEGINNING of the trail I had carried a Morgan silver dollar from 1886. The silver dollar was a gift given to me in 2002, when I went to East Timor working with the United Nations as an international police officer, Civpol. My good friend and neighbor, Ray Cole, gave me the dollar as a talisman of good fortune to keep me safe. I carried it there and back. Ray was a WW II vet and the best neighbor I could ever have.

I carried that silver dollar to Afghanistan and to Iraq when I worked in those countries as well. My promise to Ray was I would carry the silver dollar on the trail or when on any other adventure. Ray's wife, Anne, had died before I left, and just days later Ray died. In honor of such a great person I carried this dollar in his memory. I am explaining this now because my friend, Ray Cole, was from Vermont. The memory of Ray was part of my motivation to finish the trail.

Having Deb waiting for me at the end of the day brought a new strength to my legs. I hiked and ran through the woods, passing Doc Boom and Trashcan. The hill going down was steep and I used it to pick up speed. It was an easy thirteen miles from the state border and there was Deb waiting. I had made it! Folding chairs were set out for us. A Power Aide helped replenish the sweat loss from the run.

Doc Boom and Trashcan came out of the woods shortly after me. I called them over to get trail magic. They may have been a lot younger, but youngsters needed to rehydrate also. Ten minutes later, the rest of the clan appeared, ready to take off their packs. Doc Boom and Trashcan hitched into town. Deb took the rest of us to a campsite she had found. There were showers at the campgrounds. While we showered, Deb made dinner. We set our tents up in a small field. Another successful day!

The next morning, we set out for a long day. Although we were slack packing, there were no roads for the next twenty-one miles. Deb would meet us at the end of the day. The trail would take us past three shelters. There was one formable climb, but as thru-hikers, we were ready. At least with Deb at the campsite we ate a decent breakfast before we started our day.

As we headed out, the weather was cooperative. A slight overcast kept the day cool. A breeze shielded the bugs away. We each took turns being in the lead. Every stream or other water source gave us the reason we needed to stop for a break. It was a good crew to hike with and a good day to hike.

Once we finished the day's hike we all jumped back into the waiting truck. Deb was good about being there for us. We returned to find our tents had been blown around from wind gusts during the day. The mosquitoes started biting with a vengeance as we worked to upright the tents. When mosquitoes go nuts like that, it is because a rainstorm is coming, and the rains did come shortly after we got our tents setup again.

We didn't want Deb to have to fix dinner after a long day and after the rains started, so we set out for Bennington. A Subway fitted our needs for nourishment perfectly. We each ordered our subs and other foods. Normally, I would share a twelve-inch sub with Deb. This time was a little different. She ordered a twelve-inch sub and so did I. We shared her sub and I ate all of mine. A sub and a half filled me up and I slept well that night.

We had some concern for the young lad, Ruckus. Ruckus had gone by the name Forest earlier; he had changed it. He wasn't eating well and seemed to be growing a massive chip on his shoulder. His temper was growing thin, as was ours. Being depleted by hiking so long will change a person. Sometimes, the change is less than positive. If you ever want to find your true self, don't look on the trail!

Getting Sick

MORNING CAME WITH coffee and a quick study of the map. It was decided we would do a short sobo, southbound hike. Deb was to take us to Mad Tom Notch. From there, we would hike southbound, back to the road close to where we were camping. Deb drove up one road and down another. I sat up front in the middle seat; Alien was to my right. In the backseats were Shenanigans, Ruckus, and Goldie Locks.

"Turn left here, Deb." "Okay, take a right!" "We went too far, let's go back around again." The trail should be along here, everybody look for a white blaze." "Where is this Mad Tom Notch?" We each offered directions after a study of the map. Around and around we drove, eating junk food snacks. Soon, it became apparent we were not getting to the trail this day.

"Let's take a zero!" someone shouted. "All in favor say, Aye!" "Aye!" everyone yelled. We headed back to the tents then we went to see a movie. We needed a zero. Tempers were growing short and the hiking grew less fun. We deserved a fun day and we took it.

The next morning we packed up all the tents and gear. We had the back of my truck fully loaded. Deb took us back to the spot where she had originally picked us up. While we hiked she searched for places to camp. She searched the maps and called around for a spot ahead, where we would end up by the end of the day. She did great.

There wasn't much to see but we were mostly interested in making miles. A road crossed the trail two miles from our start and then in another half mile. Deb met us at both locations. We stopped to eat and to rehydrate. Every time we stopped, our shoes came off to rest our feet. It was a fine day as everything was working out for us. The zero had recharged our spirits.

We left Deb the second time and were off again. One short hill, a fifteen-hundred-foot incline, was the only hill we needed to summit. Stratton Mountain went by easily. Each of us felt strong and on top of our game. Twelve miles later, Deb sat beside the road where the trail crossed. We rested for a half hour and voted to go on. We had five miles to finish our day.

Deb was waiting, as usual, and had great news. She had found a campsite for us. We went there wondering if it would serve us well. We were all concerned about keeping the cost down. Each member paid his fair share for camping, food, and fuel. No one was taking advantage of another.

The campsite was a private campground. We were placed in the far back corner, as we had requested. No other campers were close. The grounds had showers and restrooms. We took full advantage of the showers. Deb had packed several extra towels. She always seemed to pack just right for each section. We set up our tents and started a fire. Marshmallows and whiskey made the best after-dinner delight! While consulting about the cost, we were thrilled to learn the campsite was ten dollars total each night. That came to less than two dollars for each of us; ten bucks divided six ways. We would stay here as long as we could.

I wanted to get an early start the next day. Alien, always happy to sleep in, was not eager for an early hike. We didn't clash over that difference. We each took the others opinion into consideration. We started later than what I wanted this time. Before heading out, we found a station down the road that served sandwiches, donuts, and coffee. Breakfast was a must!

The station was a quaint little place. At first it appeared to be a bait shop or some other outdoor supplier. Its rustic look had a charm about it. The people inside were indifferent to us. They may have appreciated our business but didn't seem too thrilled about serving hikers. They made no outward sign of disgust, just minimal service then happy to see us go.

I had learned times get hard and times get good again. Just as it is quick and easy to slide off a rock ledge and a struggle to get back up, the same was true for how you are feeling. Just over a week earlier I had slid off a ledge of feeling well and into an abyss in just hours. Day after day, events dragged me deeper into a depression. It had been a long struggle up. My wife and friends helped bring me back. I held on and was finally feeling the way I should. No single event brought me back to feeling well. Time and perseverance healed me.

It was surprising how reasonable the rates were for camping in Vermont. Vermont is a beautiful state and we were certainly enjoying our time there. It is a perfect place to go for a family vacation. The other hikers had become our family and we were a happy family.

We got back to the trail. All seemed to be fine. Everyone was ahead in a single file of hikers who made up our clan. Goldie Locks and I were last on the trail. After a mile or two, she fell back. I wasn't worried about her for she was a strong, disciplined hiker, a capable young lady. When I got to the first shelter I received a text from Goldie Locks' mother from Texas. She was worried. Goldie Locks had become ill.

Goldie Locks was trying to contact Deb. She wanted Deb to pick her up where she had dropped us off. Things were no longer looking good. We all tried to make contact with Deb, with the Runaways' mother, and with Goldie Locks. Our phones kept going in and out of service. We waited and debated what our best options were. We received word by text that Goldie Locks had turned around and gone back to the road. Deb was out of cell service range.

Just as we were ready to split up, half to continue on to find Deb and the other half to find Goldie Locks, we heard, "Hi, guys!" Goldie Locks walked into the shelter area. We were delighted to see her. After hearing the gory details of her illness we tried to figure out the best plan of action. We would do a short hike! Deb would take Goldie Locks to the doctor.

Our hike slowed to the pace Goldie Locks could handle. Just for the record, it was a fast pace. Once we reached the road, Deb dropped us off at the campsite, called the kids' mom, and took Goldie Locks to town in search of an Emergency Care Center. We feared she might have had Lyme or Giardiasis. Giardia is a parasite that attacks the digestive system, then moves on to other organs of the body.

When the gals returned we were happy to see Goldie Locks in good spirits. She was tired and had been given antibiotics. The doctors were not sure what was wrong with her; it wasn't Giardiasis or Lyme. She called home to report to her mom. The Runaways mother decided she was coming from East Texas to be with her kids as they finished the rest of the trail. The night ended as the sky clouded over and rain began falling.

Bathe in a Brook

THE SUN FAILED to rise the next morning as the rains continued. It was a day to take another zero. The campsite had everything we wanted and needed but the campground was getting a little run down. A group of migrant workers were also staying at the campground. They showed little respect and did not clean up after themselves.

A shower stall became clogged and dirty. One toilet was clogged with paper towels and broken glass was scattered across the floor. This was still the best deal around. We were camping away from other campers, so it was not a big problem. Later, we learned that the group of Mexicans claimed we were the ones who had messed up the restrooms.

The day after our zero came and it was time to leave our campsite. We were going to move up the trail. A hotel sounded like a pretty good idea. But first, breakfast, then the trail, and then a hotel! We were in high spirits as we headed to the station for our sandwiches, donuts, and coffee.

While in the store, a local came up to the Runaways. The local was a thin-built young man who seemed to have a chip on his shoulder. "You hikers should stop by a brook and take a bath before you come into town. Did you know you stink?" I stepped between him and the kids. The young man was trying to bully children. Goldie Locks arrived at the counter to pay for her and Ruckus' food. They went back to the truck.

I stepped out of the line for the register. The local bought his food and left. I picked out more food for breakfast and a cup of coffee. Deb had stepped outside before me. Once outside, I saw a car had stopped in front of Deb. The young man was quarreling at Deb. I approached, "Hey, what's up?" His voice raised as he stated the people of Manchester do not like hikers because they stink.

"There are brooks before you get to town; you guys could stop and take a bath before you come into town," he said. Deb responded, "That doesn't work. The long hikes and days of sweating cause the smell, and no amount of soap could take the odor away in one bath." He started yelling at Deb again, telling her we stunk. Hearing this young man yelling at my wife and knowing he had tried to bully the kids really got to me.

I stepped close to his door and said, "The way I see it, my money is as green as Manchester money, and if they don't like me being in their town . . . " I leaned in to get nose to nose and to make my words personally directed to him, "You can kiss my ass!" Then I walked slowly in front of his car, daring this fool to hit me. After seeing him berate the kids, then my wife, I wanted nothing more than to spread his battered face on the road. Needless to say, I was pissed. The jerk drove slowly away.

On another note to the people of Manchester, we came to your town and were treated poorly. Shame on you who do that! To the other people who live there, you shouldn't stand for that type of reputation. I invite you to visit Waynesboro, Virginia. Those people enjoy helping hikers and they treat them fairly. Our hike is not ours alone. It isn't our feet treading on just a path. Hikers dedicate their adventures to various causes. Some hike for the challenge of being a part of something more than themselves. More people were involved with my hike than I could have imagined.

No, this hike isn't just a walk on a trail; we were "stepping wild." We were stepping into a wild world that brought friends together as a community. We were stepping wild into an adventure, a voyage into the unknown. Most communities along the way offer support to hikers and are as much a part of our hike as we ourselves are. Deb learned she was a part of our hike by being there for us. To her, being a trail angel was rewarding.

The guy who had spoken out of line was—and most likely still is—an ass. He had no compassion, no dignity, and no honor. After he drove away, I looked across the road from the store and there sat a Veterans of Foreign

Wars, VFW. I wondered how the members there would feel about what had happened. I am a proud member of the VFW. When I came home after being deployed overseas I know I smelled as bad as I smelled while hiking. After being deployed, would that make me not good enough for this self-appointed spokesman for Manchester? That guy has a lot of growing up to do. He was rude to women and children.

The Split

GETTING BACK TO the trail with a renewed vigor was easy. We'd had a day of rest and now we were headed farther north to a town. We planned on getting hotel rooms there. That meant hot water showers, a soft bed, and a place to do laundry. We had a short hike to do and it would be quick, only twenty miles to Upper Cold River. There, Deb would be waiting for us.

We finished our hike with plenty of daylight left. In town, Rutleg, the kids chose a hotel that fit their budget. Deb and I dropped them off and would pick them up later for dinner. Alien and Shenanigans each took a room at another hotel. Deb and I went to a third hotel and stayed in a suite. After settling in, the phones started buzzing. Texting teenage-style began. It was the easiest way for all of us to communicate together.

That evening, Deb drove to each hotel to collect everyone and drive into the downtown area. We were looking for a restaurant that also had a hostel. Dinner was a delight, but young master Ruckus was being a bit cranky. He also wasn't eating well. Hiking requires an incredible number of calories. I was concerned he wasn't getting the needed nutrition for the physical efforts he was putting into his hike.

"Hey, Goldie Locks," I whispered, "I am worried about Ruckus." Goldie Locks recoiled, her facial expression turning blank. "Don't worry about us," she snapped. "What we do is none of your business!" She had immediately turned defensive. There was really no cause for this kind of response. It wasn't the response I was expecting at all, and I had had enough! Their mother was coming and she could take them. I had shown concern and got chastised for it. I would let things settle for just a while.

The suite was well worth the extra cost. Deb had earned the extra amenities. We were on the bed, propped up on top of pillows, watching Dr. Oz. Oz was listening to audience members respond to Montel Williams' claim of using marijuana for pain relief and his recommendation to legalize it for medical use. The arguments against legal marijuana use didn't make sense to me! "The studies indicate the need for more studies." And there it goes . . . more studies and more time for people to be in needless pain.

My thoughts are that if someone is in pain and the stuff works then let them have it. The alternative would be a law that requires a person to suffer pain every day. That makes no sense! Montel made rational, intelligent points based on personal experience and results. Those opposed made no point based on anything rational. Let the people suffer!

Shenanigans and Alien were ready to hike the next morning. I wanted to stay in the suite. It was nice. At the back entrance to the hotel, near the kid's room, Goldie Locks appeared. She asked Shenanigans to help her out. She wanted the room another night. Having an adult request the room gave less concern to the hotel staff. If Goldie Locks were alone, then questions could be asked and that could prove to be a hassle.

After setting the Runaways up for the rest of the day and night, Shenanigans returned to the truck. He explained that the kids had decided they were not hiking with us today and they were spending the day at the hotel. Their mother was due to arrive that evening and they were waiting for her. We three went back to the trail, Alien, Shenanigans, and me.

Our hike would be simple, go over Killington Peak and back down to Gifford Woods State Park. There, we would set up a campsite. On the top of Killington Peak was an old ski lodge. Large backhoes were tearing the building down. Two heavy machines operated in tandem. As we sat nearby to watch the destruction of the building I said, "Autobots, transform!" Alien laughed. We had our lunch and then headed back down.

We had hiked only a meager fourteen miles, but we finished a little late. The sky turned dark early and a light rain started to fall. We found

Deb at Gifford Woods State Park. We reserved a camping site and bought an ice cream at the ranger station.

Alien set up his tent, then went off to the quarter-operated showers. The showers were well worth the money. The water pressure was excellent. While Alien was away, a mouse ran through our campsite. Shortly after the mouse ran through, a skinny little fisher cat was hot on his tail. The fisher cat had a sleek, light brown body. His little ears stood straight up like little antennae.

We stood by quietly and watched as the little fisher cat sniffed the ground, searching for the mouse. He ran under Alien's tent. As if in a maze, the fisher cat went round and round, back and again. From time to time he popped his head out from under the tent looking at us, hoping we would help point out the way the mouse went.

The fisher cat came out running all around the campsite. He moved as quickly as a mongoose. That was one lucky mouse that got away. How it ever escaped was, and still is, a mystery. The cute little fisher cat was a juvenile. Heck, it may have been after its first kill.

It rained all night while we slept safe in our tents. The air grew colder. The next morning we headed out early. We wanted to make decent miles. At the end of the day we would return to the park for a second night.

A Bad Day

OUR PLAN FOR the day was simple. Deb would meet us after two miles on River Road. We would rehydrate, then head out for another eight miles to Chateauguay Road and meet Deb for lunch. After lunch, we would hike three and a half more miles to meet at Lookout Farm Road. Five and a half miles later we would meet Deb at Vermont 12. Finally, we would meet Deb at the next road four miles away to end our day of hiking.

What do they say about the best laid plans? This plan was to be no different. We made it easily to a waterfall and Thunder Brook Road. Deb didn't show up! Maybe she misunderstood the plan. That's okay, she would be at the next road, we thought. It rained harder as the day continued. We crossed River Road. Deb wasn't there, either! We moved on.

Eight miles later we reached Chateauguay Road. Signs were posted all around about a lost camera. A thru-hiker had lost her camera and all of her hiking pictures were in it. We stopped for a small snack, which we had packed for our slack pack. Deb still didn't show up. I wanted to call her, but I had forgotten my phone in the truck. Alien tried to call her but he didn't have cell service. After resting twenty minutes, we gave up waiting for Deb and hiked toward Lookout Farm Road. Chateauguay Road was a dirt road; Lookout Farm Road was almost nonexistent.

Hiking wasn't too difficult, but I started worrying about Deb. We could not get her on the phone and she wasn't at any of the roads we had crossed. I was worried she may have had an accident.

"And a random ladder in the woods!" said Alien. I looked up and a ladder was tied to a tree. The ladder was the trail. Finding a ladder in the woods was a photo opportunity. Several pictures and video were wasted on that ladder. Hey, a ladder is a novelty. A fourth hiker caught up to us, Dutch. Dutch laughed at the ladder. Dutch's pace was fast. I explained to Dutch how we had not seen my wife at any of the road crossings. He offered the use of his cell phone. His phone didn't have service either, but we were headed to a mountaintop. Certainly, we would have cell service there. We hiked together at a fast pace. Alien and Shenanigans were behind us as Dutch and I went to the top of the mountain. There was a small, rundown building on the mountain. The building had a porch, where we stood out of the rain. I tried calling Deb but got no answer. I sent a text asking her to call back at Dutch's number. I didn't know she wouldn't get his phone number from the phone that texted the message.

Alien and Shenanigans didn't stop at the building where we were. I guessed Alien and Shenanigans had passed us. It was time for me to catch up with them. A short time later, Dutch and I passed a path to a shelter and then came across a couple who were coming southbound. I asked if they had seen Alien and Shenanigans. They had. Alien and Shenanigans were only minutes ahead. They must not have stopped at the shelter. We ran to catch up with them. The faster we ran the more it rained.

Soon, we were out of the woods and facing a long trail down the hill along a vast field. I looked as far as I could trying to spot Shenanigans and Alien. They were nowhere to be seen. The rain sounded like a waterfall as it hit the trees along the field's edge. We thought we were soaked before, but walking here in the open we were really getting drenched. My feet were wringing wet. Not a spot on my body was dry. My fingertips pruned from being wet so long.

The trail was slippery as the rain came down in full force. Buckets of water fell on us, hard! Dutch and I made it to Vermont 12. Deb wasn't there! I looked back up the trail across the field. Alien and Shenanigans were not behind us. A small roof covered a bulletin board was located by a small footbridge at a parking lot. We hid from the rain under the roof. We tried the cell phone again—no service. Alien and Shenanigans were nowhere to be seen. They must have continued on for the final four miles, or did they?

As Dutch and I hid under the small roof from the rain we considered what to do next. Dutch opened his pack and withdrew a pack of cigarettes. He shook the pack extending a single smoke from the pack. Dutch reached the pack toward me, "Mingo!" "Sure," I took the smoke, and after several tries the water-soaked lighter finally lit. We smoked as the rain caused a deafening roar on the roof. Our packs were wet, our clothes soaked, and Deb was nowhere to be seen. The parking area was empty. No one in his right mind would be out here hiking today.

Dutch had information about a store that sold ice cream down the road a mile or two. Did Alien and Shenanigans go there or did they hike up the next mountain? The heavy rain continued. Deb's condition and location were unknown. Alien and Shenanigans locations were unknown. I was in a fix. After finishing our smokes, I decided to go with Dutch to the store for ice cream and on the outside chance we could get cell service there. Maybe Shenanigans and Alien were at the ice cream place. Those seemed to be my last options. We went to the store.

The store was attended by a lady, who was the owner. We tried desperately not to drip water everywhere, but that was hopeless. We were too wet to keep from dripping water in the store. I no sooner got into the store than I realized I had left my wallet with my phone in the truck. Dutch offered to pay for my drink and food. I tried his cell phone again. We barely had service, and as soon as I heard Deb's phone ring the wind would blow and I would lose service.

Inside the store was cold. Being wet to the bone didn't help keep in any warmth. Eating ice cream didn't help keep me warm, either. Dutch and I sat on the front steps and ate. The wind blew rain onto the porch, running us off the steps. The store owner announced she was ready to close the store. This was the last shelter from the rain for us. Dutch was planning to go find a barn that the owner allowed hikers to use. I was slack packing; I didn't have a tent, dry clothes, food, sleeping bag, phone, or money. This was a pathetic situation to be in. If anything could have gone wrong, it did.

A half hour or more passed. It was time to make a decision. Do I stay? Do I try to hike back to find Alien and Shenanigans? I couldn't call them. Their numbers were on my phone and Dutch didn't have their phone numbers. Do I continue to hike on, hoping to find them ahead? Do I sit at the trail crossing in the rain like a wet puppy? Night was coming soon. I shivered and shook as the wind chilled my wet clothes.

Dutch asked, "Mingo, what are you going to do?" It was time to make a final decision. I could try to hitchhike back to the campground. No, I would go back to the trailhead, wait fifteen minutes, and then hike on. That was my plan. I stepped back out of the store and headed into the rain, back to the road. The rain had not let up. I stepped off the porch, looked up, and saw Shenanigans and Alien walking through the rain, off the road, up to the store.

They were a happy sight to see. By staying at the store a little longer, half of my worries had been resolved. What a relief! Shenanigans and Alien quickly shopped for snacks and drinks and came outside to the porch. "Alien, do you have cell service?" I asked. Alien's phone went in and out of service just like Dutch's phone. The storm was interfering with connections. Alien went back inside the store.

Alien was a computer savvy sort of guy who works for Google. The man certainly knew his electronics. "Do you have a computer I may borrow?" he asked the store's owner. She did, and she had an Internet connection. Alien logged onto Google and sent a message to Deb's phone. I had no idea that was possible. Alien sent a message out. That was something we couldn't do with our phones. Now, it was up to Deb's phone to receive the message. Once she got into a cell service area she would know where we were, we hoped!

Unknown to us, Deb had driven past the store when we all walked inside for Alien and Shenanigans to get their snacks. She was no more than a mile away when her phone began beeping. She pulled over to get the text. "Deb, we are at the store on Vt 12, the ice cream sign is out front." Deb read the message and smiled. She knew exactly where we were.

Less than three minutes later, Deb drove my truck into the lot. I began counting our blessings. Deb was safe! One! Alien and Shenanigans had not hiked ahead of me. Two! I didn't have to go another four miles. Three!

We were finally out of the rain. Four! Deb was with us; we had transportation. Five! I had my cell phone and my wallet. Six and seven! I paid Dutch back for the food he bought. Now we needed to find a place for Dutch to spend the night.

The rain slowed to a drizzle. After eating and drinking, we loaded into the truck and headed back toward the trail. Dutch was going to find the barn where thru-hikers were permitted to stay. We took Dutch back to the trailhead. It was so much nicer now; the rain had stopped. He wanted to ride in the back but I wouldn't hear of it. He deserved to ride inside the truck cab, no matter how wet we were. We dropped Dutch off at the trail.

We went back to the park where we had our tents set up. Luckily, everything had stayed dry. A hot shower and a dry towel made our moods so much better. The Runaways called and wanted to get together for dinner. That was a stellar idea. It was a steak dinner kind of night. We had earned it.

New Hampshire

AFTER DINNER, WE returned to our campsite. Several new campers had moved into the area. It had been a long day and we all called it a night. This was to be our last night in tents for a while, hopefully. The next morning we showered and packed up. Everything was wet but that was okay. At the end of the day we would stay in a hotel in Hanover, New Hampshire.

We took extra time to ensure everyone was on the same plan, with contingencies. The first step: the kids and their mom would meet with us for breakfast. After breakfast, we would all return to Route 12. The kids and their mom would hike with us, leaving their vehicle at Route 12. Deb was slack packing the full crew. When the day was finished, Deb would take the Runaways' mother back to her SUV.

We gorged on breakfast as we made our plans. As the sun rose, we loaded the truck and headed out. Deb dropped us off at Route 12. After three miles, Deb would meet us for the first rendezvous. The hike seemed to be steeper than the map showed. Headed down toward the first road we crossed into the edge of a farm field. To me, everyone was going a bit too slow. I passed by them as they were standing on boards used as a boardwalk. The ground was black and shiny. I should have known to stay on the boardwalk, but I was having a brain-lock.

"Hey, Mingo, stop!" Splash! It was too late. I was in over my knees in a thick bog of rich black mud. The mud squished into my shoes and between my toes. My first thought was: *will I lose a shoe when I pull out of the bog?*

I was tugging on my legs as the other, smarter hikers passed me by. It was a chore to get out of the bog. So, that is what quicksand feels like! After escaping the mud pit, I ran down the hill past the other hikers to a creek to wash the mud off my legs and shoes. Deb was a short walk away.

We sat beside a road on our lawn chairs, which Deb kept in the back of the truck and set out for us when we arrived. An occasional car or truck came by but the road traffic was minimal. We ate snacks and rehydrated. I took my shoes off to dry. This stop was to be a quick stop. Ruckus was tired and acting a bit irritable. The hike was taking a toll on the lad, but he was hanging in there with heart. At one point, while planning the hike, Ruckus quipped to me, "You aren't on our team!" Deb heard his little comment and quickly answered, "Okay, find your own way back to your car," as she smiled in jest. Ruckus' mother quickly told him to be quiet. With my shoes back on and my pack loaded, I was ready to go.

I was saying my good-bye to Deb when we heard a disturbing noise. Thump! Thump! Ugh! We turned to see what had just happened. The trail beyond the road passed over a small, narrow log bridge. The bridge had one hand rail which was too close to the log walkway. Alien had started across the bridge first. It was wet and slippery. He was on his third step when his right foot slid off the logs. His attempt to catch his balance caused his body to turn toward the handrail. Both feet slid over the edge of the logs, under the handrail. Feeling he was falling, Alien arched his back and slid through the guardrail, down off the bridge, without any damage or injury. This was the only possible way for him to fit through the railing. The odds of him falling in this fashion were slim to none. The luck of the Irish was on his side! Alien was standing next to the bridge, hanging on for balance, with one hand overhead holding tight to the rail. His toes were barely touching the sharp rocks below. His body was arched through the only gap in which he could fit, and he was unscathed.

If trolls were under the bridge they would have run from the giant leprechaun who came tumbling down upon them. Amazed at his Irish luck, we watched Alien climb back up to cross the bridge again. He used extra caution as he stepped across the bridge. Each hiker followed, stepping slowly so as not to startle the trolls or to repeat the "Irish Bridge Ballet." If any of us fell we would be hurt, severely. Alien has a luck that just amazes those who know him.

The rest of the day went well. Deb met us repeatedly for food, hydration, and rest stops. In only twenty miles we were crossing the Connecticut River into New Hampshire. There, Deb took the kids' mother back to her car as we hiked into Hanover. We looked for the closest bar for beer and hot food. We found one that met our every expectation. We tried shots of whiskey and several types of beer. Drink specials were ordered, as we wanted to sample them all.

The Runaways went with their mother to find a place for the night. After several drinks, Alien, Shenanigans, and I jumped into the truck with Deb and she took us to a hotel. It had been a long day. We hiked a good twenty-one miles and it felt good. "Let's order in some food!" I called out. "We can go pick it up." An Indian restaurant was the best option. After a shower and cleaning our gear, the food arrived, thanks to Deb. The meal hit the spot. Being tired, I went to bed. Being young, Shenanigans and Alien went back to the bar!

We had reached New Hampshire and were proud of it. This was the next to the last state on our hike. They were going to celebrate our near victory and short distance left to hike. First, we would be in the Green Mountains, and then we would get into the Whites. The Green Mountains are steep and challenging. The Whites are usually void of trees and the trail goes over stone mountains high into the clouds. The dangers of the Whites are often underestimated. There, the hike is the hardest. Many hikers maintain that ninety percent of all the effort in hiking the Appalachian Trail is used to get through the Whites.

New Hampshire will offer some trying challenges, but we felt confident we would be ready and fit. Unfortunately, I had sent my rain gear home. The Whites are no place to be without rain and cold weather gear, anytime of the year. Mount Washington was known for having had the highest sustained winds in the world. That record has since been broken. Notably, the weather on Mount Washington is unpredictable and threatening.

Green in the Green Mountains

IN THE MORNING, I was up early and ready to go, as usual. Alien was still sleeping, but Shenanigans was green! They had drank well into the morning hours and were in no shape to hike. We opted to do a nero. A nero is near zero miles. Limited miles are what the doctor ordered. We needed a break, but not a big break. We would go shopping before going out to hike.

My feet were still hurting. They would go numb during the hike or after I slapped them onto rocks to make the pain go away. Each night, as the numbness faded, nearly unbearable pain in my feet would waken me. Getting feeling back into my feet was agonizing. Having time off this morning, we went to an outfitter to find me new shoes.

After trying on several pairs of shoes and comparing the style and durability of the soles, I settled on a pair. A lesson thru-hikers learn is never buy new shoes without buying replacement insoles. "Super Feet" is a brand of insoles which give the support desired by distance hikers. They don't come cheap, but I was tired of injuring my feet, so I bought a good pair of Super Feet insoles and a rain jacket and was ready to go hiking.

From the outfitters we went nine miles north of the trail so we could slack pack back. Shenanigans was still looking greenish in the face. The man had seen better days. He was a hiking zombie. Alien was feeling a little better. The short hike and rehydrating would do them both some good. We did the quick sobo slack pack back to Hanover and went straight back to the bar!

The nine-mile slack pack was slightly downhill the entire way. It was an easy hike. The woods were filled with bugs and hikers. Zig Zag, Ranger Bob, and Full Time were hiking northbound. We stopped to say, "Hi," and moved on. They were doing well.

Back at the bar we started our now traditional pounding of beers. Then it was decision-making time. Do we go back, shower, and then go eat, or just go eat? Three or four beers later it was decided to just go eat. A Japanese restaurant was just across the road. It had been a long time since I'd had tempura.

Once seated and ready to order drinks, we ordered beer. But being in a Japanese restaurant, we had to also order sake, and lots of it. The tempura meal was the best I had ever had in the United States. Each bite was savored and was perfectly delicious. The sushi ordered by Shenanigans was absolutely excellent. We toasted with the sake. "Here's to New Hampshire!" "Here's to the AT!" "Here's to Deb!" "Here's to my truck!" "Here's to drinking sake!" And the toasting went on. This was hands down the best tasting meal I'd had on the Appalachian Trail. We were happy to have done short miles and delighted with the foods offered in Hanover.

After dinner, we headed back to the bar like cows headed to the barn. Sitting next to a window, we made a game of waving at people who walked by on the sidewalk. Then came the next challenge, waving at people driving by. With each successful return wave, we toasted our success. It is easy to make a thru-hiker happy. The thru-hiking life becomes simplistic and pleasurable, pains and all.

Having spent most of the night partying and celebrating our successes, we were in no condition to hike far the next day. I got up at my early rising time. Shenanigans and Alien got up much later. Deb and I went for breakfast first, then went back to arouse the sleepy heads. We checked out and took the other two out for breakfast. Then, we were off to the woods, back to Three Mile Road. Feeling better, we hiked for eleven miles. Those weren't big miles, but we'd had a rough time celebrating the night before.

Deb met us at Lyme-Dorchester Road. It was a small dirt road with a parking area. We set up our tents for the night and headed into Lyme to find a place to eat. Before leaving to eat, a van pulled into the parking area.

One young guy, in his twenties, and three females jumped out of the hippie Volkswagen van. The guy said he had hiked the Appalachian Trail before. His name was Trail Dawg. They were out for a short hike and having a good day of it. We headed on to Lyme.

On the drive to Lyme we saw a yard with strange looking yard art. The art was tall, brown-rusted metal sculptures that looked like Beaker on the Muppets Show. They were funny looking. In town we found a store that sold food and ice cream. We ate and discovered they made breakfast sandwiches and coffee. We would be back in the morning.

Before leaving the store, an older man stopped us and asked if we were thru-hiking the trail. We talked about our hike for a while, sharing stories. He then said, "Hey, we have a hiking celebrity here in town. Our guy holds the record for the fastest hike." He described the famous hiker, a young man in his twenties who drove a hippie VW van. "Hey, we met him!"

On the way back to our campsite we stopped in front of the house with the cool yard art. We had to see it up close and ask about it. As soon as we stopped, we saw Trail Dawg's van was coming down the road. We flagged him down to give him trouble for not letting us know he was the record holder. Trail Dawg shook our hands and explained his record had been broken just the day before by a female hiker, Snorkel.

Trail Dawg was interesting. He offered advice, but nothing condescending or presumptuous. It was a pleasure to meet him. The yard art was also cool and interesting. The owners let us go get pictures with the art. They explained whom the artist was and how they came to buy it. The art was unique and visually fun to see.

Back at our campsite, three sobo hikers had arrived and set up their tents with us. Signs were posted all around the woods. None of the signs prohibited camping, so we were fine. The signs asked people not to shoot the bears wearing collars with radio boxes. Alien called out, "Great! Remote controlled bears." We laughed.

In the morning we found that we had to hike fourteen miles before we would be able to meet Deb. Our goal was to add ten more miles to the fourteen, giving us a twenty-four mile day. This was the beginning of the Green Mountains. The maps didn't show anything too difficult, but the maps were wrong!

After breakfast, we packed and headed up Smarts Mountain. I know now why they call it Smarts, because it did! The fourteen miles went by without any problems. We started the hike slowly, but picked up speed after sweating out most of the alcohol from the previous days.

Hikers Welcome

WE MADE IT to New Hampshire Route 25A, the first road where Deb was found waiting for us. She was excited to see us and to report whom she had there with her. Cemmeron, a trail legend, was sitting in one of our lawn chairs. He was trying to set a record as the oldest hiker to finish the Appalachian Trail. After Deb had arrived and set up the first chair, Cemmeron had stepped out of the woods and asked, "Is that chair for me?" Deb gleefully replied, "Sure."

Cemmeron was looking for his ride to a hostel, which wasn't far away. He offered to show Deb where it was so she could get us bunks there as well. Perfect! They certainly would not turn Deb away with Cemmeron sitting next to her. We hoped they had room for us, and as it turned out there was plenty of room.

Deb left with Cemmeron showing her the way. We set out for our last ten miles of the day. Later, I found out Deb had the backpacks for Zig Zag, Ranger Bob, and Full Time in the truck. They wanted to slack pack the last ten miles. I had an issue with that. They were not helping with fuel and they didn't offer to let me slack pack with them in Virginia. I let the issue slide as Full Time did get me a ride back to the trail from Waynesboro, Virginia.

We stayed at Hikers Welcome hostel. We found the Runaways and their mother there, along with Cemmeron. Soon, it was pointed out that the oldest hiker attempting a thru-hike and the youngest hiker attempting a thru-hike were both at Hikers Welcome. The two stood together for pictures, making Ruckus a star. Goldie Locks stood in the pictures as well, as well she should.

Hikers Welcome had a large tent set up with cots lined up on both sides. It had a bit of a military-style lay out. Goldie Locks, her mom, Deb, Shenanigans, Alien, and I took up the entire tent. Ruckus slept in their SUV. He had a funny way about him. He wanted to be a loner, but maybe that was his still being just a kid.

For dinner, we loaded into one vehicle and headed to a steakhouse. The food was okay and the company was fun. We always had a good time whenever we were all together. Driving back, the truck was filled with conversation. Everyone was trying to talk over each other.

In the morning, we all went out for breakfast. I tend to never miss breakfast if possible. It is my favorite meal of the day. Mt. Moosilauke was the next mountain. Everyone said to go southbound over the mountain if possible. The north side was too steep. Hiking down steep slopes are some of the worse conditions to hike; going up is so much easier. Deb took the Runaways, their mother, Shenanigans, Alien, and me to Kinsman Notch. From there we would hike nine miles back to Hikers Welcome.

Once at the top of Mt. Moosilauke, we gathered together for lunch and pictures. We had to hurry because a cloud was blowing in on us and the picture wouldn't be clear. Hiking down wasn't so bad. The map showed a steep decline, but it wasn't as bad as we thought it would be. Farther down, near the bottom of the mountain, the grade was much gentler. I was able to run some of the way.

The folks at Hikers Welcome were well informed about the Whites. They offered information and answered any questions we had. We were out of the Green Mountains now and coming into the Whites. We had a lot of work ahead of us. Cold weather, even in the summer, is a big threat in the Whites. Hikers wear fleece jackets through the Whites then shed them at Hikers Welcome. The hostel then sells the same fleece jackets for only a few dollars. It is a great deal. I bought a fleece jacket for ten bucks before I left.

The following morning we checked out of Hikers Welcome, had

breakfast, and packed. We returned to Kinsman Notch to begin our hike. The Runaways didn't go with us. Around lunchtime we stopped at a shelter to eat and read the shelter journal. I often left entries in the journals for Cargo. It would have been good to have him hiking with me here in the Whites.

After lunch, we stopped at Eliza Brook Shelter. Another couple was already there. At least, I thought they were a couple. It turned out they weren't. I needed to fill my water bottles, and wanting to do a good deed, I asked if anyone else needed water. Alien did. The female at the shelter needed water as well. She was going to refuse my getting it for her but I insisted.

Back from the creek with full water bottles that I filtered through my water filter, I gave each of them their water. On the bench area where the girl was sitting was fresh baby powder spread all around. I looked at her and in a smart-ass way asked, "What did you do, powder your ass?" She flared up, "Do you want to see me powder my ass?" She loaded her pack and headed out, defiantly.

I felt awful. It was just a joke. It was a bad joke, but a joke nonetheless. I asked the others her name, Raw Indy. Raw Indy eats raw foods and was from Indiana, so she went by the name Raw Indy.

I hiked quickly to catch up with her to apologize. She was one fast hiker. I did catch up to her and apologized. She said I didn't need to apologize, she wasn't mad. We talked together as we hiked. She was Amish, and had heard about the Appalachian Trail for the first time months ago. She had started her hike in Damascus, Virginia. She was doing a flip-flop hike by going back to Damascus after she finished Katahdin. By the way, she had powdered only her feet.

When we made it to the top of South Kinsman Mountain we found it populated by day hikers. Many of them asked about our thru-hikes. We were happy to describe our adventures—more than they wanted to know! Raw Indy showed she had what it took to be a thru-hiker; she actually Yogied a peanut butter and jelly sandwich.

When Raw Indy started to eat her sandwich, I looked at her with sad eyes. "Sure would like to have a sandwich of my own. Are you going to eat all of that by yourself?" I asked. In an excellent Yogi-master manner I was attempting to Yogi half the sandwich from Raw Indy. She looked at me and pulled the sandwich in half. I ate my half then told her, "I really didn't want it. I just wanted to Yogi from a Yogier." Now she was angry at me again. She got over it.

On the top of North Kinsman Mountain there were fewer day hikers. The trail was wide but rocky. There are no trees on the tops of these mountains. As I hiked to the top I looked down at the trail and saw two M&Ms and a peanut. A trail find! I grabbed the M&Ms and peanut. I offered to share with Alien but he refused. Shenanigans took the yellow M&M, leaving me the blue M&M and peanut. We ate them. Free food is always best, and if you could call the M&Ms and peanut trail magic, it was a small amount of magic, but magic never the less.

Death by Burger

SHENANIGANS CALLED A friend of his to arrange a room for us after we finished our hike. They had known each other as kids in Scotland. He worked at a five-star resort in the area. Deb waited for us at Franconia Notch. It was little hard to find the parking lot because it was quite far from the trail. Raw Indy found it first. She had a friend coming to pick her up and take her to a room and food.

After we all made it to Franconia Notch, we met with the Runaways and headed to the resort in Lincoln. The room was perfect. Deb and I had the master bedroom with our own private luxury bath. Shenanigans and Alien had another room with two beds and the Runaways had the living room with a foldout couch and another small bed for Ruckus. We had a kitchen and Deb had even bought food to cook.

Deb made a large pot of spaghetti for everyone. She baked bread with butter and garlic. The meal was a big hit. While sitting around, we planned the rest of the hike. Tensions were forming between the kids and us. They didn't seem to care about having me or Deb around anymore. That was fine by us. We all hike our own hike. They suggested Shenanigans might prefer to hike with them. If that was what he wanted to do it would be okay.

The games and whispers were getting old quickly. I adored the kids but I was there to hike. Shenanigans and Alien were mature enough not to succumb to the little "our team" game. Deb provided great support for the whole group and we never left anyone out. She bought food and kept records for reimbursement. The fuel was equally divided, as was the cost for camping. We worked well together and had had a great time thus far.

That night we decided to take a zero day. During the zero we washed our clothes and cleaned our gear. Alien headed out for a little alone time. He got his hair cut and cleaned up nicely! Everyone went his separate way, Deb offering rides as needed. It was a slow zero day. We needed it.

That night for dinner, Alien, Deb, and I took Shenanigans to the restaurant where his friend worked. While waiting for our meals to arrive, Shenanigans, his friend, and Alien played the trivia game held in the bar. It was fun to watch two Scotts and an Irishman get high scores in the category of American Pop Culture.

The restaurant had a burger that was called "Death By Burger." It was an eating challenge. The sandwich was made with two eighteen-ounce beef patties, tomato, lettuce, onion, and onion rings between two large buns. With the meal, a stack of onion rings came on the side, unless you wanted fries. The sandwich was bigger than a man's head. Shenanigans ordered the smaller version, only one eighteen-ounce patty, but Alien took on the challenge and ordered the "Death By Burger." He ate and ate, never stalling for a breath. He did pause for a beer. Once the beer was gone he ordered another. I guess the burger wasn't enough for him.

Thru-hikers can eat. But we had slack packed enough and ate well enough with Deb cooking for us that I no longer had the appetite of a thru-hiker. Alien worked on the meal without the slightest hesitation. After finishing the challenge successfully, a bar employee took his picture and posted it on "The Wall of Fame." The wall of fame is for those who met the challenge. The wall of shame was nearly full. That's where your picture goes if you fail eating the entire meal in one sitting.

Alien also received a T-shirt, a mug, and bottle opener and other stuff. He also won items from the trivia game. Shenanigans and his buddy told stories of days back in the old country, Scotland. I felt as if I were working for the United Nations again. Deb and I were the only two "English-speaking" people at the table. We had a blast.

The next morning we loaded the truck and packed for a two-day hike.

The next time we would meet Deb would be in two days. We planned to remote camp if we didn't find a place to stay at Galehead Hut. When we pulled up to Franconia Notch, Alien went to the outhouse. The meal from the night before was passing through. Later, when he caught up, he reported that he had clogged the outhouse.

In the Whites there are no shelters. That entire part of the Appalachian Trail is managed by the AMC. I think they call the AMC the Appalachian Mountain Club. We called it the Appalachian Money Club, because everything costs money and lots of it. They have huts throughout the Whites. The huts are sort of like a hostel, but the cost for a bunk is too high for a thru-hiker. Plus, you have to have reservations. The huts offer activities, games, and informational tours. They do serve a purpose, but they are not what a thru-hiker usually plans during his hike and the cost is prohibitive.

Thru-hikers may sometimes work for a stay at a hut. You don't get to sleep on a bunk but you may sleep inside on the floor. That is good enough. The food is expensive, but what isn't eaten must be carried out. There is no trash service, so they sometimes offer thru-hikers the leftovers. It is a win-win situation.

We made it to Galehead Hut only to find the kids had made it there before us and other thru-hikers were there also. They were the ones getting to work. We were being sent away.

Rain had started falling. Remote camping was not permitted in the Whites. Camping along the trail or even in the woods was prohibited. There were campsites in some areas farther north, but none existed where we were.

Because there was a shortage of work-for-stay—and since some Hut Masters (the person in charge at the hut) show no love for thru-hikers—we knew our reception could be unfriendly, so we were prepared with a secret list. I probably shouldn't reveal this secret, so don't tell anyone! There is a secret list of remote spots to camp for thru-hikers only. We keep the areas clean and make sure we have minimum affect.

Armed with the secret list, we searched for a site to stay for the night. We found the secret mark along the trail, paced out the required distance, and turned into the woods. Soon, we were away from the trail and in a small opening that provided a safe place to set up. This wasn't quite remote camping. Remote camping is camping along the trail. We were stealth camping, hiding from the long arm of the AMC.

Early in the morning we were back on the trail. Our campsite was sterilized, showing no sign we were ever there. While we were stealth camping, Deb slept in our truck at Franconia Notch. The kids' mother slept in her SUV parked next to our truck. Sometimes we all roughed it a little.

Deb waited for us at US 302. We hiked down to meet her. After seeing how easy the trail was, we were disappointed we didn't hike the full twenty-eight miles in one day. We loaded our gear into the truck and went to find a motel. We found one with a large parking area and lawn. We needed the open space to spread our tents and gear out to dry. The Runaways came by but they opted to find a different place.

Thru-hikers have a set way of doing things to make their life easier. We hang our sleeping bags and other gear out to dry in our hotel rooms. A thru-hiker takes his shoes off and leaves them outside the door of his hotel room, with the insoles pulled out. We usually use a zip lock bag for a wallet. It is lightweight and keeps everything dry. Best of all it is cheap and easy to replace when worn out. These are just a few small tricks or traits of a thru-hiker.

While talking to Deb, she told me she had slept the night before in the truck. I asked her to find a hostel and stay there and not in the truck while we were out on the trail. The next section was going to take two days again. It was going to be rough. We were headed up Mt. Washington. I wanted Deb to be safe and comfortable while we were away.

The Dungeon

NORMALLY, WE COULD hike twenty to twenty-five miles a day. But we were not so fast in the Whites! It was hard to believe someone at some time looked up at a cliff and said, "Hey, there is a trail." A trail? What were they thinking? I'm thinking I'm not a goat! We were able to hike nine to fifteen miles a day there, and those were big miles in the Whites. We left early to get to Lake of the Clouds on Mount Washington. Mount Washington is absolutely breathtaking, both for its scenic views and for the difficulty of the climb. We wanted to get to the Lake of the Clouds Hut early to be first in line for getting work-for-stay.

Upon arrival, however, we were shunned by the Hut Master. He would not offer us work-for-stay. Oftentimes, hikers are offered work-for-stay, but he decided we had arrived too early to get that offer! That was just the opposite of what had happened at Galehead Hut. He did offer to let us pay to stay in the dungeon. Regular bunks were around one hundred ten dollars a night. Thru-hikers are permitted to stay in the dungeon for ten dollars a night. We were spending the night in the dungeon and happy for it.

The dungeon was a small, stone-wall area, twelve foot by twelve foot, with a walk out basement; it is an emergency shelter, under the hut. I was standing by the door inside the dungeon talking with two other hikers who were also staying in the dungeon. The Hut Master was giving a tour to tourists. They were standing outside the door just as he was explaining that they let thru-hikers stay in the dungeon. They asked to see inside.

The Hut Master opened the heavy steel door by lifting the weighty steel bar off the hooked latch. The door swung open with a loud creak and there I stood in the doorway. I glanced out at the crowd and in unison the crowd recoiled. Their mouths gaped open as they all gasped for air. Shenanigans was in the crowd and laughed at the people's response to seeing me. I scared them?

After explaining we were in the room because we were thru-hikers, the hut master closed the heavy steel door and latched it closed with the large steel bar. It opened from both sides. One of the ladies had a question about the thru-hikers, asking the host, "Do you keep them confined?" She must have thought we were like wild animals. I guess I made a good impression on her. We all laughed our butts off at that. But in her defense, I must have looked a little wild, and she thought I might be dangerous to "real" people.

Later that evening we went to the dining hall. The paying customers get fed for a high but fair price. We waited for the scraps. What wasn't eaten must be carried out, because there was no trash service at the huts. Once all the paying "real people" have finished, the staff gathers plates for the dungeon dwellers and we get to eat all we can just to get rid of the excess. For us it was a real score. We ate and ate. It was excellent and the cost was free; it couldn't have been better.

The next morning, we headed to Mount Washington. The hike was uphill one mile. We were the first hikers headed up the mountain. The sky was clear and the air chilled. Looking one mile up to the top we could see the observation building and several antennac pointing skyward. The trail was marked well enough. There were no trees, just rocks upon rocks. We hurried because the weather could change in a minute and the landmarks disappear. With a clear sky, we were assured of good views.

The weather cooperated and the scenic views remained crisp and clear. Mother Nature was spectacular. I visited the other parking lots to take in more distant views. Panoramic views could be seen in every direction. I wanted to take in the full three-hundred-sixty-degree view.

As I was exploring the area, more tourists began arriving. One lower parking lot was almost totally empty. A couple was there before me, taking photos. The gentleman was leaning on his motorcycle, while his companion was standing a few feet away. She was taking a photo of him next to his Harley Davidson.

The couple was clad in heavy leather. As "knights of the road," "asphalt warriors," "modern day wild ones," they were armored up in their black leather. He sported a beard not quite the degree of a ZZ Top beard, but one you would expect from a biker. His jacket bore colors. Colors are the insignia on the back that states the name of his local and national bike club. He appeared to be a true biker.

The lady with the camera was equally covered in leather. She had a rough look about her. She walked as if her legs were permanently bowed by riding on the bike. Other tourists came to the parking area, but they would not come near this couple. It seemed odd that so many would walk in their direction then turnaround and walk away. Bikers must be a bad breed of folks?

I walked up and said, "Hi, would you like me to take a picture of the two of you together?" She wheeled around, extending the camera. Then her eyes landed on me and snapped to the size of saucers. A grimace crossed her face and she scowled at me, "No!" She jumped on the bike and they drove off rapidly. She looked back to make sure I was not following them. It was easy to read the fear in her face. I bet her friends love playing poker with her. Her face showed she was afraid of me.

Shunned by the bikers, I walked with my head hung low. Feeling like an outcast, I returned to the only people on this mountain who understood me, Shenanigans and Alien.

The delis had begun opening, so I found Alien there. We had breakfast and explored the visitor's center. Looking out the large windows we saw the clouds blanketing the valleys. We enjoyed a couple cups of coffee and relaxed.

While admiring a wall map, I commented that Deb better not show up in my truck. "The road up here is very narrow. I'll kick her ass if she brings my truck up here." I said, jokingly. The next moment Deb walked in, "Hi, honey!"

Deb laughed about driving my truck to the top of Mt. Washington.

The truck could easily make the drive up; that wasn't the problem. The road was narrow and larger vehicles were not permitted to be on the road. The rangers below had folded the side mirrors in on my truck so it would be narrow enough for traffic to pass coming down the mountain. I would have guessed the truck was too large, but it ended up being barely small enough.

Vote for Jackson

WE STOOD IN a long line to wait our turn to stand by the sign stating we were at the top of Mount Washington. People stared at us and gave us plenty of room. They either didn't care for our looks, or the way we smelled, or both. Shenanigans laughed that the line to get a picture of the sign at the top of the mountain was mostly made up of the people who drove up the mountain. We were stuck waiting to get our picture and we had walked to get there. We had climbed the mountain. We had even walked well over a thousand miles to get to Mt. Washington. That's okay; we would wait our turn.

We got our pictures and walked away, leaving the site to the hordes of tourists who drove up the mountain. Deb asked if we were going back to the road below today. I told her yes, we were planning on it. She reminded us we could slack pack. Our spirits lifted quickly as we headed off to the truck to lighten our backpacks. I was happy Deb had brought my truck up the mountain!

At the truck, we emptied our packs of everything except the bare essentials. Then, as if she were Santa Clause, Deb surprised us with presents. "Hey, guys, I found a new type of candy bar." These bars were large, peanut-covered, with caramel and icing filled. Shenanigans quipped, "Nut jobs!" The best part, they contained nearly eight hundred calories each. We quickly ate one of the bars and loaded our packs with the others, along with more candy, jerky, cheeses, and other snacks Deb had brought us.

We were now satisfied. Life was grand and we were at a high that couldn't be topped, or so we thought. But, Deb topped that moment. She not only topped the moment, but instantly became a legend to us and our hike. "I brought you guys another gift." She smiled ear to ear, proud of what she had brought us. She extended a plastic grocery bag. The three of us stood in a small circle, each grabbing an edge of the bag to peer inside. We raided the plastic bag like a pack of puppies after a bowl of milk. Small bottles of whiskeys and rums filled the bag. Our hearts leaped with joy! Small things please thru-hikers, but this, this was big!

We were also happy to have Deb with us because she loaded most of the weight from our packs into the truck so we could hike down comfortably. We upgraded our food and drink supplies then started down. The trail was difficult. Did I say difficult? It was hell! We had some of our toughest climbing ever that day. I have video of clouds rolling in on the mountaintops as we went over them. I swear I saw snow! That was bad, because I usually wore swim trunks and a T-shirt for hiking clothes.

Before going too far, we crossed railroad tracks used by the cog train. The cogs enable the train to climb the steep mountain. We took turns laying across the tracks for a picture. Then, while climbing a cliff and going around large boulders with nothing but lichens  growing on them, I spied a small, lone flower. I had to stop and address the flower with a kind, "Hello." Then, I took a few pictures and wished it well.

The trail led to a sign with an arrow that read, "Jefferson Mountain Summit." We needed to stay on the AT to get down off the mountains. "I am not going to summit Jefferson. I didn't vote for the guy," I said jokingly. Without missing a beat, Alien answered, "That's because you were seventeen." Oh, an old joke? Shenanigans laughed. I smiled and answered, "Aw, dude, I am so totally getting you back for that!" Alien's quick comeback was, "Mingo, if you are going to kill me, do it now—not after I have hiked all these mountains." "Oh no, I will wait for the right opportunity." I smiled at my answer. We joked on as we hiked.

On the Presidential Mountains the trail and surrounding area is nothing but rocks. The rocks were large and small. Usually the small rocks stayed in place. The larger one-ton rocks would shift under foot. Since the trail was marked by piles of rocks known as cairns, we really had to pay attention to ensure we stayed on the right path.

The sights were astounding. The views were as far as one could imagine. We looked back and saw where we had hiked. It was both beautiful and painful to see. Our legs were throbbing and our backs aching and now my feet were burning, but we were at the top of the Presidential Mountains, the mountains named after our presidents. The hike, we had guessed, would be over at four o'clock. We were wrong. We called Deb and told her it would be six that evening before we could reach the road.

We made it off the mountains and into the woods. The woods had white blazes marking the trail. When the trail was smoother we would hike faster. Often times the trail seemed to fall off the face of the earth. A straight drop over the mountain was our path. Carefully, we climbed down the steep route. Alien, who could hike fast uphill, had a rough time with the downhill trails.

Alien wore long black shorts and a black t-shirt. He kept his black hair cropped short and seemed to always need a shave. Despite being a large man, Alien was impressively agile when on a dance floor. The man had moves. He could dance like Fred Astaire. It was shocking how nimbly his feet floated him across the floor, and when it comes to hiking uphill, Alien picked up an alarming amount of speed. He could fly uphill.

However, in contrast, Alien sucked hiking downhill. He was worse than a drunken buffalo. The man fell like an imploded building, falling to the ground dozens of times nearly every day. Downhill was this Superman's kryptonite.

Over and over, Alien would fall. At each steep descent we hoped to find Alien had made it to the bottom okay. He was a trooper, taking on each descent without hesitation. We made our way down the gantlet of steep drop-offs. Then, the trail became easier as it leveled off, but the white blazes stopped appearing. Since there were no other trails, we were assured of our path.

Then, the trail came to an intersection. A sign pointed to the right and read, "Mount Washington." There were no signs for the trail to the left. We had come from Mount Washington and didn't want to return, but there were no white blazes to show the correct direction. We tossed our packs off. I studied my map. It was difficult to decide which way to go.

In an attempt to find a white blaze I headed down the trail to the left for a reconnaissance. My map still offered no help as there wasn't any distinguishable terrain. After a mile or so, I went back, reporting an unsuccessful recon. We studied the map then made our best guess. We went to the right. Then a mile later we hit a trail with a name. This was the trail that was also the AT. We were on the right path again.

We had guessed our time at the road would be six o'clock. We were wrong again! I called Deb and told her we would be late—very late. Confident we were on the right trail we hiked faster as night began falling. Dusk was not what we had hoped for; it came too soon. We hiked as fast as our feet would allow. Then a small stream crossed the trail. In the lead, I stepped on a rock to keep my feet dry. My footing was not good. The rock was slippery. Alien was close behind me. Not trusting the slippery rock, I announced, "Nope, not worth falling. That rock feels slippery." I stepped into the creek for a flat footing. I was across the creek.

I continued on when all of a sudden I heard a commotion. Wheeling around to see what was happening, I saw Alien out of control. He had heard me say the rock wasn't worth the risk. He decided he could step on the rock and stay out of the water. His foot had slipped. Sliding down the side of the rock, Alien twisted and turned to catch himself. He had attempted to balance himself and maintain an upright position.

While twisting and spinning down the rock, Alien fell backward. His feet flew into the air and his entire body was airborne. Alien's head went downhill while his feet were facing uphill. He landed flat on his back in the creek among large rocks. He landed a full body length downhill from where he had been walking.

This fall by Alien wasn't just a *trail-ending* fall, it was a *life-ending* fall. My stomach jumped to my throat. Shenanigans and I both threw off our packs to begin life-rescue procedures. Alien lay on his back in the creek, his arms and legs extended upward looking like a dead bug. We leaped to his side and were instantly shocked at what we saw. Alien didn't have a single scratch or bruise. He had landed between two large rocks. His pack was pinned between the rocks and took the full impact of the fall. It was a miracle the man even survived.

After getting up, Alien stated he had only a bruised ego. "I heard Mingo say the rock was slippery. I thought I could do it. I guess I was wrong." We laughed our asses off at the great escape from a tremendous fall. "Alien, that was karma getting you back for the comment you made about me being seventeen and not voting for Jefferson. I guess we are even." I laughed in relief.

The woods grew darker. I tried calling Deb, but there was no cell service. My pace slowed because we were tired and starting to make mistakes with our footing. Then out of the dark, flying through the woods like a knife being thrown at my heart, a bee flew into my chest and stung me! I did not know the types of bees in the area, but typically, I am allergic. Pain started in my chest and it began swelling.

Making several attempts to find cell service finally paid off. I got Deb on the phone. I asked her if she would meet us on the road leading up to Mount Washington. The road is a few miles before the parking lot. She tried. The park service from the Appalachian Mountain Club was less than understanding. They would let her in to get us because she had already paid for entry that day, but if we wanted to be brought back to the same spot the next day it would cost each of us an additional entry fee. We decided to finish the hike to the parking lot. That would take another hour of hiking in the dark.

Soon, we reached the road to Mount Washington. Thankfully we had only a few more miles to go as we were spent. Onward, we marched toward Deb and the truck and out of the woods. Deb began worrying about us, so she started hiking into the woods to guide us to the truck. She was a half mile into the woods when we first saw her. "Don't stop, Deb. Don't break our momentum." I called ahead. "Turn around and lead the way back." She dutifully turned and went back toward the truck. Our pace was still quicker than most, but slow for us. We caught up to her and she informed us we were getting close to the truck. We slowed our steps even further. We got back sometime late that night. We were smashed, way past tired.

The Dark Abyss

WE WERE AT Pinkham Notch. Deb had pizzas and beers waiting for us. The energy generated by the calories was most needed. We ate and told her about the adventures that day. My bee sting had stopped swelling, but still hurt. Finally safe for the night, we laughed and teased each other about the day's follies. Alien's spinning like a top, flying through the air like

 a gymnast, and landing flat on his back was the highlight. What a hike that was!

Deb took us to a hostel, Hiker's Paradise. We slept in bunk beds. Shenanigans and Alien stayed in one room, Deb and I took another. The hostel had cabins that were being rented as well. We looked but found there were no other thru-hikers around. That night as it rained we were safe inside.

The next morning we stopped in at the front desk and learned that the hostel served breakfast. The owner came out and talked for a bit. He was a friendly Polish man. While eating breakfast we spoke a little in Russian. The Hiker's Paradise was a relaxing place. We decided to take a zero. This was going to be Deb's last day with us. After this, we were on our own, again.

During our zero, Deb took us to the next hostel in Gorham. That hostel was close to the trail. Our hike was headed straight for it. The hostel was full of hikers. Freight Train and Plan B were there, as well as several other hikers we knew. We had a friendly reunion. Shenanigans announced, "While on Kinsman, Mingo found two M&Ms and a peanut. It was a good trail find. We ate them." I added, "I shared one M&M with Shenanigans but Alien turned the other one down, so I had the M&M and peanut." Freight Train laughed and informed us she saw the same M&Ms and peanut two days prior to our seeing them. She thought about picking them up and eating them but decided against it. Lucky for us!

Before leaving the hostel, we decided to have dinner with several hikers that evening. The hostel's host allowed us to leave gear there so we could reduce the weight in our packs. The next day wasn't a real slack pack, but it was going to be close. We had only the essentials for two days, nothing more. Deb was leaving to go home, so we had to make the best of our last slack pack opportunity. Dinner was fun as we said our good-byes to the other hikers.

The following morning we had breakfast with my new Russian-speaking Polish friend. Deb took us back to Pinkham Notch. We started out from Pinkham and headed up Wildcat Mountain. The start of the hike seemed a bit too easy, but that changed in less than a hundred yards. Although we were in the woods, the ascent was abrupt. The mountain was so steep that we had to climb hand-over-hand for much of the way. We came to several spots were we had to wait for each other to clear the trail just to see if we could all make it. The climb was hard going and seemed quite slow for us. We stopped several times to rest and rehydrate.

The trail turned away from the woods and out to a ledge of exposed rock. From the ledge, Pinkham Notch was in plain view. Across the way, Mount Washington stood next to the other Presidential Mountains. We had climbed those mountains on our previous hike. It was surprising to see how far we had traveled in one day. Looking across the valley at the mountains, I was amazed we had hiked over that mountain range.

An old man who looked too frail to be climbing was hiking up the mountain in front of us. His pack was full and seemed to be really weighing him

down. It was obvious he was not a thru-hiker. Sweat poured down his face as he panted for air. He took a step, rested, took a couple of breaths, and then took another step. He was slow and was holding us up. The path was too narrow for us to pass him. The man did not offer to step aside to let us go around him. We had to wait until he reached a spot wide enough for us to go by. It was a wonder he had made it up this high on the mountain.

The higher we climbed the more difficult it became. There were several places where it seemed almost impossible for the old man to make it up the mountain. I worried if he would be okay. It would be worse for him if he tried to get down the same way he came. Climbing up is hard but going down is more dangerous. It would be several hours before he could make it as far as we went in only one hour. There was no place to set up a tent on the steep ascent, so the old guy would have to keep climbing.

We reached the top of Wildcat Mountain. There was a gondola ski lift at the top. A small building for maintenance supplies was close by. We sat on the steps of the small building for lunch. Several tourists were hiking around the mountaintop. They had all rode up in the gondola.

A small Canadian family was shocked after we told them we hiked up the mountain. Then, when they found out we had hiked all the way from Georgia, they were really amazed. Instantly, the mother started giving us food and water. "Here! We have to feed you. We have food in our camper. Eat our snacks." The young boy was getting ready to drink his water when his mother snatched it from his hands and gave it to us. They offered lunch cakes and other snacks with drinks of water. Another good trail magic score!

The daughter, Olivia, proudly announced she was having her birthday in two days. I offered, "Hey, we will be in Maine in two days. Tell you what: in two days, during your birthday, as we reach the border of Maine, deep in the woods, I will yell out, 'Happy Birthday Olivia!' That is my present to you." Olivia cherished the idea of my promise to her.

We finished our break and returned to the trail. These mountains were mostly wooded and the shade helped keep us cool. Our path was in better condition than it had been. Some steep climbs up and down were as rough as any other, but none were as challenging as the hike up Wildcat Mountain. I wondered if the old man had made it up the mountain or if he had to be rescued.

After leaving one mountain top and climbing over to another, then another, we reached a site where we could look down and see the rooftops of a hut. Then, we looked across the valley to another high mountain, Carter Dome. We were going down to the hut, Carter Notch Hut, then back up and over Carter Dome. While at the hut, we stopped to eat and relax for a while. The staff at Carter Notch was much friendlier to us than the folks at Lake of the Clouds had been.

A few miles after Carter Dome, we stopped near Imp Campsite to remote camp. I found a spot that was relatively flat and had enough room for three tents. Only seven more miles and we would have made it to the hostel. But, we had planned on staying in the woods overnight, so we did. After the fact, we realized we could have made the hike in one day, from Pinkham Notch to Gorham. That distance was only twenty-one miles, but they were all up one mountain and down the next, like a steep roller coaster all the way.

On top of the mountains we got into "alpine zones." Alpine zones are above the tree lines and often are covered with wet bogs. The bogs are delicate regions protected with walks made of boards laid across and along the trail. The boardwalks do get slippery. I stepped onto one boardwalk with my left foot while my right foot stayed firmly planted on the ground.

My left foot slid on the walkway and I could not stop it. I did a full splits, then fell back to ease the tension in my legs. That hurt!

Hiking down to Gorham was a breeze after that incident. We arrived during the midday. It was only a short seven-mile hike from our camp site. Upon arrival, we checked into the hostel. After a quick shower and a cold beer, it was time to relax for the rest of the day. Four southbounders arrived for a "quick stop." They had great pictures on their phones. Three of the four were brothers. For the length of time they had been on the trail they were doing great. They also had some awesome stories to share.

One of the brothers had gotten stung by a bee and another brother had carried his pack for miles. Now that is brotherly love. They stopped for a short time to resupply, then continued south. The time they were making was impressive, due no doubt to the young men being in great shape. It was fun meeting and sharing trail adventures with them.

That evening, all the hikers sat around a fire and drank a few beers. We each told tales from our past. Shenanigans told the tale of the guy I kicked out of Delaware Water Gap Hostel. He told a couple other stories of things that had happened on the trail as well. Then the host asked about my background. I told him I was a retired police officer.

I sat quietly and listened to the others tell their tales and hiking adventures. Alien took the lead in the conversations. He was more talkative than he had ever been. He had everyone laughing. He was a delight.

Morning came and we ate breakfast. This was to be a special day. This day, we would arrive in Maine, the final state in the Appalachian Trail. Prior to leaving the hostel, a section hiker arrived. He warned us that we needed to leave early. Being overconfident, we did not heed his warning. "You don't want to get to Carlo Col Shelter in the dark. There is a steep rock climb down that you really don't want to do in the dark." We scoffed, "It won't be a big deal. We made it this far. We can do it."

After a slow start and long good-byes, we were back on the trail headed to Maine. It was only sixteen miles away. We left the hostel around noon, and that was a bad idea. The trail was steep, but not too bad. We passed a pond that was huge. Then we passed by a lake that looked smaller than the pond. Then large rocks began blocking our path.

A huge descent down, over, and around giant boulders slowed our progress. The stones were moss covered and slippery. "Hey, this must be the spot that the section hiker was talking about. I wouldn't want to do this in the dark." I called out. We laughed at our difficulty. Not because it was funny but because the trail was almost impassable in the middle of the woods. Dusk was falling and we were still in the woods trying to stay on the trail.

We could barely see the trail as night overtook us. Our goal was to get to Carlo Col Shelter, so we kept on hiking. Then, in the deep darkness of night, we stumbled upon a large, white sign, "Maine." We each took our turn posing for the camera next to the sign. "Happy birthday, Olivia!" I yelled into the woods as soon as I officially reached Maine. "A man of his word," responded Alien. Not only were we in the state of Maine, but also in a state of jubilation. We had arrived. What next?

Should we remote camp, or head on for the shelter? We decided it was shelter or bust. It was only a half mile away. As we climbed higher and higher the woods turned into thin evergreens that grew in thick stands. Each tree was only a few inches from the others, forming a nearly impenetrable wall of evergreens. The trail narrowed as the trees closed in on us. There was no place to remote camp. We wouldn't be able to step off the trail if we wanted to!

We went to the top of a peak that had a large stone outcropping. We sat down and studied the map. Carlo Col Shelter should be only a couple hundred yards away, but the maps were often wrong. We could see the hillside across a deep crevice or ravine. The trail appeared to drop off the face of the earth. Clouds covered the moon, preventing any light that might have helped us.

We put on our lights, attached to straps, that we wore on our heads. The lights would help us find and see the trail. I sat on a ledge between two large stones sloping steeply downward. The light from my headlamp faded into nothing in the dark abyss below. There was no telling how far of a drop awaited me. If I fell, the rocks below could be slanted and I could break my legs. Worse even, if my pack hit a rock and pushed me forward, I could tumble head first over the stones and die.

This was a bad situation! We couldn't see where to go. We could not see what was below us. There wasn't any way to see how to get down. As far as we knew, we were on a cliff's ledge. This was bad. Alien suggested we go back a bit and remote camp, but there wasn't any place to set up our tents or sleeping bags. Then, accidently, I slid a couple of inches downward!

"Oh no! We are going down here!" I called out. There was no recovery to my slide and I wasn't going to risk my friends' lives by trying to get me back up to the ledge. "I'm going." And I slid off the ledge. My mind raced and I was hoping to not break a leg or ankle or anything.

My feet landed, oddly, but safely. The fall was only ten to twelve feet. My heart was pumping ninety miles an hour, not from working but from the anxiety of facing the risks. "I'm okay!" I turned to shine my light on the rock wall to guide the others to good footing and hand holds. Alien came first then Shenanigans followed.

Another ledge blocked our path. Risking my luck again, I tried the same method of falling and hoping for a safe landing. This was repeated again and again until we were all down on the lowest part of the pass. That section hiker was right. This was not a section of the hike we wanted to do in the dark, but we had made it. Barely!

Soon, we found the trail that led to Carlo Col Shelter. On shaking legs we hiked down to the shelter. It was packed, but a few tent sites were available. We set up our tents while wondering how we had made it over the cliffs. Before bed we had a quick meeting, ate snacks, and drank a shot of whiskey in celebration of our day. We were in Maine! We were safe! We had a place to sleep!

In the morning we were covered by heavy fog from a low cloud that brought a thick mist of rain. As we packed our tents and backpacks, several weekend hikers came over to our camp site. "We wanted to meet the hikers that came down those rocks in the dark," they said. Shenanigans smiled and replied, "Oh yes, we are legend." I laughed at his response. Shenanigans had a way of saying the oddest things.

Another Tough Day

WE INTENDED TO head out early that day because we were hiking the most notorious spot on the Appalachian Trail, Mahoosuc Notch. No one wants to attempt getting through there in the dark, not even us. It was only six miles away, but we wanted to be fresh to get through it.

We made it to Mahoosuc Notch early enough. The notch is a series of giant boulders. To get through the notch hikers usually takes about an hour. That may not seem untimely, but it was only a half-mile long. To be slowed down that much for a short section is something unique; the trail goes around boulders, over them, and under them, and so do the hikers.

The day heated up as we reached the notch. As we climbed down we were met by an instant drop in temperature. It was like walking into a walk-in cooler. The temperature dropped to thirty degrees. That was a far cry from the upper eighty degrees in the higher elevations. The boulders were huge. In several spots we took our packs off and passed them forward to each other. Our hiking poles were useless.

Down low, between the boulders, were large chunks of ice. This ice never melts. I chipped off a small piece and ate it. I don't know why, I guess I wanted to try ice that could be hundreds of years old. We climbed, crawled, and scurried around the boulders. Finding our way was like solving a large puzzle or going through a maze. Here, you boulder. There is no such thing as hiking through the Mahoosuc Notch.

At the end of the notch we heard water flowing under the boulders. I climbed down deeper between the boulders to reach the water. We needed to refill our water bottles. Shenanigans handed the bottles to me one at a time. As soon as they were full the bottles formed a mist around them. The water was near freezing, yet, thankfully, refreshing.

After Mahoosuc Notch, we faced a climb called the Mahoosuc Arm. The Arm was reportedly incredibly difficult. However, we found the Arm to be much easier, even though it was wet and slippery. The Arm and Notch took most of our day and all of our strength. The next campsite was Speck Pond, where we stopped for the night. The day was a complete adventure on its own and we enjoyed the challenge and fun of getting through Mahoosuc Notch and Arm.

We'd had enough hiking to last us for a while, even though the day took us only a whopping nine miles down the trail. It was a short hike, but we were pleased to have survived and made it this far. Speck Pond campsite was a pay site. There was a caretaker for Speck Pond. We paid to set up and called it a day. It was a tough day for all of us.

The maps showed we were facing a steep three-hundred-foot elevation climb, followed by a drop of twenty-five hundred feet. After the descent into Grafton Notch, we were facing another steep 2,550-foot climb. The short miles had hurt our average and we needed to finish by September first. Our plan was to get up early and make big, long miles—climbs and all.

We did get up early, and we were off. The hike was going well. It was still morning and we had already descended into Grafton Notch. We stopped to eat snacks and prepared for more climbing. Our climb was up Baldpate, a long climb. Then, the skies turned ominously dark. Rain started falling as we started up Baldpate.

After hiking two miles more into the woods, the rain started falling harder. And rain it did. Buckets of rain came down as we approached the steepest part of our climb for the day. Luckily, there was a shelter in the woods. We hid from the onslaught of the downpour. Stuck in the shelter, hoping to stay dry, we waited several hours.

Other hikers arrived at the shelter during the pouring rain. As one hiker came into sight, everyone jumped up in anticipation of meeting an old friend. Chicago walked into the shelter. Months ago he had left the trail and gone home. Now, he was back on the trail going southbound. He and the other hikers warned us about the trail ahead. It was weird seeing Chicago again. I had first met him in Hot Springs, North Carolina, during breakfast. Alien and Shenanigans knew him well and were both delighted to meet him again.

Around two o'clock the rain stopped, but the wind continued and clouds were still all around. We said our good-byes and good lucks then moved on. Our climb was steep and the rocks still slippery. Slippery rocks were common, but the waterfalls now forming on the rocks were not so common. It was as if we were hiking up a creek without a paddle. And the actual creeks we crossed were swollen, making them difficult to cross.

I arrived first at the top of our highest peak for the day, Baldpate. The trail up was nothing more than a giant rock slab, tilted at an angle that made climbing difficult, even on a dry day. One slip and you found yourself sliding down a waterslide, getting soaking wet and hurt. Then you had to try climbing up again, hoping not to fall again. To make matters worse, the clouds were thick and we were in the middle of them. Visibility was twenty feet at best, at times even less. Finding the trail on a giant flat rock was nearly impossible, but we did it! The trail was marked by cairns, large rock piles. Most of these were more than twenty-feet apart, allowing the trail to disappear. Walking too far the wrong way off a cliff could be the result.

After reaching the top of Baldpate, I waited for Alien and Shenanigans, hoping they had kept on the trail. The wind blew more clouds and moisture all around. As the wind howled by, I crouched low behind the rock pile marking the summit. I used the pile as protection from the shearing wind.

My body heat was lowering at an alarming rate. In my current condition I knew I could wait for only ten to fifteen minutes. I recorded the event on my camera.

After thirteen minutes, I saw a shadow moving through the fog. Shenanigans was making his way up to the summit. He had fallen hard and broken one of his hiking poles. It had snapped in half during his fall. Then, a second shadow appeared, Alien. This was great; we were together again. Quickly, I put my pack back on when they arrived and over the hill we went. The way down was no easy task. We were soaked to the bone and the wind was causing great loss of body heat for all of us. Trying to hike faster to get warm was not an option; the way was too steep, too slippery, and too dangerous.

Our goal now was simply to get to the tree line for protection from the winds. Heading down, we were met by waterfalls like the ones we had encountered hiking up. Water was everywhere. At one point, I thought I might see two giraffes, two hippos, and two monkeys come marching by in pairs! The rain had stopped but its results were still with us. There was no trail, only a small, fast moving stream, pushing us around as we sloshed downhill.

The tree line was a wonderful sight. It provided some protection, but was limited. We decided we needed to get out of the woods. The next road showed a hostel fairly close but too far to hike. We needed to get a ride, perhaps by the shuttle service offered by the hostel. I called the hostel to arrange for the shuttle. It stopped running at seven o'clock; our estimated arrival time was half past eight. We agreed with the hostel's host to be at the road by eight o'clock. That gave us just two hours to hike six miles. This was going to require running and pain.

We stumbled and tumbled down the mountain, splashing into swollen creeks, ignoring the pain, as we ran through the woods like fugitives with dogs hot on our trail. Time was short and the trail was not friendly; we slipped and slid, we kicked and ran. My heart beat like a drum out of sync; my breath was hard to control. Cold was no longer a factor. We wanted to be out of the woods and into a hot shower, then warm and dry. We needed shelter and that required speed and getting to the road on time.

As we got to lower elevations the rushing water still followed. There was no escape from the flooding. But all that didn't matter, because we were going to be dry soon. The youngest in our small band, Shenanigans, arrived at the road first. He made the descent fifteen minutes quicker than the other two of us. Hey, he was young, just twenty-seven years old. Alien and I arrived two minutes before eight. We had done it. We had made it. It was one hell of a run. Exhaustion took over as I lay on the road waiting for my breathing to slow down. This had been one tough day.

After arriving in town via the shuttle, we went to a small store that doubled as a local fryer. I got the large double-bacon cheeseburger. Calories—and lots of them—were needed by all of us. While waiting for our food orders to be cooked, we walked through the store. As we passed through the aisles of food, we ate. Passing the chips, I grabbed a can of Pringles and ate them. Next, I went to the candy bar section and downed three Snickers. After a quick trip to the cooler, I chugged a Gatorade and started on a large Mountain Dew. Our dinner orders were ready, so we went to the register with our empty wrappers and bottles to pay for the appetizers we ate. Then we sat down to eat our meals. After filling ourselves, we walked to the hostel and took our showers, did laundry, and were ready to sleep.

Before calling it a night, we met and talked with another hiker. He had gone over Baldpate before us. Alien said that climb had scared him. The other hiker scoffed at Alien's comment and claimed the hike over Baldpate was a "piece of cake." His arrogance just didn't serve any good purpose. Beyond his making little of our day's accomplishments, he may have crushed Alien's confidence.

We calculated it would take seventeen miles each day on average to finish the hike by September first. Completing those short, difficult miles the previous day had seriously delayed our targeted finish date. Still wanting to make a run for it, we packed, ate breakfast, and loaded the SUV, ready to be taken back to the trail. We hoped to get at least twenty-three miles in by the end of the day. It would be a long hike, but the weather was friendlier, which was a good thing! "We are legend," as Shenanigans would say.

Losing a Friend

WE WERE NOT going to make twenty-three miles that day. The trail had different plans for us. As we headed up the first steep incline we were forced to take a detour. Landslides had closed the main trail. The new route went to higher elevations and was steeper than the older trail. It also added miles to our hike. Energy reserves were being depleted rapidly from our tired legs.

I stopped at a shelter for a quick snack. Alien and Shenanigans were somewhere behind me. The hiker who claimed Baldpate was an easy climb was already at this shelter. He was an odd sort, a tall, thin young man. Before I arrived, he had changed into a black mini skirt.

A spring was close to the shelter, so we went to get water. While hiking to the spring I let him know he was wrong to contradict Alien's statement about how difficult the hike over Baldpate was. I told him others would think less of him for making those comments. Everyone hikes his own hike. Some folks have little-to-no-experience in the woods and each climb is an accomplishment. To belittle or diminish someone's effort was outright rude. Seeing his mistake, he politely recanted and apologized.

Alien arrived at the shelter in time for lunch. The other hiker had moved on before Alien's arrival. I loaded my pack and was ready to go as Shenanigans arrived. We made a quick plan where we would meet again and I left. Shenanigans and Alien could always catch up with me easily, so I tried to get a head start.

The trail proved more difficult than we expected. I stopped for dinner and Shenanigans and Alien arrived soon after. We studied the map, making plans for how far we could go the rest of the evening. The detour had added miles, ruining our plan for big miles that day.

Unable to make our big miles, we decided to remote camp that evening. I hiked ahead looking for a suitable location to set up three tents. For mile after mile, nothing was available. Then, I found a trail that went off to the right. Hidden inside the thick woods was an opening with a nice, level clearing. Another hiker was already setting up his tent. Being considerate, I asked if there was room for three more tents. He sharply said, "No." He obviously wasn't a thru-hiker.

Another couple miles later the woods opened up enough for three tents. There was just enough room for our tents to be set up close to each other. Another spot not too far away would have been better, but someone had "soiled" the ground surface and contaminated the site. We were fine where we were. We had gone only sixteen miles, but that was okay for now.

Alien was not as happy as he had been. The hike over Baldpate had emotionally drained him, and rightfully so. It had been a dangerous situation and we were lucky to be past it. Normally, Baldpate might not be such a challenge, but because of the weather when we hiked through it had been as rough as it could be. Additionally, the run to meet the shuttle for the hostel took more out of us than we cared to admit.

Our bodies were both emotionally and physically drained. We were not recovering well. The hike had become more of a chore and less about enjoyment. The need to meet a completion date was another demand making the hike more difficult. Alien was showing signs of being tired. His energy and motivational levels were getting low. He said he was going to quit hiking. That was a bad idea! We tried talking with him to change his mind. That evening we went to sleep early.

Rangeley was the next town. The road to it was twenty miles away. That was our new goal. When morning arrived we were greeted by great weather. Maps indicated there were no rough climbs or difficult trails ahead. Miles went by rapidly. Then, in the middle of the woods was a large street sign: "Detour Ahead." Then, another sign showed up on the trail, "Warning: Blasting Zone." The trail skirted around the area where a road was being built.

I crossed the road under construction several minutes ahead of Alien and Shenanigans. Alien reached the road next. He flagged down a van. Shenanigans exited the woods as Alien was just about to get into the van. Shenanigans stopped him. Alien was attempting to leave the trail, forever. After his escape was stopped, Alien managed to Yogi a bottle of Gatorade from the occupants of the van. However, Alien had made up his mind; he was getting off the trail.

Four miles later I spotted a large bull moose eating weeds in a pond. He was huge, but most bull moose are huge! I paused several minutes taking pictures and video, hoping Alien and Shenanigans would catch up to see the moose. They never made it and the moose walked off into the woods.

A short distance later I stopped at a pond with a sandy beach. I took off my pack and had a swim in the pond. The water wasn't deep; the shallows extended about a hundred yards out. The swim was refreshing as I waited for Shenanigans and Alien. They arrived about a half hour later. They did get to see the moose also. That was good news.

Alien again announced he was finished hiking the trail. We discussed it for a few minutes, hoping to talk him out of quitting. He was adamant about stopping. Seeing there was no changing his mind about getting off the trail, the only thing left was to support his decision. We decided to go to Rangeley and there we would take a zero to see him off properly.

Rangeley had a hotel with a price that was excellent for thru-hikers. But, before we got a room, we hit a pizza place for food and beer—lots of beer. We had a bond, the three of us. Seeing Alien leave wasn't going to be easy. In the back of our minds, Shenanigans and I both hoped he would stay on the trail. The hike would never be the same without him.

During our zero day, we rented kayaks to go out on the lake. We floated around for over an hour. Next, we had fun walking around, doing laundry, and eating at as many different restaurants as possible. It was a relaxing send-off for Alien, who was going to be sorely missed. Of all the trials and tribulations I had endured on the trail, I hated losing Alien the most. But he was doing what he felt was right for him and that was how it was to be.

Alien arranged a ride to another town and from there was set to get back to New York City. Shenanigans and I were set to resume our hike. Since Alien was off the trail, Shenanigans was going to use Alien's hiking poles. Shenanigans had broken a pole and none of the outfitters had new poles for him.

Once back on the trail, Shenanigans and I were hiking slower, feeling the loss of our dear friend, Alien. But we were determined to finish our hike. We were closing in on the two thousand mile marker. We were in Maine, within reach of a finish, our bodies spent but still hiking.

Saddle Back Mountain was just ahead. We looked up and climbed to what we thought was the summit. Once at the peak, we were faced with the reality that we had to go higher to what looked to actually be the summit. Then, once we reached that "summit" we could see there was yet another, higher climb. We climbed higher and higher until the summit was beneath our feet.

Just ahead was a climb down, followed by another climb up. The trail was void of trees. We pushed on, speaking little. It was a somber time for reflection. We thought about our time hiking with Alien. I wondered how Deb was doing and about where my friend Cargo might be.

Just before dark we reached Spaulding Mountain Lean-to. We had hiked a solid eighteen miles. It was a good day. The hike wasn't easy, but the miles went by without incident. Big mountains were ahead of us.

A fire was smoldering in the fire pit at the shelter. As I entered the shelter area, I remarked, "Hey, a fire." A female's voice came from the shelter, "Leave it alone and let it go out." I thought, *who the heck was ordering me not to get warm by a fire?* Shenanigans arrived and saw the smoldering fire as well and had the same idea, "Let's start the fire and get warm."

I remarked loudly so the female could hear me. "Oh no, we aren't allowed to have a fire." I said, as I threw wood into the fire pit. Shenanigans laughed at me for being silly and admonished me with a single word, "Mingo!" Soon, the fire was burning high; the heat was needed. We found a tent site close by.

Below the campsite was a stream. I went to get water. While there, two college students, a guy and gal from Harvard, walked into the creek upstream from me. They were no more than a few feet away from me, muddying the water I was collecting. Their rude behavior and lack of respect angered me. The guy made a comment to me, bragging about how he was from Harvard—as if that gave him special permission to ignore common courtesy. The girl expressed her superiority over me by stating how dirty I looked. Actually. she called me "nasty looking."

I had seen this couple for only a few seconds, but they were really pushing my buttons. I wasn't going to say anything to them, but now they had pushed too far. In my "Mingo" format, I quipped back, "Oh, you must be from Harvard, because all the cute chicks go to Dartmouth." I hoped they would respond. They didn't. I smiled inwardly at my own true wit. Maybe they got smarter and got the message!

The rest of the night went by without event. We slept and awoke early to head off for a good eighteen-mile day with steep climbs. The day promised rain, but it was a light rain.

We were headed to Horns Pond Lean-to. The caretaker at Horns Pond was a young man who had done a thru-hike before. Jonathan was his name. He was a super kind guy. We settled in to spend the night and set up alone in one of two shelters. Jonathan explained that a group of college students were due to arrive later but would stay in another shelter building. They were from Dartmouth.

At the shelter, Shenanigans briefly read the journal. He then went to the privy. I also read the journal. There was an entry from a section hiker. The section hiker wrote a full page of rhetoric that was kind of preachy. It was difficult to continue reading the long passage about how God had served them. At the end of the journal entry the hiker noted they had left trail magic in the large box used to keep animals from food. I quickly went to the box. Eureka! Candy bars and snacks were nestled in the box. I left it there untouched and waited for Shenanigans. He returned to the shelter.

"Hey, Shenanigans, did you read the journal?" I asked. "Yeah, I looked at it." I quickly instructed, "Oh no! Read it." He looked at me as I sat there, looking pensive. He knew I was up to something, so he quickly consented to read. Then, as Shenanigans got to the end of the entry, he looked up like a kid opening a Christmas present. "Is it still there? Did you look?" he asked. I smiled, "Oh, yes!" We retrieved the magic and split it up between the two of us. It was wonderful receiving trail magic where no magic was expected to exist.

Low clouds hid the next day's climb, Bigelow Mountain, from our view. We went over to the site manager's tent to hang out with Jonathan. He fixed food for us and shared fresh bread. Again, he was a super kind man and we really enjoyed talking with him. He asked if we saw the dead moose in the water at Mahoosuc Notch. We said, "No." But, we did drink the water.

Wind and rain lowered the temperature that evening. The night air was as cold as it could be. I remembered a lesson Cargo had taught me about staying warm. I put my tent inside my sleeping bag to add an extra layer of thermal protection. The trick worked.

Up late the next morning, we were pleased the day was drier than the previous one. I hiked ahead and kept a good, fast pace. From time to time I stopped for snacks and rehydrating. Each time I stopped, Shenanigans would catch up and we would take pictures and discuss our hike. We both missed Alien.

The Rubber Chicken Rescue

AT THE BOTTOM of Bigelow Mountain I met two hikers hiking south-bound, sobo. The guy said he recognized me. He looked familiar to me also. I told him my name was Mingo. He told me his name, but I didn't recognize it. They were doing a flip-flop. That means they had started down south and hiked north then jumped north to Katahdin and started southbound.

"Hey, when I started I was called Hooker," I said. "Hey, Hooker! I remember you. I was called Thigh Master. I gave you the moonshine in the Smoky Mountains." I certainly remembered Thigh Master. We talked about our hikes until Shenanigans arrived and he knew them, too. It was good seeing Thigh Master again, but sadly, he didn't have moonshine this time! That would have been totally awesome. It was still pretty darn cool

meeting him again.

Two miles later, Shenanigans and I were still hiking together when we arrived at a road. In the middle of the road was painted "2,000 mile con-grats!" We took turns tak-ing each other's pictures lying on the road by the numbers. We had hiked, run, crawled, and slid two thousand miles and only had one hundred eighty-one miles to go. It was exhilarating to acknowledge we had reached this mile marker!

Back into the woods we hiked talking about a variety of things. Soon, I was a few yards ahead of Shenanigans as we started up a hill. Shenanigans yelled, "Shit! Oh shit!" I quickly turned around, expecting to see him with a twisted ankle, as he sounded as if he were in pain. He was still on his feet, hiking rapidly toward me. "Are you okay?" I asked. "No!" he responded.

Shenanigans had been stung several times by a swarm of bees. To make things worse, he was stung once in the face. Shenanigans was in pain. To keep track of the swelling we began taking pictures of his face around the sting area. Three miles later we opted 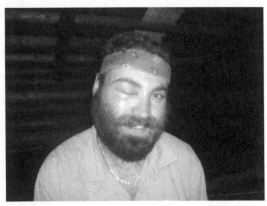 to stop and camp for the night at West Carry Pond Lean-to. It was apparent Shenanigans was allergic to the bee stings. His face was really swelling.

The next morning I awoke early, as usual. "Shenanigans, are you ready to go?" I shook his tent. "No, Mingo, go without me," he softly answered. "Are you okay?" I asked. "Just go! I can't open my eye." There was no way I was going to leave Shenanigans alone in the woods with a swollen face and only one good eye. He had helped me when I had lost motivation; I refused to leave and decided to let him rest a while longer.

While waiting, I mapped out a new hiking plan for Shenanigans. Typically, we could have hiked three miles or more every hour. I marked my map to hike only two miles each hour, and then marked the locations with our planned arrival times. There were no major climbs, not even a thousand-foot elevation increase. We were in luck; at least some luck.

If we started at eight thirty and hiked an easy pace of two miles an hour we would reach a road by four in the afternoon; then, we could hitch a ride to Northern Outdoors, an outdoor resort. Once there we could get ice for his face and have a warm, dry place to stay. That was my plan and I was willing to help in any way needed, but I wasn't going to leave Shenanigans alone.

At nine thirty we stopped for a short break. We had made the two miles as planned. My concern was that the swelling would get worse because blood was pumping harder from his exercise. Shenanigans needed rest, but more importantly, we needed to make it to civilization. The pace we set allowed us to stop each hour for a short break.

The next rest stop at ten thirty was at East Carry Pond. While standing along the trail giving Shenanigans a rest, I looked at a stump along the trail. Inside the stump was a rubber chicken. Shuffle's rubber chicken, Sheng Wei, was sitting alone in the tree stump. It seemed odd she would leave her beloved Sheng Wei. I took the chicken and secured her to my pack. Shuffle would want her chicken back.

Each hour we dutifully hiked the planned two miles. After each hour, we stopped for a short break. The hours passed. We were making our schedule as planned. At one thirty in the afternoon we were taking our break at Pierce Pond Lean-to. Shuffle had left a note in the journal. She had lost her Sheng Wei and was offering a reward for her return. She sounded heartbroken and I was certainly happy to help get her chicken back to her. I was rescuing a rubber chicken! That is something I would have never guessed I would get to do when I started hiking the trail.

Toward the end of our hike to the road we came to a river. We waited on the banks of the river for a boatman to row a canoe over to us. After loading the gear into the canoe, I helped row us across the river. At four o'clock we made it to the road at Caratunk. There was reportedly a box at the post office that held trail magic. We didn't go for the magic. We needed a place for Shenanigans to rest. Even though he was strong and was holding up well, he needed to get ice on his eye, which was swollen shut.

We walked several miles along the road. The traffic was scarce and when a car did pass they refused to offer a ride. Shenanigans and I were making our way slowly to Northern Outdoors. Northern Outdoors is a resort-type place that had cabins. They have tent sites as well, but we wanted a cabin. Finally, a vehicle stopped and the driver was going to Northern Outdoors. The driver was shocked at the sight of Shenanigans. His face was severely swollen.

While checking in at Northern Outdoors we were told there were no more cabins available. As we stood there, our hopes dashed, the lady behind the counter said, "Wait, there were a couple of hikers that said if other hikers came in they would share their cabin for help with the cost. Are you interested?" Oh yes, we were interested! We went to talk with the hikers about sharing the cabin. They were superb and were section hikers.

The next order of business was to get a resupply. We were told about a place called Berry's. The lady who checked us in offered us a ride after she got off work. We sat and waited. After a longer than expected wait, she came and got us. She drove us directly to Berry's.

Berry's is a gas station and grocery store. They had limited items but they had enough. I collected food as carefully as possible. We bought beer for the guys who were sharing the cabin. I bought a half-pint of whiskey for the trail. Shenanigans paid for his food first, then I paid for mine. We bought about the same amount of food and supplies. Then, we headed to the road to hitchhike back.

While standing on the side of the road I commented about how expensive the food was in Berry's. Shenanigan's agreed. Shenanigan's bill was half the cost I had paid. We discovered that after Shenanigans had paid for his food the store clerk did not clear the register and had charged me for his food again, along with my food. Shenanigans paid seventy dollars and I paid one hundred fifty dollars.

I was about to go back inside, but a couple pulled up in a car and offered us a ride back to Northern Outdoors. My guess was the clerk did not try to cheat me. It was an honest mistake. I let the overcharge go, since we had a ride back. It was way too hard to get a ride here. That was one expensive mistake, and a lesson learned.

Back at the cabin we showered and cleaned our gear. There was a kitchen in the cabin. A large cooking pot was under the sink. I put the large pot on the stove and stuffed Sheng Wei into the pot. Using my phone, I took a picture of poor Sheng Wei in the pot and sent it to Shuffle. Shuffle's

response was legendary, threatening to cook me in a pot. It was good we were out of her reach; we laughed. Shuffle was happy Sheng Wei had been found.

The other hikers in the cabin took the upstairs area and we had the downstairs. We scattered our gear throughout to dry the tents, clothes, and sleeping bags. The inside of the cabin looked like a hobo laundry. Gear was scattered and hanging everywhere.

By the next morning we had a few beers left. I decided to sneak two beers into my pack. I planned to give Shenanigans a beer at the next shelter. There is nothing better than a beer at a shelter to end a long day's hike. I stuffed the beers in the bottom of my pack. The secret surprise was ready, and after being stung in the face, Shenanigans could use a shelter-beer.

A pickup truck came to take us back to the trail. We tossed our packs in the back and hopped in for the ride. Being driven back to the trail was a service Northern Outdoors offered for free. That was kind of them, and was really appreciated.

Upon arrival at the trail, we unloaded the packs and prepared for another long day of hiking. The beginning of the hike was uphill. I started out first. I wasn't ten minutes into the hike when I realized something was wrong. A cold burning sensation was running down my backside. My butt was wet and the smell of beer was filling the air.

Shenanigans stopped as I was taking off my pack. I opened the bottom of the pack and pulled out the spraying can of beer. He laughed until I told him it was for him at the next shelter. Sadly, the beer was gone! Slyly, I hid the unbroken beer can deeper into my pack, covering it with my sleeping bag, hoping it would not burst also. We moved on. The beer chaffed me with each step. And here I was, clean when I started, but now I smelled like a bar stool after midnight.

We shared the surviving beer at the next shelter during lunch. It would have been nice to have one each, but things just don't always work out as planned. However, we were doing well and were on time. Our goal was to summit Katahdin on the first of September. We missed our friend, Alien. Most importantly, though, we were still on the trail. It would have been better not to have beer down my backside. By the way, if you hike, try not to get beer butt. That burns! First, I had monkey butt in Virginia, and now, I had beer butt in Maine.

Hiking in bad weather day after day had been difficult. Finishing brings a new set of emotions and challenges. Total exhaustion was setting in. Not many hikers quit close to completing their hike; our bodies were simply wearing out. Eating the high number of calories needed by our systems for this long was difficult. But, we still had a hundred and fifty miles to go; we kept on hiking.

The swelling was going down in Shenanigans' face. He could see out of his eye again, but he still looked awful. Even with a bad case of beer butt, I made it to Moxie Bald Lean-to. It was a good nineteen-mile hike. The site was pleasant. There were a few section hikers there, but they were far enough away not to be a bother. We found a flat spot near the Bald Mountain Pond with a great view. As Shenanigans began clearing some fallen limbs for his tent, he noticed a large bee's nest among the limbs. The bees were beginning to get agitated, as he had disturbed the limbs around them. We found another spot farther away. He didn't need to be stung again, and that had been a close call.

Shaky

UP EARLY THE next morning we were off with a little more pep in our step. Shenanigans' swelling was going down. The day's hike was mostly level, with hardly an incline at all. We made great time hiking quickly through the woods. Then, my right foot slid on a slippery rock and I fell, landing solidly on my butt. The shock wave hurt my back again. This was the same pain I had felt when I went through my several days of hell. Then, just as we were so close to our destination, Monson Maine, the rain started again. It rains in Maine!

I called the Lakeshore House and scheduled a ride to pick us up once we reached the road. It was an easy fifteen-mile hike for the day. At the Lakeshore House Hostel we did all of our laundry. The hostel was on the second floor of a two-story building. They have spare clothes for hikers to use while doing their laundry. That was an unexpected surprise.

Down the road was a store and gas station where we could resupply our food. I checked my food bag and it was still pretty full, but I bought enough food to top it off. Downstairs at the hostel was a restaurant. We met another thru-hiker, Shaky, who joined us for dinner. He was a fun sort. He had a full, thick beard, which looked like Dutch's. He sort of looked like Dutch. We easily became friends.

The next part of the trail was called the Hundred-Mile Wilderness. It was one hundred miles with no roads for access, and one of the most remote places in the lower forty-eight states. I weighed my food bag carefully and was certain I had all the food I needed. It is recommended a hiker carry ten days' worth of food out to the wilderness. I suspected I had a good four to five days' food supply.

I woke up at the hostel with a serious sinus infection. Throughout the night I was restless, and my back was getting sorer as time went on. I was not in a physical condition for a good, long hike. This was the most miserable I had felt in a long time. To make matters worse, I had twisted my left ankle and it had swollen. My knees had seen better days and were swelling also.

Meeting Irene

SHENANIGANS, SHAKY, AND I went out in the morning for breakfast at the local gas station. After some coffee and a sandwich we were shuttled back to the trail. Let the fun begin! Despite my poor condition, we set out for the trail. A sign warned hikers about the rigors of the Hundred-Mile Wilderness. We scoffed at the sign. We stopped for water at a creek, and then hiked on. The day started with a light shower but had cleared. The air still held a chill from the morning rain and a light breeze kept finding its way through the trees. Periodically, the sky would shine bright blue as sunrays stabbed through the clouds.

We were only a few miles or so into the wilderness when we met several day hikers. Three ladies were sitting by the trail and asked us if we had a first-aid kit. Well, we didn't carry kits, but we had all that was needed in a pinch. The ladies claimed they needed an ace bandage or tape. I had tape—a small amount of duct tape wrapped around one hiking pole. My tape was to make bandages, to cover blisters, to fasten down toe nails that are just hanging on, to patch gear, and any other need as it arose.

The ladies were so excited I had duct tape. I showed them the small amount wrapped around the hiking pole. Their faces went from elation to despair. I asked to see the wound where the tape was needed. To my surprise, one lady held her foot up for me to see that the sole on her eight-dollar bargain brand shoe had come loose and was flapping like a hound dog's tongue. "That's it? That's the big emergency?" we all exclaimed.

They had less than a mile to hike to the parking lot. Their hike was on a smooth surface that seemed to be wheelchair accessible. Even if she went barefoot she would be better off than us by the end of the night. We could not believe they were asking thru-hikers to give up their medical supplies for a shoe repair when they were that close to their car.

I quickly rescinded my offer. My two friends explained what we have is what we need to just keep us alive. We don't carry extra or miscellaneous junk for two thousand miles just in case a shoe sole comes loose. The ladies were not pleased with us, but we had our priorities. If she had been wounded I would not have hesitated to help and give all I had, but, lady, please!

We encountered a couple hills that surprised us by their difficulty. Hills or no hills, we were making good progress. To our surprise, we came across more day hikers than ever before. I thought this was the wilderness? Shenanigans got stung by a bee again, this time on his hand.

We stopped at Cloud Pond Lean-to. A couple there asked if the rubber chicken was mine. My throat being sore and my spirits low, I looked at the hiker and answered plainly, "No." Shenanigans explained it more politely. I wasn't in any mood to be nice or to talk. We camped that night and started early the next morning.

We were hoping to make it over White Cap, but didn't make it. We stopped just before White Cap at Carl A Newhall Lean-to. I felt like crap. My sinus infection had moved to my ears and that really hurt my balance and enthusiasm. A sobo, southbound hiker, stopped at our site and we talked about the weather. The last he had heard, three feet of water was coming our way in the form of heavy rain. We asked about the fords. High water plus fords equals trouble. Big trouble was a coming and her name was Hurricane Irene.

We decided we needed a contingency plan in case the fords were not passable. We might need to wait a day or two after the hurricane before continuing forward. That was no problem. We inventoried our food supplies and planned to eat less, just in case. I dumped my food out to make an accurate plan. My jaw dropped, my heart missed a beat, and my mind went spinning. I remained silent to hide the dismal condition in which I found myself.

When I had weighed my food bag before the resupply, I had forgotten one thing—I didn't take the trash out of my bag first. I weighed the trash as if it were food. Now, I found I had a new problem, a new set of circumstances to deal with, and I needed to make big decisions fast.

The circumstances were simple. I had a sinus infection that was getting worse with no medication. Next, my back was giving me fits. Oftentimes I could not get my right foot in front of the left. I was hiking like Igor. "Yes, Master, Igor is good servant," I would say to myself. I dragged my foot through the wilderness with pain shooting down my right leg. My left ankle was still swollen, but less so. I walked slower to keep from twisting it again. And now, I had screwed up the resupply like a rookie hiker. I was down to a half bottle of whiskey, a tube of toothpaste, and two zip lock bags of powdered Gatorade. Oh! And a massive hurricane was closing in on us. The hurricane was certain to flood the fords we needed to cross. My shoes were shredded, and my gear was getting damp—which was not good for down-filled bags. Distance wise, I was thirty-six plus miles into the wilderness.

Those combined circumstances could prove to be rough. I had a couple of choices. I could turn back now and try again later. Not! I do not retreat well. The next choice was try to make it all the way through. That would be rough, but possible. The third choice was hike to White House Landing Hostel and pay high prices for a resupply.

The hostel was forty-five miles from the end of the wilderness. Hikers had to walk a mile off the trail to a lake where they would find an air horn hanging on a tree, which they had to blow just once. The owner of the hostel would come out in his boat to pick you up and take you across the lake. Once across the lake, the hostel has items you can buy for a resupply. The items are at premium prices to cover the costs of getting the supplies there in the first place. That is fair. Plus, when you are down to one half bottle of whiskey, a tube of toothpaste, and powdered Gatorade, any price is fine!

Going to the hostel seemed to be the best option. It was only a mile off course, but would change the speed at which we hiked. Things were going to get a little tougher, so we would need to hurry. I had to inform my two hiking buddies of the dismal shape I was in at that time. They had a good laugh on me! Our goal was reset. We were headed to White House

Landing Hostel. But, Hurricane Irene was going to hit us first. I needed to survive two days on my sorry rations. No problem!

It was 4:42 a.m. when the rain came. Our plan was to get up at five, leave at six, and hike fast and hard. We stuck to our plan. The rain came down violently and kept on coming. Often, we would stop to see the scenes and take pictures, but not this day. Well, there was one exception. While hiking up White Cap, I saw a cow moose grazing in a pond in the heavy rain. We stopped, tried to take pictures, and hiked on. We climbed higher and higher.

At the top of White Cap there were no trees; it's an Alpine Zone. Shaky slipped on a bog bridge and fell in. He went waist-deep into the bog before he caught himself by grabbing the boardwalk. He never hit bottom! The bogs can be well over one's head. Falling in was always dangerous. Shenanigans got a great picture right when Shaky hit the water. The timing was both accidental and perfect. Shaky climbed out of the bog, covered in mud.

The rain continued as we expected, growing even stronger. We had to be the only three hikers on the Appalachian Trail hiking that day. The first shelter we reached was being used by thru-hikers hiding from the rain, the smart ones. We pushed forward. Water lay in puddles on the trail and  they grew deeper and wider. The fords were not an issue yet, not as much as we thought they would have been. Flash floods were a growing concern. The trail, as it passed around ponds and swamps, became the issue. The water levels swelled over the trail, and the rain kept coming.

A hiker had died a week earlier somewhere up here. It was believed he had fallen and hit his head. That's not too hard to believe. I had fallen several times and left my share of blood on the trail. We all had. Hiking the Appalachian Trail might sound like a simple walk in the woods, but it was not. Another hiker was crossing a stream a couple of days earlier, fell, and went down to her neck. She quit. We had already crossed that river. The water was cold and the rapids were fast. She was lucky.

My sinuses, ears, and now my throat were hurting and I developed a bad cough. The cough was at times uncontrollable and would gag me. Leading the way, I tried to stay well ahead of my hiking friends. My thought was not to make them suffer by seeing me suffer. Besides, this was kind of fun. Well, "fun" may have been the wrong word.

We hiked nineteen miles in high water and rain. Much of the hike was through waist-deep to knee-deep water, splashing water with each step. We made it to Cooper Brook Falls Lean-to. Freight Train and Plan B were in the shelter. We stopped, soaked and worn out.

I had once promised Freight Train I would never make her stay in a shelter with me again. The last time I ran her out of the shelter with my loud snoring she had to set up her tent in the rain to get away from me. But now, the situation required a need to break that promise.

While talking with Freight Train and Plan B, it was decided we would all hike to White House Landing the next day. Our goal was get up early and hike fast and hard to get to the air horn in time for lunch. Lunch was between eleven and one o'clock. We had to make big miles quickly. There would be no stopping for water crossings and trying to keep dry. We would just push straight through any water obstacle. I was already soaked and badly chafed, but food, hot food, was calling me.

The pain was almost unbearable. I could not sleep. Sitting up hurt my back. Trying to lie down hurt my ankle and constricted my breathing. There wasn't any position that brought relief. Then, I was offered some relief from the pain. The offer came by way of a "medication." It was common to take someone else's pain pill or some type of antibiotic to relieve pain and illness. But what I was being offered was different. This "medication" was legalized as a medication in some states, including Maine, and is smoked. I had watched Montel Williams talk about it with Dr. Oz.

Suffering beyond my tolerance level caused me to make a decision to accept the help. After only two tokes, my back stopped hurting. I could breathe without pain and was able to swallow. I drank a copious amount of water before lying down. As I relaxed, I reveled in being pain free for the first time in a long time.

The next morning I felt well rested. That was the first time I had been able to sleep the entire night through without waking up because of my tossing and turning. It was my best night of sleep ever. Legalize the stuff already. Make it legal and easier for those in pain to find relief. I swear it worked wonders for me. I don't think I would have survived to see the next day without it.

Morning came and I needed breakfast. I swiped my index finger with toothpaste and dipped it into the powdered Gatorade to eat it like a pixie stick. After several dips into the powder, it became sour in my mouth. I drank some of the whiskey to wash out my taste buds, and then repeated the pixie stick process again. Drinking lots of water filled my stomach and I was ready to go. I started packing as the others were waking up.

We had only fourteen miles to go to White House Landing. Shortly after starting, we saw a cow moose with her calf. We took a short break to stand and enjoy watching the moose. The torrential downpour had eased to a heavy shower. Then, we were off again. We hurried to make it on time for lunch. Freight Train and Plan B were lagging behind us. We made it to the air horn to signal the hostel. Freight Train and Plan B caught up to us as the boat was just approaching to take us across the lake. Lunch was still available! At White House Landing the food was great, the beds were dry, and of course, the weather cleared.

Freight Train and Plan B decided to spend the night at the hostel as well. Getting dry and sleeping in a warm bed was what I needed. My throat and ears were feeling much better. My ankle was no longer swollen and my back stopped hurting as much.

White House Landing was an interesting and picturesque place. The buildings were scattered throughout the property. They were small wooden buildings and had everything hikers needed. The lawn was fresh mowed and well groomed. The lake water was clear and reflected as a mirror to the sky. White House Landing was a paradise in Maine.

The owner seemed less than thrilled with thru-hikers. He particularly disliked hikers who didn't have money. He was a nice guy, and his wife was polite, but he was not shy about expressing his feelings about hikers wanting his services for free. His hostel was more for tourists and naturalists and to be fair it was a business not a charity. He had an idea to raise his rates "to keep the hikers out." I was not thrilled with that idea.

I bought more than enough food to finish the trail, and we ate tons of food there. The owner prepared our meals and did a great job. He wanted to sell the hostel and I certainly would have liked to have bought it, but the price wasn't agreeable to me. I loved the place. I would love to own it. But then, I would not enjoy having a business tie me down. Others see owning a business differently. That kind of person should own White House Landing. Most anyone would love the place.

Katahdin

THE MORNING AT White House Landing brought about new plans. We were forty-five miles from Katahdin and before that was Abol Bridge. That was close. My knees were fit. All chaffing was gone. My throat was clear. My ears were no longer infected. My ankle was no longer swollen. My back didn't hurt. I was physically ready to finish my hike. Deb would be waiting in two days at Abol Bridge. Shenanigans would have Fancy Pants, his fiancé, waiting for him there as well.

We were taken by boat back across the lake to the trail. We needed to hike only a short distance and it would all be over. Only two days more! The rest of the trail was an easy path. That night we stopped early and camped. We wanted to be fresh when we arrived at Abol Bridge.

The next morning we hiked quickly to Abol Bridge. It was just a handful of miles away. We found Deb and Fancy Pants waiting for us. Shenanigans, Fancy Pants, Deb, and I went inside a store to eat lunch. They sold subs that were delicious. After eating, Deb took our gear for a slack pack and drove ahead to Katahdin Stream Campground to wait for us. Fancy Pants hiked with Shenanigans. I hiked alone and that was just fine. Time for reflection was needed.

After finishing our day's hike, we set up at a campsite. Shenanigans had the campsite reserved for us at Katahdin Stream Campground. We went to Millinocket for dinner. We arrived so late that nearly every place we went to was closed. Finally, we found a spot that was open. It was a dark, dimly lit pizza shop. We ate copious amounts of food and drank plenty of beer. Back at the campsite we went right to sleep. A herd of thundering horses couldn't have woken me. I really slept well after a good day on the trail and with a full stomach.

I awoke to my last morning in a tent. This was also my last day hiking! Shenanigans and Fancy Pants were going to hike together. Freight Train and Plan B were hiking together. Deb was here to support us all. I planned to hike to the end of the Appalachian Trail at the top of Katahdin, then down the Knife's Edge to Roaring Brook Campground. There, Deb would be waiting for me. She would drive me back to Fancy Pants' car and I would drive it back to Roaring Brook.

I had planned to summit Katahdin with Shenanigans, but now I was less willing to wait for him. Also, Shenanigans had his fiancé to hike with him and that was cool. This whole adventure was about being "my hike" and today I was "hiking my hike." I started the Appalachian Trail alone, and now, alone, I was climbing Katahdin. The hike onto Katahdin started easy, but once Katahdin got steep, the inclines remained steep. There were places where iron rods were implanted into the rocks for hand and foot holds.

On a false summit, the trail twisted and turned as a labyrinth made of rock outcroppings. At one point, I met a couple who said they were "headed to the top," and they were hiking in the opposite direction! It took some time convincing them they were headed down, not up. They were on a special adventure—hiking to the top of Katahdin so the gentleman could propose marriage. He carried a ring for the occasion.

Soon, and it seemed much too soon, I saw the top of Katahdin. My steps slowed as I approached. Several day hikers crowded around, blocking my approach to the sign for the summit. I squeezed in, walked past the sign, reached out and touched it, then walked a few steps more and

sat down. Some of the tourists posing for a group picture were not pleased that
I walked through them to
touch the sign. They got
over it.

After the area by the
summit sign was clear, I
went up for my turn to get
pictures. The day hikers
were friendly and helpful, taking pictures of me. I took Sheng Wei, the
rubber chicken, out of my pack and carefully placed her on the top of the
summit sign, taking pictures for Shuffle. Sheng Wei made it to the summit
at Katahdin! I sat down, ate lunch, and waited for Shenanigans. Freight
Train and Plan B arrived, but there was no sign of Shenanigans. Time
passed. I knew Deb was waiting for me. The hike was coming to an end.

It was time to head
back down the mountain. It
was time to end my hike. I
felt as if I had lost a friend;
my heart was heavy. An
overwhelming urge filled
me with the desire to turn
around and hike back to
Georgia; I resisted. Deb was
waiting at a parking area be-

yond the Knife's Edge. The Knife's Edge was a series of ridges formed from
sharp boulders with a steep drop off on each side. A fall could mean certain
death. A person could potentially fall hundreds of feet before stopping.

Day hikers covered the Knife's Edge like locusts on a cornfield. They
were crawling all over the area, making my hike an obstacle course. I must
now dodge the day hikers. Clouds periodically rolled in, blocking the view
of what was to come. As the clouds blew past, the sun's rays radiated warm-
ly and the wind blew with contrasting cold air. There was no vegetation on

the Knife's Edge. There was no trail. The way was marked with painted blue blazes on large boulders along the top of the razor back ridge. I had seen the last of the white blazes marking the Appalachian Trail.

I started down, leaving Freight Train and Plan B behind. My frustration started growing as clumps of day hikers prevented me from progressing at my own pace. Several times I went low, traversing rocks along the ledge, leaping from one stone to another, passing the slower tourists. They commented about my speed. They admired the agility and strength in my legs. I wondered why they admired my strength because all the while I felt weak. It was strange to me. But I kept going, passing person after person. Occasionally, I looked back to see the people I had just passed. They appeared to be far away.

A traffic jam blocked the pathway ahead. Four men, hiking together the same direction as I, were waiting for three women making their way down a steep rock face. The women coming from the opposite direction were attempting the climb up Katahdin by way of the Knife's Edge. The climb was difficult for them. It took at least ten minutes for them to clear the small area. I could have been a half mile farther along by now. I tried to be patient, but desired to be back with Deb. I waited.

The women were all middle aged and were struggling with their hike. I applaud their attempt and for being there in the first place. It was my misfortune that we met at a location where I had to wait. They were making progress. Patience was what I needed. If there was a problem it was mine and I knew it.

After the women passed us, one of the men started up the steep incline. Another man suggested he wait to let me pass, but he was already clinging to the rocks and committed to the climb. It seemed there was only one way up, or so it appeared. I used a couple of boulders to leap upward and onward to another boulder. Three leaps later I was standing a full body length above the hiker who started the climb ahead of me.

Now the way was clear of other hikers and climbers. I was off, leaping, bounding, and scrambling up and down the sharp-edged stones. I put a great distance between me and the other hikers. Deb was waiting and I wasn't going to waste any more time.

In the distance, I saw a couple hiking in the same direction. They were at least a mile away. My pace quickened. I jumped and leaped. The views were spectacular. I would leap upon a rock, landing on both feet at the edge. My knees were bent for balance. My eyes would gaze downward over the rock ledge at the drop hundreds of feet below. One slip and I was a goner! This made the effort so much more fun.

Within twenty-five minutes, I had caught up with the couple ahead of me. They didn't seem to notice they were so much slower than me. They didn't yield to let me pass. I waited for a place to pass them. It never came. They were enjoying their hike, as they should; I wanted to be finished with my hike, as I should. To pass them I had to find another route; that meant harder climbs and more dangerous leaps. It was worth it!

The blue blazes went low and to the right of the ridge. The ridgeline boulders might have been too large to climb or jump, but I had trail legs. Up I went like a spider on a wall. I scurried to the top of a giant stone only to discover it was the apex with nothing close to leap on. I scurried down into a deep crevasse. Pushing on both sides of the rocks, I made it back up to another ledge. Leaping from that ledge back the way I came gave me the footing and force to make a huge leap forward. I was bouncing around on the rocks like a pinball in play.

The way became clear as I bounced around, leaping from rock to rock. I made a new path through the area. The slower hikers were behind me now. My final leap was almost straight down onto the sharp edge of a boulder. If I missed, I could slide to one side and break a leg or hip. If I missed on the other side, I could break an ankle. Worst of all, if my legs split apart I would end up straddling the stone's edge with dire consequences. I would be singing soprano! None of those choices were appealing. I leaped downward. My toes gripped through my shoes to the edge of the stone. I was safe!

Two small leaps later and I was back on the marked trail and the way was clear to make real time. Looking below, I saw no one was in my way. I ran the boulders, faster and faster! I paused to look back. The couple was almost at the same spot where I had passed them, back a half mile or more. My knees were screaming and sore. I came to a tall stone. The path now was a jump down about five feet, but the success of this jump depended on the landing spot. That spot was between two large, flat, parallel stones standing on edge. The distance between the vertical slabs was quite small.

I jumped. My knees were weakened and strained from all the climbing and jumping. As I landed, my knees failed to hold my weight. They bent! Crack! Pain flooded my mind as my left knee hit the stone. Damn, I was still making mistakes on the trail! The hit had the sound of a baseball being hit by a bat.

Walking out from between the rocks should have been easy, but my knee could no longer hold any weight. If I were still hiking the AT, I would have stopped and set up my tent to spend the night, but Deb was waiting for me. My hiking was soon to be finished. Completing my hike was emotionally painful, and now more physically painful than before.

But, it was time to rest. I hopped to the edge of a cliff to pee, then hopped back. I sat on a flat rock to snack on the last of my food. I grew thirsty as I rubbed my swollen knee. The question in my mind: "*Is the thirst from the hike or from shock setting in?*" I decided it was both and drank, but only small sips.

While sitting and resting, the other hikers started coming closer. There was no way I would allow them to catch up to me. My only course of action left was to walk off the injury. That was easier said than done! I loaded the pack on my back then headed off. My steps were small, mincing. The tree line was close. It was my hope the tree line would bring an end to the rocks. It did.

The trees opened a pathway into the woods. Following the blue blazes in the woods along the trail was easy, but from time to time the trail took a steep decline. It was the climbs down that hurt. Slowly, I made my way, farther and farther downward. The woods were growing thicker.

As time stretched out, my strength grew and my knee became less sore. More people showed up on the trail. A man with two young boys came hiking up the hill. This was encouraging. If small children were around here on the trail, the parking lot should be closer. Pain slipped further from my mind. My steps grew faster; Deb was close by.

Soon, the woods gave way to an opening. In the opening was a building. Beyond the building was a parking lot. My heart jumped. This was it. The end of my hike! The end of the pains! Deb stood by her car. We hugged. She had water, beer, and food. I took my pack off for the last time. Deb set up a folding chair for me.

The hikers whom I had passed came by to compliment the speed of my hike. "He is a thru-hiker just finishing the AT," Deb proclaimed. They all came by asking questions about my hike. They each wanted to shake my hand and congratulate me. I was treated like a celebrity and it felt good, sore knee and all.

Now came the hard part: coming home. Once back, I was trying to find my orientation at home. It was odd not sleeping in a tent. I was quickly losing my identity as "Mingo," as I put my gear away. The adventure was not totally what I had expected, but the hardest part of any adventure is coming home. That is difficult for our soldiers overseas as well. Life at home is never the same. Fitting back into home life is a process mixed with time.

My time was spent catching up with friends and family. The best support came from friends made on the trail. Cargo and Pony Express came and stayed for a visit. Socks, and a friend she made on the trail, Hoops, came to visit as well. When friends finished their hikes they sent pictures at the top of Katahdin. I wished I were there!

At home, I was welcomed by groups of friends. Settling back into a routine seemed strange. My feet hurt every day. My hunger was never satisfied. I shaved and went to the local, small-town barbershop, Dave's, to report my "finish" and to get a haircut. People there were more interested in the hike than I expected them to be.

Difficult questions were expected and would be asked. The hardest question would be, "How was it?" Now answer that question in less than five minutes. Beyond five minutes everyone would be bored. Or try to answer these questions in a few words: "How was the trail?" "How was the hike?" "How were the last five months on your adventure?" *Hmm, how do I answer that?*

It was . . . <u>stepping wild</u> . . . it was a life of its own . . . it was the Appalachian Trail!

The End

CPSIA information can be obtained
at www.ICGtesting.com
Printed in the USA
BVHW04s1838240518
517299BV00001B/53/P